THE
CASE OF
ROSE BIRD

*Gender, Politics, and
the California Courts*

KATHLEEN A. CAIRNS

University of Nebraska Press   LINCOLN AND LONDON

Library of Congress Cataloging-in-Publication Data
Names: Cairns, Kathleen A., 1946– author.
Title: The case of Rose Bird: gender, politics, and
the California courts / Kathleen A. Cairns.
Description: Lincoln, Nebraska: Bison Books, 2016.
| Includes bibliographical references and index.
Identifiers: LCCN 2016024936
ISBN 9780803255753 (hardback: alk. paper)
ISBN 9780803295421 (epub)
ISBN 9780803295438 (mobi)
ISBN 9780803295445 (pdf)
Subjects: LCSH: Bird, Rose Elizabeth | California.
Supreme Court. | Judges—California—
Biography. | Political questions and judicial
power—California. | BISAC: BIOGRAPHY &
AUTOBIOGRAPHY / Women. | BIOGRAPHY
& AUTOBIOGRAPHY / Lawyers & Judges.
| HISTORY / United States / State & Local /
West (AK, CA, CO, HI, ID, MT, NV, UT, WY).
Classification: LCC KF373.B527 C35 2016
| DDC 347.794/035092 [B]—dc23
LC record available at https://
lccn.loc.gov/2016024936

Set in Sabon Next by Rachel Gould.
Designed by N. Putens.

CONTENTS

ILLUSTRATIONS

Following page 140

ACKNOWLEDGMENTS

Thirty years ago, as a newspaper reporter, I covered Chief Justice Rose Elizabeth Bird's unsuccessful 1986 retention election. It was a depressing and brutal affair, and shortly after it ended I happily put it behind me. Little did I know that decades later I would revisit Bird and her tortured tenure atop the nation's premier state supreme court. I have many people to thank for helping me reconstruct the life and times of this complicated, enigmatic, and remarkable woman.

Wallace Kaufman and Edwin Gauld grew up in Sea Cliff, New York, and helped me immeasurably in my efforts to understand the geography and cultural landscape of the town where Bird lived during her teenage years in the 1950s. Gauld went far beyond simply providing a snapshot of Sea Cliff. He located acquaintances of Bird's who knew her before she became quite so reluctant to share personal information. Bird always asserted that she had grown up poor and an "outsider." Information about her youth in Sea Cliff revealed the accuracy of these statements.

At UC Berkeley I thank Boalt Hall librarian Bill Benemann for providing a list of the law school's class of 1965—nearly two hundred men and only eight women, including Bird—and a poem Bird wrote for a student publication. Also at Berkeley I thank the Bancroft Library staff, specifically Crystal Miles, for helping me navigate permissions for photos at Bancroft and for the personal reminiscences of state supreme court justices at the university's Regional Oral History Office.

Members of the Commission on Judicial Performance kindly gave me permission to wade through voluminous records of the 1979 CJP investigation into the state supreme court; I am grateful for their courtesy, particularly Fran Jones of the California Judicial Center Library and Amy Ladine, administrative assistant at the CJP. Steve Greenberg graciously allowed me to use one of the many wonderful cartoons he penned depicting the turbulent court during the hearings.

I also thank my colleagues at Cal Poly, San Luis Obispo, who have enthusiastically supported my work during the decade I have worked there, and my great, good friends Kathy Olmsted, professor of history at the University of California, Davis, and Dorothy Korber, reporter extraordinaire. Kathy read the manuscript that became the book and invited me to join her on a panel for the Western Association of Women Historians to discuss Rose Bird and her role in shaping California politics. During my research trips to Sacramento, Dorothy provided me with welcome respite—riotous reminiscences about our days as young journalists and about politics and life in general. My good pal Donna Schuele, an alumna of Boalt Hall, read all of the chapters focused on legal cases. Her input saved me from more than one embarrassing omission and interpretive error. Any remaining errors are mine.

Finally, I thank members of my family for their patience and ability to refrain from visible eye rolling whenever I wax poetic about whatever project I'm working on. All of the dance and piano recitals, soccer and basketball games, the lunches, dinners, and trips to Santa Barbara and San Francisco serve as constant reminders that there is more to life than work. My husband, Larry Lynch, has always been my rock and my port in every storm. He is truly a man for all seasons.

Introduction

In fall 2010 former eBay chief executive Meg Whitman was the Republican candidate for governor of California. At campaign stops across the state, she accused her Democratic opponent, Edmund G. "Jerry" Brown Jr., of being "soft on crime." As evidence Whitman cited Rose Elizabeth Bird, whom Brown had appointed chief justice of the state supreme court thirty-three years earlier in his first iteration as governor.

Whitman could be forgiven for believing that her audience would understand the reference. For more than two decades, beginning in the late 1970s, Bird had been California's most controversial figure, responsible, according to critics, for keeping vicious killers alive and making it hard to do business in the state. Even after she left the court and became what friends deemed a tragic recluse, Republican candidates continued to use her as a "perennial bogy-person," useful for stirring up fear and anger among voters. But ten years into the twenty-first century, relatively few people still remembered Bird. "What a pretty name," one young woman responded, shaking her head in puzzlement. In the end, Brown easily defeated Whitman.

Rose Elizabeth Bird was forty years old when Brown tapped her to become California's first female supreme court chief justice in February 1977. She already had a history of firsts behind her: first female law clerk of the Nevada Supreme Court, first female deputy public defender in

California's Santa Clara County, first woman to hold a cabinet position in California. Bird also had finished near the top of her class at Boalt Hall, the University of California, Berkeley's storied law school, where she was one of only a handful of female students in the class of 1965.

She had bruised egos and made enemies on her way up. Nonetheless, Bird was utterly unprepared for the outrage that accompanied her court appointment. She was too young; she had never been a judge; she was arrogant, aloof, and controlling. One person called her vindictive. Many said a sitting justice should have received the plum job. In fact, long-serving associate justice Stanley Mosk had expected to get the nod.

After a bruising confirmation hearing, Bird barely won approval from the Commission on Judicial Appointments. It was not an auspicious beginning, and it went downhill from there. She squeaked by in her first retention election in 1978, receiving fewer votes than any previous justice. Disappointed opponents initiated recall efforts, featuring direct-mail solicitations, letter-writing campaigns, and a thudding drumbeat of "soft-on-crime" allegations.

The recall attempts failed, but anti-Bird forces viewed them as training exercises, a prelude to the real battle in 1986, when she again had to go before voters, this time for a twelve-year term. Opponents understood that the notoriously media-averse chief justice would be an inept candidate and that, in any event, judicial ethics would severely restrict her ability to mount an effective counterattack.

After a sophisticated campaign that cost more than $10 million and garnered national attention, in November 1986 Bird earned another first, this one humiliating. She became the first chief justice in California to be removed from office by voters. Two other justices were defeated as well: Joseph Grodin and Cruz Reynoso, both Jerry Brown appointees. "They were just in the wrong place at the wrong time," said campaign consultant Bill Roberts.[1]

What was it about Bird that engendered such widespread and pervasive antipathy and outrage? The level of public attention and scrutiny she received was unprecedented. Historically, few voters knew the names of any sitting justices, periodic retention elections drew disinterested yawns, and jurists routinely won election by wide margins. In reality the battle over Bird was always about more than one individual. It represented the opening salvo in what has become an ongoing, bitter, and expensive war over control of the nation's judicial system. In this, as in so much else, California stood in the vanguard.

In the two decades before Bird's appointment, the U.S. Supreme Court overturned segregation and miscegenation laws, barred illegal searches, banned prayer in public schools, abolished the death penalty, and granted women the right to terminate pregnancies. Conservatives and even some moderates railed against many of these rulings as judicial activism and "social engineering." In the 1950s and 1960s ultraconservative groups such as the John Birch Society went so far as to erect billboards alongside the nation's highways urging motorists to "Impeach [U.S. Supreme Court chief justice] Earl Warren." Federal judges had lifetime appointments, however. Once confirmed by the U.S. Senate, barring extraordinary circumstances, they enjoyed airtight job security until they died or chose to retire.

In reaching high-profile decisions, the U.S. high court often was persuaded by rulings made earlier by the California Supreme Court, considered the nation's most prestigious and pioneering. Unlike their federal counterparts, California justices had to face the voters in periodic elections, but they had long enjoyed an exalted status that made it virtually impossible to mount effective campaigns against them, no matter how thoroughly their rulings may have angered various interest groups. Solidly entrenched members of the political and legal establishments, these male jurists went to the best schools and often went on to practice law in prestigious firms or teach at elite institutions. They belonged to exclusive private clubs.

Bird had been a criminal defense attorney and an advocate for migrant workers and other underprivileged individuals. She possessed none of the prerequisites that ordinarily conferred prestige and status. She might have gone to a good school, but she was an outsider, not a member of the political elite. Opponents cited many reasons for going after Bird with such a vengeance, but underlying all the explanations was the fact that they saw her as vulnerable. After years of pent-up anger, to opponents of the judicial status quo she was a godsend.

None of her opponents ever publicly uttered the word "woman" as a factor in their opposition, but gender significantly enhanced her vulnerability. With women historically excluded from the upper echelons of the legal profession, she had no long-established network of allies and colleagues ready to rush into the breach and declare that an attack on a sitting justice represented an assault on the judiciary itself. In fact, many male judges and lawyers resented the notion that an inexperienced female should occupy the same seat once held by such towering figures of jurisprudence as former chief justices Roger Traynor and Phil Gibson.

Bird partisans charged her opponents with sexism, but critics denied that gender had anything to do with their opposition. Instead they cited her abrasive, uncompromising personality, her proplaintiff rulings, and her refusal to uphold death sentences. Bird did possess an abrasive and uncompromising personality, she consistently ruled in favor of plaintiffs, and she voted to overturn every death sentence that came before her. But Roger Traynor had been characterized as a "prima donna," the pre-Bird court was notoriously plaintiff friendly, and her predecessor as chief justice had written the decision that eliminated (at least temporarily) capital punishment in California.

Her lack of judicial experience also did not set Bird apart. Neither Traynor nor Gibson had spent a single day as a judge before their high court appointments. And one associate justice, William P. Clark, appointed by Governor Ronald Reagan in 1973, had flunked out of both college and law school before passing the state bar exam on his second attempt. No one talked of removing Clark from the bench. California's first female supreme court justice obviously was required to play by different rules.

Gender may have been the elephant in the room, but timing holds the key to understanding how it enabled opponents to derail Bird's career. Her appointment came just as second-wave feminism stood at its peak in terms of accomplishments. In the 1970s Congress passed the Equal Rights Amendment, Title IX of the Civil Rights Act, and the Equal Credit Act. With *Roe v. Wade*, the Supreme Court cited the right to privacy in granting women the right to abortion. More women had begun to enter previously off-limits professions, becoming police officers and firefighters. They took advanced degrees in high-paying, male-dominated fields like law, medicine, and finance.

Many women and men celebrated these gains, but others voiced fears that the women's movement had gone "too far," that a "radical" feminist agenda might topple longstanding institutions and threaten "traditional" values. As a woman sitting atop a court system known for setting precedents in a wide range of areas, Bird automatically became the focus of significant media attention. Additionally, by the 1980s a strong backlash had emerged, with feminists regarded as man-hating lesbians and sad and bitter spinsters. "Just when women's quest for equal rights seemed closest to achieving its objective," wrote Susan Faludi, "the backlash struck it down."[2]

Never married and childless, Bird was an easy target. Opponents recruited mothers of murdered children to appear in television ads holding photos of their dead offspring. They proclaimed Bird responsible; she had overturned death sentences of vicious male predators. Because she was not a mother, the ads implied, she could never identify with those who had lost children. Bird tried to convey sympathy with victims' families, but her response that she was required by law to follow the Constitution rang hollow. The constant assaults led her to utter some impolitic comments, such as calling her male opponents "bully-boys."

Following her ouster Bird retreated to the Palo Alto, California, home she shared with her mother. Exhausted emotionally and physically, she withdrew from friends and former colleagues. Fellow justices Joseph Grodin and Cruz Reynoso quickly landed positions at prestigious law schools. Bird faced a bleaker future. Law schools did not queue up to hire her; neither did law firms—clients might object. A stint as a television commentator did not last long. Stations had touted her as "the most controversial woman in California," but her commentaries turned out not to be controversial enough.

Without a job, California's first female chief justice lived on a small pension and turned to volunteer work. One day she walked into a legal aid clinic and offered to copy documents. The young lawyers had no idea who she was and handed her a stack of paper; they were mortified when they discovered her identity. They asked her to work as an attorney, but she declined; she had let her state bar dues lapse.[3]

In the mid-1990s Bird experienced a recurrence of the breast cancer that had first appeared two decades earlier, and she died of the disease in December 1999 at the age of sixty-three. Obituary writers recalled her as a trailblazing pioneer but also the victim of what had become a new kind of politics that relied on sound-bite slogans, high-powered campaign consultants, direct-mail solicitations, and prodigious fundraising.

During the campaign to oust her, Bird and others had warned of the dangerous, precedent-setting potential in targeting a sitting supreme court justice. "Political forces have been unleashed that will return to haunt us," said Santa Clara University law professor Gerald Uelmen. CBS *Evening News* anchor Dan Rather predicted that anti-Bird forces would take their talents "far beyond the California judiciary and make judges nationwide think twice about politics, pressures, and principles." And activist actor and director Warren Beatty warned that "political ideologues" would "push to apply an ideological litmus test to judges all over the country."[4]

The accuracy of these predictions soon became apparent. Less than a year after Bird's defeat, President Ronald Reagan tapped federal appeals court justice Robert Bork for the U.S. Supreme Court. Confirmation by the Senate would guarantee Bork a job for life. Critics pounced: he opposed civil rights and women's rights; he would take the court backward, into the antediluvian past. After a bitter battle lasting several weeks, in October 1987 the Senate turned down Bork's nomination. Four years later court of appeals judge Clarence Thomas became the focus of a bitter Senate confirmation hearing. Allegations of sexual harassment nearly undid him, but he ultimately prevailed by a narrow margin.

The battle soon moved back to the states. Some lower-court judges were targeted, but big-money donors saw high-court justices as much more valuable prey, given their power to shape law policy on the macro level. In 1992 Mississippi justice James Robertson was targeted and went down to defeat over a ruling mandating murder as a prerequisite for the death penalty. Four years later "tough-on-crime" proponents successfully targeted Nebraska justice David Lanphier and Tennessee Supreme Court chief justice Penny White. And back in California, in 1998, two justices were targeted for a ruling that allowed minors to obtain abortions without parental consent. Both retained their seats.

In 2008 Mississippi voters defeated Justice Oliver Diaz, long a target of the state's chamber of commerce and other business interests who viewed him as too sympathetic to plaintiffs. Opponents had previously tried unsuccessfully to get Diaz convicted of corruption and tax evasion. In 2010 Iowa conservatives defeated Chief Justice Marsha Ternus and two male colleagues after a high-stakes campaign targeted them for voting to legalize same-sex marriage in that state. In 2012 three Florida high court justices barely held their seats after opponents of "Obamacare" fueled voter outrage at the judges' decision upholding its constitutionality. And in 2014 two Kansas Supreme Court justices held their seats despite a campaign by victims' groups angered by a ruling that overturned two death sentences.

Every election season seems to feature new and ever more expensive campaigns aimed at justices who anger powerful constituencies, though opponents' motives often remain hidden beneath rhetoric that leans heavily on hot-button cultural issues. Often it takes only one controversial ruling to put a target on a justice's back. Since 2000 judicial retention elections have cost upward of $275 million, with corporate representatives and trial lawyers among the biggest contributors.

The implications of this phenomenon have fueled intense discussion and debate. "If the day comes that judges make decisions as politicians or theologians, this society and our democracy are in serious trouble," Iowa justice Marsha Ternus said after her defeat.[5] Former U.S. Supreme Court justice Sandra Day O'Connor warned that "the public needs to understand that the notion of independence is not only for the benefit of judges, judicial independence is for the benefit of all society."[6]

Polls suggest that most Americans agree at least philosophically with legal experts about the dangerous influence of large contributors to judicial elections and the ability of justices to retain independence in the face of constant political threats. As one retired chief justice declared, "It's pretty hard in big-money races not to take care of your friends. It's very hard not to dance with the one who brung you."[7] But solutions have proven elusive. Suggestions have included the establishment of nonpartisan campaign conduct committees possessing sanctioning power; single fixed terms for justices; and official tracking of donations to judicial campaigns, with the names of contributors posted online.

The clock cannot be rewound to a time before state supreme court campaigns became relentlessly partisan slugfests, but closely examining the place where it all started offers some insight into how canny campaign operatives honed their skills by shaping public perception and then used the fears and concerns of ordinary people to hijack the California Supreme Court. The confluence of gender and politics doomed Rose Bird, and neither she nor her allies possessed the tools to mount an effective counterattack. Long after her defeat, she concluded, "At least three-quarters of the battle is looking the part. Nobody knew what a woman justice was supposed to look like."[8]

Today everyone knows what a woman justice looks like; virtually every state has had at least one. California currently has a majority of four women on its seven-member court, including Tani Cantil-Sakauye, the state's second female chief justice. Partisan judicial attacks have become "equal opportunity" affairs. As more women joined the judiciary, voters, it seems, became comfortable with ousting judges, no matter what their gender.

As she ascended the career ladder, Bird could never have envisioned what awaited her at the top rung. She always hoped, she said, to make a difference in the world. She accomplished this goal, though surely not in the way she had hoped. "The legacy of Rose Bird," one journalist wrote following her death, "is not outlawing the short-handled hoe or bolstering tenants' rights, but embodying the warning that henceforth, beneath the robe of a jurist, there better beat the heart of a politician."[9]

The First Woman 1

In September 1999 Rose Elizabeth Bird telephoned a female reporter to arrange a lunch date. She dressed carefully in a blue blouse and black slacks, but the clothes hung on her thin frame and she could barely eat. She was dying of breast cancer and had only a few more weeks to live. The phone call had been unexpected. Bird was notoriously risk averse when it came to the media. As her life slipped away, however, she wanted to revisit the past and set the record straight before it was too late. It had been too late for a long time—for two decades, in fact.

She was almost sixty-three, and hers had been a remarkable life. From an impoverished girlhood in Arizona and New York, she had risen to heights no woman in California had then achieved. It had all unraveled. In 1986 she became the first chief justice removed from office by California voters. Even in her final months, she seemed not to entirely understand how it had all gone wrong.[1]

But the beginning of her journey held clues to the end. Bird always claimed to have learned her life's most valuable lessons at her mother Anne's knee. Chief among them: that women had to take care of themselves; that education, hard work, and perseverance were keys to a life free of physically taxing, low-paid labor; and that a career aimed at helping others less fortunate would bring psychic satisfaction along with remuneration. "She probably more than anyone else influenced me in understanding that you had to rely on yourself—that you couldn't rely on a husband to financially see you through life," Bird once said.[2]

But her father also played a profound role in the person Bird became: obsessively self-reliant, deeply untrusting of others, and possessing a nearly pathological need for control. She was also extraordinarily cautious, and she prized loyalty above all other traits, remnants of an early childhood with a parent who seems always to have had one foot out the door. Harry Dalton Bird left his family when Rose was small. As a teenager, she apparently revealed to a friend that he had been an alcoholic. As an adult, she never spoke publicly about Harry. She pointedly omitted references to him in all of her "Who's Who" entries. If asked by journalists, she offered a terse response: "My mother married a much older man, and as a result my father died when we were very young."[3]

Harry Bird was born in New Jersey in 1873 to parents who had emigrated to the United States from England just two years earlier. His first marriage took place in 1894 in Manhattan, and according to U.S. census records his first child was born less than six months later. Harry and his first wife, Charlotte, eventually had five children.[4]

In April 1918 Harry signed up for military service, though at forty-four he was too old to fight in World War I. The enlistment form described him as tall and slender, with blue eyes and light hair, and it listed his occupation as salesman for a New York City company that made sandpaper. He also worked for at least one company that made glue.[5]

Although Charlotte maintained that her marriage lasted into the 1930s, by the end of the previous decade Harry had left his family and was living in a rented apartment in lower Manhattan with a new wife, Anne Walsh Bird.[6] When Harry and Anne's first child, Jack, was born in August 1930, they had moved to Nevada; by the following year they had relocated to Tucson, Arizona. Three more children would be born there: an infant daughter who died in late 1931; a son, Philip, born in June 1935; and a second daughter, Rose Elizabeth, born in November 1936, four decades after her oldest half sibling.[7]

Anne was more than thirty years younger than her husband, though census records suggest that he may have misled her about the age difference. Anne was twenty-five and Harry claimed to be forty-two at the time of the marriage, though he was really fifty-seven, about the age of Anne's own parents, James and Hannah Walsh. Her reasons for marrying Harry are unknown, but Anne grew up in a farming area in central New York that provided limited employment and marriage opportunities for young women. She surely did not marry for money, however; the Birds struggled financially throughout their marriage, which ended about the time the United States entered World War II.

By the time of his youngest daughter's birth in the depths of the Great Depression, Harry was no longer a salesman. Instead, the family eked out a living on a chicken farm they owned in a rural and run-down section of Tucson. At some point in late 1941 or 1942, Harry left Anne and their children. Sources later suggested that he died soon afterward, but he lived another decade, dying in Tempe, Arizona—about one hundred miles from Tucson—on May 21, 1953.[8]

Rose Bird was clearly sensitive about her family background. Once, when a journalist suggested her father had abandoned his family, she snapped, "My parents separated." In any case, Anne Bird never remarried, and Harry Bird seems to have been deleted from the family narrative soon after his departure. At the time of Harry's death Rose was nearing the end of her junior year in high school and no longer lived in Arizona.[9]

In some ways the timing of his departure was fortuitous. World War II had opened up the job market for women, particularly in the defense industry, and Anne found work at Tucson's Davis Monthan Air Force Base, installing Plexiglas windows on T-47 transport planes. With their mother at work all day, the three children were responsible for keeping the house in order: cooking, cleaning, and doing laundry. "It was hard," Rose Bird once noted in an interview. "I tell myself I was 80 when I was 5." She offered no specifics to explain this bleak depiction of her childhood, but a story told by her mother provided a glimpse at how it must have seemed to a young girl left to fend for herself.[10]

In one of the rare interviews she gave, Anne Bird recalled her children's youth as generally happy, one in which they amused themselves playing ball and climbing trees. The neighborhood held few other children and no girls Rose's age, so she had only her brothers as playmates. Jack was almost six years older and Philip less than two years older. They generally tolerated their younger sister, at least according to their mother. But the boys often enjoyed visiting the military base, where they fraternized with mechanics or with "an occasional tolerant pilot." Rose was not welcome to join them.

One day Anne returned home just as her sons were headed to the base. When they saw Rose running to catch up, they turned and started throwing stones at the dirt in front of her to keep her from coming closer. "I can remember her standing there crying. But you know when I was working there was a limit to how much I could discipline the boys. I wanted them to take care of Rose and I didn't want them to get angry at her so that when I wasn't there she'd suffer for it. And I think by and large they were pretty fair to her."[11]

Anne Bird remained at Davis Monthan until soldiers began returning from the war, and she eventually was let go. Advertisements, magazines, films, and the new medium of television depicted white women of the late 1940s and 1950s, with few exceptions, as happy housewives eager to replace their rivet guns with roasting pans and to exchange their work clothing for shirtwaist dresses and aprons. This lifestyle may have been claustrophobic for some ambitious women, but for Anne Bird—and millions of others—it was unattainable, a fact that her daughter implicitly understood, even as a young girl.[12]

Anne needed full-time work, but postwar opportunities were scarce to nonexistent for women, at least in fields that paid wages sufficient to support families. To make ends meet she took in laundry and cleaned houses. In 1950, having exhausted her options and her limited resources, Anne decided to leave the southern Arizona desert for the rolling hills and farms of her childhood home in New York.[13] The job search there proved as fruitless as it had in Tucson, and after a few months, Anne moved with her daughter to Sea Cliff, New York, situated on a scenic spit of land on the north shore of Long Island, twenty-five miles from New York City. Rose was fourteen at the time, and she must have experienced extreme culture shock.[14]

Tucson sprawls across more than two hundred square miles of rugged desert terrain sixty miles north of the Mexican border. It is surrounded by mountains and held a population of nearly fifty thousand in the late 1940s. It also was a diverse place, counting Anglos, Latinos, Native Americans, and a few African Americans among its residents; the neighborhood where the Birds lived was mostly Latino. The Papago Reservation reflects the city's Native American roots while the Mission San Xavier de Bac, built in the late 1600s and situated nine miles south of Tucson, recalls the city's origins as a Spanish settlement. The OK Corral, about an hour's drive east of Tucson, reminds visitors of the city's connection to the wild and untamed West of lore. Later in her life, Rose Bird recalled attending segregated schools and having a Native American woman as a babysitter.

Sea Cliff is an incorporated village inside the boundaries of the larger town of Oyster Bay. It got its start in the mid-1800s as a campground for Methodist revival meetings and later became a resort town attracting tourists who sought the Victorian and gingerbread flavor of old-time Americana. Today it is still the kind of place that visitors refer to as "quaint." Its small downtown seems designed for walking rather than driving. A few residents refer to Sea Cliff, perhaps with a touch of irony, as "Mayberry"—the bucolic, fictional town from the *Andy Griffith* television show. In fact, tourists eating lunch at the deli across the street from the town library are treated to black-and-white reruns of the *Andy Griffith Show*, complete with its distinctive whistled theme song and laugh track.

As its name implies, Sea Cliff sits high above a bay, which can be accessed by driving down a winding road or climbing down wooden stairs. Today, as in the 1950s, the town's population of nearly five thousand is virtually all white and middle to upper-middle class, with a smattering of wealthier and poorer residents. The former live in large homes with expansive gardens, and the latter reside in a small number of rental apartments. Sea Cliff might have been more monochromatic than Tucson, but in the 1950s, it seems to have been more inclusive in some ways. Two of Bird's classmates—both girls—were African American, and both were prominently featured in the high-school yearbook.[15]

Rose and Anne Bird lived in one of the rental housing units. A long-ago acquaintance remembered Anne as "nice" and the Birds as "rather poor." Rose was viewed as friendly, though intellectual rather than emotional; for example, she was not particularly interested in gossiping or hearing about other people's problems. She was, however, empathetic when it came to ethnic or religious minorities. A photo in her high-school annual depicts Bird with an arm around Valerie Gordon, an African American classmate. And she had Jewish friends, though at least one family member apparently was antisemitic. On a train trip to visit relatives in upstate New York, Bird suggested that a traveling companion not divulge her Jewish background.[16]

Bird herself undoubtedly felt like an outsider. Anne's status as a single parent in an era that extolled nuclear families automatically placed her—and her daughter—into a separate category from more "traditional" women. It is impossible to know how, or if, Anne explained her marital status to others. In a list of parent sponsors of the 1954 high-school yearbook, Anne referred to herself as Mrs. A. W. Bird. The use of her own initials might suggest she revealed her status as a divorcée but also that she fudged her status, since she used only initials, rather than her full name.[17]

And Anne was a working mother at a time when most mothers stayed home. Her job at a plastics factory was physically draining and the hours long, but at least it enabled her to provide her daughter with a modicum of financial security. It was in Sea Cliff that Rose Bird began to reveal a set of values that would come to shape her life and worldview: an intense dedication to hard work, a fierce independence, and a highly developed sense of outrage at what she perceived as injustice.

Photos of Bird during her high-school years depict a tall, slender, and very attractive girl who wore her long blonde hair in a braid wrapped around her head or pulled high into a chignon, a popular style in the 1950s. Her eyes held the camera in a steady gaze. "She must have had lots of beaux," a reporter once suggested to Anne Bird, who replied, "Not as many as you would expect. I think basically she was rather shy."[18] Her list of activities belies that assessment, however.

Rose entered Sea Cliff High School in her sophomore year and almost immediately signed on to the campus yearbook and newspaper. She also joined the Pioneers Club, the glee club, and the Alpha Math Club. She acted in school plays. In fact, she had the lead role in the senior play, *Mother Was a Freshman*. She played sports, including tennis, volleyball, softball, and basketball. Her involvement in so many activities seems to contradict her later depiction of herself as a plodder and a grind, a girl who stayed home "to do the shopping on the weekend and bake bread for the following week."[19]

A life filled with constant activity did not signify parties, dances, and sleepovers, however. Former classmates recall Bird generally as "a loner." In group photographs, she often held herself somewhat apart from her classmates. And comments beside her senior photo reflect her classmates' view of her as serious and somewhat aloof. Other girls were "fun-loving," "always on the go," "vivacious," and a "small-sized package of pep and energy," but Rose held "ardent discussions with [English teacher] Mr. Palmer" and "munched on her favorite blackstrap molasses and yogurt."[20] Despite her attractiveness, stellar grades, and accomplishments, she was not voted best looking, most athletic, or even most likely to succeed. And she did not win prizes in either English or history, her favorite subjects.[21]

She was not reticent about revealing her political leanings, even at such a young age. The yearbook also characterized her as "our energetic political fiend" and "a definite opponent of certain politicos."[22] Offering a hint of what her partisans would later depict as courageous and her detractors would refer to as excessively ideological, she sailed against the prevailing winds.

In fall 1952, at the age of fifteen, she went door-to-door campaigning for Democratic presidential candidate Adlai Stevenson. Sea Cliff "must have been about 99 percent Republican and I was about the only one in my school who supported him," she recalled later. This might have been a bit of an exaggeration. Current residents refer to Sea Cliff as historically more liberal than its neighbors, and one former resident recalled that the town also attracted a few "bohemians," such as artists and those with somewhat unconventional lifestyles.[23]

Bird's straitened economic circumstances made it necessary for her to work during the summers, and here, too, she showed remarkable assertiveness for one so young. One of her first jobs as a teenager was at a company that made metal plates for Addressograph machines. The work space was small and stifling; she later characterized it as "kind of a sweat shop." The workforce was made up entirely of women, who stamped out the plates for low pay and with few breaks. Rose soon discovered, according to her mother, "that if all of them stopped their machines and then started them up at the same moment, they could usually manage to blow a fuse, thus allowing them a comfortable ten- or fifteen-minute respite while repairs were made."[24]

After graduating with honors from Sea Cliff High School in 1954, Bird won a full tuition scholarship to Long Island University (LIU). She lived at home and commuted more than fifty miles round-trip each day, biking to the nearest train station and then riding the train to Brooklyn and back. Anne Bird once tried to explain to a journalist how her daughter had come to be so ambitious: "Even as a youngster in high school she realized that if you don't have a good education, you were at the mercy of the economic system. Of course, you are anyway, but maybe less so."[25]

She began as an English major hoping eventually to work in journalism and follow in the footsteps of her heroes, newspaper reporter Elmer Davis, who had headed the Office of War Information during World War II, and radio and television journalist Edward R. Murrow. Her interest in both men reflected her determination to make a difference. They were "crusading" reporters who used their respective platforms to oppose Wisconsin senator Joseph McCarthy's red-baiting; Davis also had opposed Japanese American internment during World War II. "When my classmates would have crushes on movie stars, I would have them on news commentators," Bird remarked.[26]

LIU was an ideal place to pursue this career goal, since the university sponsors the prestigious Polk investigative journalism awards, given annually in honor of George Polk, an American foreign correspondent for CBS News murdered in 1948 while covering the Greek Civil War. And the college counted noted journalists among its former students, including New York reporter and raconteur Jimmy Breslin, who attended LIU a few years before Rose Bird.

It was also during her undergraduate years that Bird found the first of several mentors. At LIU journalism professor Len Karlin played that role. He later recalled Bird as "a very lovely, sweet, caring person. I would have been very proud if she had been my daughter."[27] Karlin also described his former student as "naive" and possessing what he deemed "an idealistic view of the world." In one interview he compared Bird to Billy Budd, the ill-fated protagonist of Herman Melville's novel of the same name. This seems a somewhat prescient assessment.[28]

Even with a male mentor, in the 1950s journalism was still a man's business. A lucky few women wrote "hard news" stories about crime, politics, or foreign affairs that appeared on newspaper front pages or in weekly newsmagazines, but most female journalists toiled in suburban or society sections of newspapers, where they wrote about school carnivals, Little League raffles, fashion, and parties—not the kinds of stories that appealed to a young woman who had her eye on the brass ring.[29]

At some point Bird decided to focus on political science, which seemed to offer more career options, including the possibility of advanced study. At her graduation she received the Alumni Association Award as outstanding senior in the class of 1958. She was on her way, it seemed, having been offered a scholarship in the University of California, Berkeley, graduate program in political science.

Her scholarship did not cover living expenses, however, so Bird remained in New York, working as a secretary to a research scientist at the Polytechnic Institute in Brooklyn. The job must have reminded her yet again of the limited options for women in the workplace, even those with college degrees. In September 1959 she finally set off for Berkeley, the crown jewel of California's vaunted university system and her home for the next six years. Though not yet the center of explosive youthful protest it would become by the mid-1960s, Berkeley nonetheless provided a yeasty intellectual environment.

Students read Jack Kerouac and Allen Ginsberg. They listened to music by Woody Guthrie, Phil Ochs, and Pete Seeger. They discussed nuclear disarmament and closely followed the burgeoning civil rights movement in the South, where young African Americans put their lives on the line challenging Jim Crow and white racism in lunch counter sit-ins. It was a heady time to be at college—particularly at a politically aware campus like Berkeley. Bird had strong opinions, but as a career-focused graduate student, she had little time to participate in student activism.[30]

Seeking the broadest range of experience available, she chose to reside in International House (dubbed I-House), a campus residential facility built in 1930 with an endowment from John D. Rockefeller Jr. that housed Berkeley students from all over the world. In fact, instilling appreciation for diversity was the objective of I-House, and thus it can be inferred that students who chose to reside there were already politically and culturally aware and engaged. Students had to submit applications to be considered for residency. Bird's cited the "ability to meet individuals from different nations," which afforded "one an opportunity to get a new perspective on one's own country."[31] Students who lived in I-House also were willing to buck tradition with regard to living arrangements. Most campus dormitories in the early 1960s still had strict rules and segregated men and women in different facilities. In I-House they lived together, though not in the same rooms.

Previous and future residents included famed economist John Kenneth Galbraith, attorney and civil rights activist Pauli Murray, Google CEO Eric Schmidt, astronaut Drew Gaffney, and political writer David Brock, along with nearly a dozen Nobel Prize winners, politicians, and scientists. Bird's fellow residents included Cho Soon, later deputy prime minister of the Republic of Korea; Pete Wilson, future governor of California; and Edmund G. Brown Jr., the son of California governor Edmund G. "Pat" Brown. Bird knew Brown only as an acquaintance at Berkeley, and she later recalled the future governor as "a very quiet rather serious person, quite reserved. A lot of us were very interested in politics, but he didn't seem very interested at all." For his part, Brown later told a reporter that he had no strong recollections of Bird at Berkeley. "If I saw her more than a few times . . . I'd be surprised. I saw her, I met her, I knew her. She was not a close friend."[32]

In her single-minded pursuit of success, Bird sought every opportunity that came along. In 1960 she competed for and won one of ten Ford Foundation fellowships given to graduate students from four California universities: Berkeley, Stanford, UCLA, and the University of Southern California. Each fellow received a nine-month assignment to work as an intern for a state lawmaker in Sacramento and earned a $500 monthly stipend. Bird was assigned to Democrat Gordon Winton, who chaired the state Assembly Education Committee. The task Winton assigned her: determining how many states had student testing programs and then working with him and his committee to draft a legislative bill for a California plan.

If Winton expected Bird, as a neophyte and a young woman, to take a cautious approach to her assignment, one destined not to ruffle feathers or challenge conventional wisdom, he was in for a surprise. "When she started out, she was in favor of [statewide student testing]," an assessment approach then gaining favor among lawmakers. "But then she read a critical report" suggesting that poor and minority students were adversely affected by the practice.

"So Rose and I—Rose did most of the work—came up with a compromise bill that said there would be testing, but gave districts choices of three or four different tests. Well, she did a beautiful job." The final bill contained language mandating that scores be released to the public only on a district-wide basis. That way schools enrolling large numbers of poorer and minority students did not suffer by comparison to their more affluent white counterparts. When the chaptered bill was published Winton gave Bird a copy of it, with the inscription "To the real authority."[33]

On her last day in Sacramento Bird informed Winton that she had decided to apply to law school at UC Berkeley's Boalt Hall. Many members of the state legislature, including Winton, were attorneys, and Bird told him she believed practicing law would give her the opportunity to make a difference and to do interesting work. He encouraged her ambition, telling her that "the law is beginning to open up to women."

It was not happening with any speed, however. Law schools had long been reluctant to admit women, but after World War II, schools had begun to use the Law School Aptitude Test (LSAT) for admissions, and it became more difficult to exclude women who earned high scores. By the early 1960s women still represented less than 5 percent of admissions, but at least they had a foot in the door. Bird was one of eight women in the class of 1965, out of an enrollment of more than two hundred.[34]

Her tenure at Boalt dovetailed with the emergence of a nationwide student protest movement focused on civil rights and the beginning of the Vietnam War. Berkeley played a pivotal role at the center of the Free Speech Movement in fall 1964. The law school was not immune to challenges. Some faculty felt compelled to defend protesters while others were frustrated by their growing antiauthoritarian bent. One observer noted that "there was a lot of hostility and anger openly expressed against anyone in authority, including the most sympathetic and indulgent faculty members."[35]

Only the best and the brightest taught at Boalt, according to Frank Newman, who was then law dean. Being editor of a law review and clerking on a prestigious court were among the required criteria.[36] The law school did have one woman professor. Herma Hill Kay arrived at Boalt in 1960, four years after graduating from the University of Chicago Law School. She taught family law, including marital property rights. Sho Sato, one of the first Japanese American law professors in the United States, taught government law and taxation at Boalt. In addition to his administrative duties, Newman taught legislative and administrative law, and Preble Stolz—a professor only five years older than Bird—taught civil procedure. Newman was Bird's favorite professor and later became her colleague on the California Supreme Court while Stolz ultimately became a vocal critic of his former student.

Bird did well at Boalt. In her third year she won the moot court competition, in which students prepared and argued simulated cases before a panel of judges, made up of faculty members and prominent jurists. She also won the law school honors prize, the first woman to do so, thus beginning the string of firsts that came to characterize her professional life.

Bird had swapped one profession dominated by men—journalism—for another, a fact that she ruefully addressed in a poem dedicated to Professor Herma Hill Kay that appeared in *The Writ*, a Boalt student publication. It read:

Oh, we're just eight women lawyers
Who just want to practice not preach
Oh, we're just eight women lawyers
Who just want to practice not teach ....
We'll stand near the seats of the mighty
Contributing our little bit.
And if there's a gentleman present
Then one day we even may sit.[37]

By May 1965 she had attained enough prominence to be featured in a *Mademoiselle* magazine article about female law students. The article's title, "The Case for Girls in Law," suggested how far women still had to go to be accepted. "To the Hollywood director, the neat attractive girl walking up the courthouse steps might be the judge's daughter," the author began. "To the jurors or witnesses who pass her in the busy corridor, she might be a secretary returning from lunch, or a housewife scurrying to pay a traffic fine." However, the "girl" in *Mademoiselle*'s article was "one of the fast-growing breed of young professional women, graduates of America's top law schools."

Bird was one of a dozen women featured. The writer described her as "a tall honey blonde, who swims a quarter of a mile each day to break up the sedentary student routine." Bird understood "there would be tough sledding ahead," she told the reporter, but, she added, "if you want to have an impact, law is the key." She told her interviewer that she wanted to work in a government agency "on behalf of indigent defendants." Trial work for private law firms, she acknowledged, was "a fairly remote possibility" for women.[38]

Bird was twenty-eight when she graduated from Boalt, years past the time when many if not most women of her era usually married. Yet she was still decidedly single. In college Bird had been romantically involved with an Englishman, according to one friend, but she worried about citizenship issues so had broken off the relationship. Nearly a decade later she undoubtedly had different concerns, understanding that marriage usually proved to be a serious disadvantage to women seeking professional careers, and she most definitely sought a profession, not just a job.[39]

Employers justified discrimination against married women by claiming that men needed money to support families while women worked only for "pin money," and that women lost interest in careers once they had children. But as Bird knew from bitter experience, husbands and fathers could walk away from their families, leaving them destitute, or close to it. Later in life she expressed occasional regret at not marrying, but by then she had established herself in a successful career and had little time to search out a mate. She may have had intimate relationships, but if so, they remained under the radar of all but her closest friends or family members.[40]

Her closest relationship was with her mother. Anne Bird had remained in Sea Cliff during her daughter's first three years in California. The summer before she started law school Rose asked her mother to move west to live with her in Berkeley. Anne agreed. Nearing sixty, she still needed to work, so she took a job with the *Oakland Tribune* newspaper, answering phones and typing classified ads. The two women would live together, with brief separations, for the remainder of Anne's life.[41]

Asked much later if her sons resented their sister's success, Anne Bird replied cautiously. "I would say they have mixed feelings. It is, I suppose, a sort of an attack on a man's masculine feelings if his sister runs faster than he does." But her daughter had "always kept going toward the same goal," she added. "The boys might seem less successful because they've been more diverted. Things of immediate value seemed more important to them, whereas Rose looked at the long term." Left unsaid was the notion that men of the time could be "diverted" from singular career paths without worrying that an opportunity once ignored might never emerge again. Thus Philip could attend law school at Santa Clara University in his late thirties and begin practicing law in his forties. Jack worked at a variety of jobs throughout his life, which he spent in the Tucson area.[42]

Graduating from law school might have seemed a sterling accomplishment for women in 1965, but law firms, as Bird had suggested to *Mademoiselle*, were not clamoring to hire them. A year earlier Congress had passed the Civil Rights Act. It barred employment discrimination based on race, color, religion, sex, and national origin. Yet most law firms still refused to hire women; less than 20 percent employed them.

A *Harvard Law Review* headline put it succinctly: "Women Unwanted." The author of the accompanying article had asked potential employers, on a scale of plus 10 to minus 10, what kind of candidates they sought when hiring. The respondents rated women at minus 4.9. Asked to explain, they declared that women couldn't "keep up" with men, that they were subject to "emotional outbursts," and that they had "responsibilities at home."[43]

To succeed in the masculine field of trial law women often had to go it alone, engage in attention-garnering behavior, and represent clients few others were willing to take on. California's most famous female lawyer in this period may have been Los Angeles's Gladys Towles Root, who defended sexual "deviants" and appeared in court in flamboyant costumes and outrageous hats, often purple—her favorite color. Sometimes she dyed her hair to match her clothing. She also employed a chauffeur, who transported her to court in a flashy Cadillac.[44]

Root's strategies definitely did not suit Rose Bird. She initially struggled to find work despite a résumé that, as one of her law school classmates put it, "would knock the eye out of any potential employer." It included a summer stint as a parole officer for the California Youth Authority, where her caseload consisted of teenage boys.[45]

Fortunately a male mentor emerged. Gordon Thompson was an associate justice on the Nevada Supreme Court. He had helped judge the moot court competition at Berkeley, was impressed by Bird's performance there, and invited her to clerk for the Nevada court during its 1965–66 term. She quickly accepted the job and moved with her mother to Carson City, Nevada. Thompson later recalled Bird as "an outstanding law clerk. She was very bright, full of energy and she exhibited keen awareness" of legal issues applicable to the appellate process.[46]

Bird also clerked for David Zenoff, chief justice of the Nevada Supreme Court, who described her as "intellectually marvelous, personally charming, industrious and a hard worker." He had had "only one other law clerk like her since," he said, "and that was a man, now well established in the profession." Zenoff did offer one observation that hinted at Bird's increasing willingness to challenge authority. When Bird disputed a point, she became "physical in expressing herself. She was a very physical woman—tall and blonde."

But disputes did not lead to hard feelings, and under Zenoff's instruction, she also came to understand something about how the "game" of office politics worked in a male-dominated workplace. "During the noon hour we would go out and throw a ball around," Zenoff said. "She could toss a ball half a block." Apparently her older brothers had taught her a useful skill.[47]

In 1966 Bird passed the California bar exam. She and her mother returned to the state, and Rose began an intensive job search. She first applied to a Sacramento law firm, but the interviewer told her that he had "never met a good woman trial lawyer." The Santa Clara County public defender's office had an opening but had never hired a woman deputy; attorneys there were not anxious to break new ground. Public defender Sheldon Portman was impressed with her résumé, but when he polled his deputies, only two out of ten voted to hire her. Fortunately one of the two "yes" votes was Donald Chapman, Portman's chief deputy, who overcame his colleagues' skepticism, earning Bird another first for her gender.

In going to work for a public agency Bird was following the same path as the majority of her female counterparts. Since law firms seldom hired women, ambitious law graduates often cut their legal teeth in state and federal agencies. Even so, "the men were much concerned about having a woman come in," she said later. Their reluctance had less to do with fears that she could not handle the work than with concerns about whether she would try to stifle the sometimes ribald and raunchy office atmosphere, which included profanity and liquor-laced celebrations following successful trials. But Bird proved adept at playing this game as well. And once again, her brothers' tutelage came in handy. Her colleagues "even let me play on their softball team," she said.[48]

In many ways the Santa Clara public defender's office was a good place for Bird to start her career. It was small and, since it depended on county funding, often operated with fewer staff than needed to handle the workload. She quickly had to become adept at a wide variety of cases, including both misdemeanors and felonies—even homicides. Portman called the environment "very intensive, very active," offering training that "very few lawyers get." Bird "immediately showed signs of being very capable," he said. The office had "a very high reputation with the appellate courts and it stems in large part from the work Rose Bird did, the excellence of her presentations, particularly."[49]

The office also allowed her to represent the kinds of defendants she sought to help—indigents and working-class people. At one point she successfully defended a Native American woman arrested for prostitution. Afterward the woman had no money to return home, so Bird invited her to stay the night and then gave her money for bus fare. She may have graduated from an elite law school, but as one acquaintance said, "She still sees herself as being from a different class than most lawyers and judges."[50]

Bird spent six years working full-time as a deputy public defender, years that coincided with the height of protest against the Vietnam War, the emergence of a radical wing of the civil rights movement, and second-wave feminism. It was a heady time to start out as a lawyer. As Bird acquaintance and fellow attorney J. Anthony Kline explained in an interview, "Many of us saw the law as a way to effectuate progressive social change. We were inspired by the possibilities the legal process represented. We saw the law and change through the law as the great victory of our society."[51] However, this period also saw the beginning of a backlash against what conservatives deemed youthful excesses, including antiauthoritarian values, drugs, and the sexual revolution.

Bird made more than eight thousand court appearances in Santa Clara County and eventually rose to become chief of the office's appellate division. Her professional success meant that her mother no longer had to work, and Anne Bird often showed up to watch her daughter in court. The job also gave Bird the opportunity to write briefs for cases argued before the California and U.S. Supreme Courts. One involved a police search for illegal drugs. Officers found no drugs in the defendant's home, so—without a warrant—they rummaged through his trash cans. As Bird later described it, "The question was whether an individual had a right to privacy in his garbage can. At the trial level it was decided that he did not."

On appeal the California Supreme Court disagreed and reversed the lower court ruling. The state's attorney general appealed the reversal to the U.S. Supreme Court, which agreed to hear the case. Bird, representing the California Public Defenders Association, successfully argued that the California Constitution should take precedence in this particular case.[52]

Over time her colleagues came to see her gender as a useful attribute, helping to disarm opponents in the courtroom. In an interview Santa Clara County prosecutor Ulysses Beasley described the first time he tried a case against Bird. "The way she spoke, it was so soft I thought she was crying. I guess it had an effect on the way I was handling the case, because the judge took the clerk aside and told him I was acting as though I wanted to give the case to Rose."[53]

Though many if not most of Bird's contemporaries described her—then and later—as reticent and private, she sometimes loosened up at parties. "She could have half a beer and get real happy," Beasley told one reporter. "We would go to a party and Rose would be there laughing and having a good time and somebody would say, 'she's in a good mood tonight.' And someone else would say, 'she must have had half a beer.'"[54]

But Bird was not always so easygoing, according to Beasley, who claimed that she occasionally exhibited a "hair trigger" temper. "I didn't want to set it off," he told a reporter. Beasley also suggested that Bird, even early in her legal career, had a judgmental side to her personality. "She was a very high, moral person, but there was something about Rose. I can't put my hand on it. She was just wrongheaded when it came to understanding people. I always felt she thought I should be a very liberal person because I was black."[55]

By the early 1970s Bird's reputation as a talented trial lawyer opened a new opportunity—a joint appointment with the public defender's office and Stanford Law School. She taught two classes a semester at Stanford as part of a clinical program that gave students real-world experience in both criminal and civil cases. Her connection to the public defender's office "enabled my students to handle trial cases in the courts of Santa Clara County," she said. Stanford law professor Anthony Amsterdam worked with Bird on the criminal cases.[56]

Amsterdam later described the clinical approach as "having students handle actual cases instead of simply sitting in a classroom."[57] Students were recruited from both the Stanford and Santa Clara University law schools. Many touted the program as extraordinarily valuable for their future career endeavors. John Cruden, a deputy assistant attorney general in the U.S. Department of Justice, recalled being a student of Amsterdam and Bird. "Tony and Rose led us through lectures, role-playing, practice sessions and then videotaping with daunting critique sessions. The interviewing, plea negotiation and in-court work was superb."[58]

The program proved so popular that other universities, including UCLA, adopted it. William Warren, dean of the UCLA School of Law, described Bird as "a stern taskmaster, a very hard-working, intense person who could be ruthless in critiquing student performances."[59] But many of her students appreciated her toughness. Scott Sugarman later became a staff attorney for Bird. She was "widely regarded as one of the best teachers on the faculty," he said, committed "to teaching her students to be real lawyers."[60]

Cruden said that Bird went above and beyond simply teaching, frequently meeting with students outside of class. She ultimately "became a friend and mentor. She was quick to hold our new baby daughter" and at law school graduation "congratulated each one of 'her' students."[61] One participant in the program, Stephen Buehl, continued working with Bird after she left Stanford, eventually becoming her chief aide, a job he held for her entire career.

These contrasting views hinted at Bird's complexity. She possessed an utter lack of subtlety and nuance. She could be abrupt and brutally honest, and yet she devoted herself to her clients and her students. Work was her lifeblood. She may have been willing to participate in office sporting events and an occasional party, but she lacked the ability to stroke egos or tell white lies. She was intensely hard on herself and on other people. But her heart was in the right place; virtually everyone who knew her at the time said so.

She also cared little for popular trends in fashion, perhaps intentionally. As a college student she had expressed dissatisfaction with her looks—particularly with her small and crooked teeth, a friend recalled. As a young professional, however, she wanted to be judged on her ability, not her appearance. By her midthirties her hair had grown darker, and she usually wore it pulled high off her forehead and wrapped into a loose French twist. Sometimes she added ribbons or bows. Wispy curls framed her face, and she wore little if any makeup. In photos she looked more like a prim schoolmarm than a pathbreaking attorney. Her work attire generally consisted of print or striped blouses, shapeless skirts or dresses, low-heeled shoes, and chunky jewelry. Within a few years she would begin wearing pantsuits, but in the 1960s and early 1970s women lawyers were not yet allowed to wear pants in court.[62]

Bird was not the first woman to teach at Stanford; that honor had gone to Barbara Babcock, a graduate of Yale Law School, former director of the public defender system in Washington DC, and a committed feminist who taught criminal procedure. Bird's life and work clearly reflected feminist principles, at least the brand of feminism focused on getting ahead via individual accomplishment. She did join women's professional organizations; she was a founding member of California Women Lawyers, for example. But she was not an outspoken advocate of women's rights in general, nor was she necessarily drawn to other women whose overtures suggested a focus on or desire for female solidarity. Thus her personal and professional lives remained separate, and each night when she left work she went home to the small Palo Alto home that she shared with her mother.

Anthony Amsterdam may have been the person who most influenced Bird at Stanford. He cotaught in the clinical program, but more important he was a leading strategist in the national fight to end capital punishment, the issue with which Bird would come to be closely identified. Working with the NAACP's Legal Defense and Educational Fund, Amsterdam and other lawyers came to focus on the "vagueness" and arbitrary nature of capital laws. Since juries were mostly made up of white, middle-class citizens, they did not necessarily identify with impoverished individuals and minorities, who thus were far more likely to be condemned and executed than whites who committed similar or even worse crimes.

By the late 1960s Amsterdam and the NAACP had begun to make headway with the U.S. Supreme Court in getting justices to overturn individual cases. But he and other abolitionists sought a national ban on capital punishment. In 1972 he successfully argued *Furman v. Georgia* before the U.S. high court, convincing a majority of justices to end capital punishment, at least for the moment, and to require states to rewrite death penalty statutes.[63]

Bird had to this point in her career focused little if any attention on capital punishment, though people who worked with her said later that they assumed she would be against it. Nevada chief justice David Zenoff said she had never expressed an opinion on the death penalty while clerking for him, "but from talking to her, I knew she would be the kind who would be philosophically opposed to it." Stanford law professor John Kaplan, who worked with both Bird and Amsterdam, said, "I don't think she would look with favor on the death penalty because she knows a lot about it."[64] Amsterdam's perspective undoubtedly led Bird—steeped from youth in the notions of class and racial privilege—to ponder the impact of both factors on capital cases.

In spring 1974 Bird left Stanford. As an adjunct faculty member she had no chance of earning a tenured position; in any event she had become increasingly critical of the ivory-tower nature of legal academics, which, she believed, did not adequately prepare students for the real world. She had always wanted to have her own law firm, saving money toward that end. She planned to open a private practice after taking the summer off, her first vacation since moving to California fifteen years earlier.[65]

As it turned out her life veered in a different and wholly unexpected direction. Jerry Brown, Bird's old Berkeley acquaintance, had become interested in politics after all. In 1970 he had run successfully for California secretary of state, and Bird had volunteered in his campaign. In 1974, at the age of thirty-six, Brown decided to run for governor; with time on her hands, Bird decided to volunteer again. At first she worked in his San Mateo campaign office stuffing envelopes, but soon she became his chauffeur, driving him around the San Francisco Bay Area for campaign appearances.

Even though they came from vastly different backgrounds and still could not be called friends, Brown and Bird shared a few personality traits. Both tended to be loners who kept their own counsel, guarded their privacy, and were frugal, prickly, and disinclined to suffer fools gladly. Both claimed to prize directness and honesty in themselves and others, though some acquaintances and colleagues of both called this assertion disingenuous.

But Bird's blunt manner served her well when it came to Brown, at least in the short term. In an interview long afterward she recalled driving Brown and his campaign manager to a debate with Brown's Republican opponent, State Controller Houston Flournoy, shortly before the November 1974 election. Brown casually asked Bird how she thought he was doing. "Apparently his campaign staff had kept from him the fact that he wasn't doing real well. I said, 'I think you'd be lucky if you win.' I thought [campaign director] Tom Quinn was going to explode because it was not something that was useful to have him be told right before a debate."[66]

Brown ultimately won a narrow victory and asked Bird to serve on his transition team; she agreed, thinking it would only be a matter of weeks until she returned to practicing law. That time never came. Just before his January 1975 inauguration Brown asked her to join his cabinet. He initially planned to name her resources secretary because, as she later put it, "He thought that women were sort of the symbol of Mother Earth, and to have a woman head up that agency would be a symbolic recognition of that."[67] Ultimately he decided to appoint her secretary of the Agriculture and Services Agency.

When reporters asked Brown why he had selected Bird, who had no experience working in state government, to head California's largest and most important agency, the new governor called her "a very well organized, very intelligent person. . . . She is extremely honest. And I think she's committed to the kind of society I think we ought to have." Anthony Kline, another Brown aide, suggested a different motivation. During the period between Brown's election and his inauguration he had given each aide a different assignment; Bird's was to investigate issues related to agriculture, so it may have seemed like a natural fit.[68]

Bird accepted the position even though it meant moving to Sacramento during the week and returning to Palo Alto on weekends. In doing so she added to her growing list of firsts, becoming the first woman to serve in a gubernatorial cabinet in California and the first nonfarmer to head the sprawling agency. She took the job, she told a reporter at the time, because "the way women advance is by showing that they can do the job the same way anyone else could." But she worried about losing her privacy.[69] She could not have foreseen in January 1975 just how profoundly her decision to join Brown's cabinet would affect her, beginning the process of altering the life she had so carefully constructed.

2 *A Woman in Charge*

When Jerry Brown chose Rose Elizabeth Bird to be California's secretary of agriculture and services, he fulfilled a pledge he had made during his campaign to include women in his administration. He was reminded of this promise shortly after his election, when representatives from the National Women's Political Caucus (NWPC) visited him in Sacramento. They knew they needed to move quickly because Brown's transition team, with the exception of Bird, was composed entirely of men. Ann Renner, head of the NWPC's Sacramento branch, told the governor-to-be that she was "urging women to submit their résumés, so that Brown couldn't say he is 'not receiving applications.' Gov. Brown needs to affirmatively screen in women," Renner added, "because women in the past have been screened out."[1]

Renner and her colleagues were pleasantly surprised, therefore, when Brown eventually named two women to high-profile cabinet positions. In addition to Bird, he tapped Claire Dedrick, an environmentalist, to head the state resources agency. Dedrick became an activist, she told one interviewer, during the battle over a road extension in front of her Bay Area home, when a county engineer ordered her to "get back to your kitchen, lady!" Brown also named the first Latino to head a state agency when he tapped community organizer and lawyer Mario Obledo as secretary of health and welfare. During his first term as governor,

Brown made more than two thousand appointments, and nearly half went to women and ethnic minorities. All of Brown's cabinet secretaries, including Bird, earned the same salary: $43,404 annually.[2]

He named women to high-profile non-cabinet-level jobs as well. Adriana Gianturco, whom Brown knew from UC Berkeley, became director of the Department of Transportation, and Carlotta Mellon, a women's studies professor at Pomona College, became his appointments secretary. People often saw her title and thought she was a clerical assistant, Mellon recalled much later. But part of her job was to find and vet female candidates for Brown to interview.

"Jerry showed an early interest in women and minorities," Mellon said. Since she had been active in the Orange County chapter of the NWPC, she "was asked to go out and recruit women into government." Brown also suggested that Mellon talk to Bird to get ideas for potential candidates. He "thought that she was terribly bright and able. I remember him saying, 'you should meet Rose Bird.'"[3]

By including women and non-Anglos in his administration, Brown strongly signaled his intention to be a very different kind of chief executive than his predecessors. They included his father, Edmund G. "Pat" Brown Sr., who led the state from 1959 to 1967. Pat Brown was a liberal Democrat who thought big, particularly when it came to projects he hoped would make California the envy of the nation. He promoted a massive statewide water project and a vast network of freeways, and was instrumental in shaping a world-class higher education system, "where a young man or woman who has the ability can go from kindergarten through graduate school without paying one cent in tuition."[4]

Pat Brown also opposed the death penalty, appointed liberal judges, and supported minority rights. But as the progeny of a time when few women sought careers outside the home, he was a decided traditionalist in matters involving gender. All of Pat Brown's top appointees were white men, though he did appoint women to some prestigious positions. For example, he appointed Shirley Hufstedler to the Los Angeles Superior Court bench.[5]

People who knew Jerry Brown should not have been surprised at his inclination toward upending tradition. Rose Bird clearly recognized this trait when she agreed to join his administration. "I had a strong feeling that he was going to be different . . . and that it might be exciting to work with him."[6] In fact, Brown had been an iconoclast and rebel for much of his life. He was the third of four children and the only son of Pat and Bernice Brown. The family had deep roots in California, extending back to the 1850s, unusual for a state famous for its vast population of newcomers. Born in April 1938, Jerry spent his childhood in San Francisco as his father worked his way up the political ladder, from district attorney of San Francisco County to California attorney general and finally to governor. While Bird's disadvantaged background had made her extraordinarily cautious, focused, and diligent from a very young age, Jerry Brown's experience was markedly different. As the product of a politically powerful family, and the sole male "heir," he could afford to make mistakes and to change course when the mood struck. He attended a private high school in San Francisco. After graduation, he enrolled at Santa Clara University. A year later, he decided to become a Catholic priest and entered Sacred Heart Novitiate in Los Gatos to train for the priesthood. "Sometimes I'm not really sure I know Jerry," his father told one writer.[7] After three years at Sacred Heart, he decided he did not want to be a priest after all; he wanted "to get into the world."[8]

He never cited capital punishment as a catalyst for his decision to abandon the monastic life, but he had urged his father in spring 1960 to commute the death sentence of Caryl Chessman, convicted of kidnapping in 1948 and still awaiting execution. Jerry undoubtedly understood he could be a more effective advocate for ideas and issues he cared about outside the seminary.[9]

Back in the world, Jerry found that doors opened easily. He was, after all, the governor's son. UC Berkeley was just fifty miles up the road from Los Gatos, and in fall 1960 Jerry enrolled. He moved into International House, where he met Bird. Following graduation in 1961, he headed east to Yale Law School. He was twenty-six when he completed his studies at Yale in 1964.

Two years earlier, Pat Brown had appointed a longtime friend, labor lawyer Mathew Tobriner, as an associate justice on the California Supreme Court. Tobriner had written a letter of recommendation for Jerry to Yale, and following graduation, he asked Jerry to become his law clerk. After a brief stint as an attorney, Jerry's interest in the law began to wane. "I didn't find the problem solving that interesting, that exciting, or that challenging," he said. Politics was the family business, and he was willing to start at the bottom. In 1969 he ran for, and won, a seat on the Los Angeles Community College District Board. Soon he was on the fast-track. In 1970 voters elected him California's secretary of state. Four years later, at the age of thirty-five and with limited political experience, he decided to run for governor. Money and media attention soon followed.

In November 1966 Pat Brown had been defeated in his bid for a third term as governor. By the mid-1960s, Brown's brand of liberalism had come under attack from a public grown weary of campus protests over Vietnam and exploding racial violence in places like Watts, an impoverished, racially charged section of Los Angeles. Ronald Reagan, a Republican and political neophyte, had successfully harnessed voter anger, branding Brown a "big spender" who "coddled" privileged students by giving them a virtually free education while ignoring the concerns of ordinary, hard-working citizens.

By 1974 Reagan was nearing the end of his second term as governor. He had his eye on a bigger stage—national politics—and Pat Brown, practicing law in Los Angeles, leaned on his former associates and contacts to back his son for the Democratic gubernatorial nomination. Jerry soon proved his political mettle. His idiosyncratic personality drew as much attention as his political platform. He would not "cut ribbons, kiss babies, christen freighters . . . give out pens at bill signings or ride in motorcades."[10] These were things his father had reveled in doing. Since Jerry was unmarried, some Republicans subtly suggested that he might be gay. The charge failed to stick and was inaccurate to boot, though other observations—that he was "flaky," had a short attention span, and was inordinately self-centered—dogged him for decades.[11]

Brown's "flakiness" did not extend to the women he appointed to high positions in his administration, however. His decision to include them can be viewed from several perspectives. As a product of the 1960s, and that decade's emphasis on breaking down ethnic and gender barriers, he honestly thought women deserved high-level jobs; he wanted to declare his independence from the political establishment, including his father; and female appointees could serve a useful purpose, since they would undoubtedly work overtime to advance Brown's political agenda and be grateful for the opportunity. When their diligence paid off, they would be quick to give Brown the credit. When his agenda proved unpopular, he could count on the women to quietly take the heat.

His decision to appoint Bird to head the Agriculture and Services Agency was extraordinarily significant, whatever his reasons for doing so. Agriculture was the largest entity in state government, and the agency's reach extended far beyond farming. The "and services" portion encompassed eleven separate departments, some of which seemed to be at cross purposes with others, or at least catered to different constituencies. They included food and agriculture, industrial relations, consumer affairs, the Franchise Tax Board, the State Personnel Board, and the Public Employee and Teacher Retirement systems.

Agriculture was the agency's preeminent focus, however. In the 1970s, as today, food crops represented a significant slice of California's economy. The state's mild climate and long growing seasons enabled virtually every region to cultivate at least one product for export. California produced almost all of the country's artichokes, avocados, olives, and tomatoes, and many of its other fruits and vegetables. It produced nearly 60 percent of all the domestic wine sold in the United States. As a result, agribusiness had long enjoyed unparalleled political clout in the state.[12]

Farmers and ranchers donated to campaigns, sponsored and promoted legislation, fought against regulations, and set their own terms on hiring and working conditions for the vast population of migrant workers who planted and harvested their crops. Efforts to improve working conditions for farmworkers over the decades had been met with violence and arrests amid charges that organizers were communists.

Any proposed legislation nearly always died before it could be passed by lawmakers. In 1960, for example, agribusiness interests beat back an effort to include farmworkers in a proposed minimum wage bill. One grower got so "carried away with the debate, he claimed the proposal . . . had been conceived in hate."[13] Even liberal politicians like Pat Brown feared reprisals from growers if they appeared to favor farmworker rights, though they privately sympathized with the laborers.[14]

In ordinary times, growers might have expected to continue with business as usual. But political sentiment was shifting toward farmworkers by the time Jerry Brown became governor. This might seem counterintuitive, since public tolerance for government-sanctioned civil rights efforts was waning, but California's population growth occurred mostly in cities. Urbanites had little emotional investment in agricultural politics; they just wanted reasonably priced and easily accessible food. Additionally, the emergence of attractive, media-savvy activists such as Dolores Huerta and Cesar Chavez raised the profile of farmworkers. Both Huerta and Chavez had led community organizations in rural areas of California. In the mid-1960s they joined forces with other workers' groups to create the United Farm Workers of America (UFWA).[15]

Both came from backgrounds that rendered them particularly effective spokespeople for what came to be called "la Causa." They were young, articulate, and committed to bettering conditions for farm laborers. Huerta had been a teacher in Stockton, California, where she worked with migrant families, and she was the daughter of farm laborers. Chavez had worked in the fields from a young age and had firsthand experience of the deprivation and degradation migrants experienced—hours of "stooped" labor for low pay, lack of clean water and toilets, traveling from farm to farm, living in shacks with no plumbing and unsafe working conditions, constantly being sprayed with pesticides.

"We had no money at all and had to live on the outskirts of town and under a bridge and dry creek," Chavez told Studs Terkel for *Hard Times*, Terkel's oral history of the Depression.[16] He told another writer that "probably one of the worst jobs was [harvesting] broccoli. We were in mud and water up to our necks and our hands got frozen. We had to cut it and throw it on a trailer; cut and throw, cut and throw." This went on for three months, December to March. Afterward, the workers moved on to harvesting other crops on other farms, an endless cycle of spirit-killing, mind-deadening toil with little downtime.[17]

The UFWA, like other civil rights organizations, utilized strikes and sit-ins and espoused nonviolent tactics. The group first captured public attention in 1965, when it joined a strike organized by the mostly Filipino farmworker group Agriculture Workers Organizing Committee (AWOC) against grape growers in Delano. By the 1970s, UFWA and AWOC had merged and added a new strategy—boycotts against grape and lettuce growers and secondary boycotts that targeted grocery stores and other outlets that carried and sold the produce. The boycotts, particularly secondary boycotts, devastated growers financially, leading many to decide to drop their opposition to organizing workers.

To thwart the more "radical" UFWA, however, farmers turned to the International Brotherhood of Teamsters, an established union under the jurisdiction of the National Labor Relations Board that forbade secondary boycotts.[18] Farmers believed—accurately—that Teamsters would prove friendlier to grower interests. Teamsters had never tried to organize farmworkers before the 1970s but entered the fields with a vengeance, unleashing a brutal war on the UFWA. Teamsters patrolled the fields, beating UFWA organizers with clubs, bats, brass knuckles, and pieces of irrigation pipe. They ran down UFWA members with cars. The UFWA retaliated by burning down storage facilities.[19]

By 1974 the struggle had exhausted both growers and labor organizers, many of whom pronounced themselves ready to accept collective bargaining rights. Both sides hoped to control the process and its outcome. Growers hoped to ban secondary boycotts. UFWA leaders had long resisted legislative remedies, viewing them as unduly bureaucratic, but Jerry Brown's election signaled new possibilities, as did the election to the state legislature of men like Howard Berman and Richard Alatorre, Los Angeles Democrats and farmworker allies.

Brown strongly supported farmworkers and had marched on picket lines with them. As secretary of state, he blocked a progrower ballot initiative after determining that many signatures had been obtained illegally. The first order of business of his new administration, he announced in his January 6, 1975, inaugural address, would be to compel growers to deal fairly with their workers.[20]

As secretary of the Agriculture and Services Agency, Rose Bird stood on the front line of this battle. Brown would remain in the background, while she led negotiations certain to fuel acrimony, disagreements, and resentment among all parties. As Brown arm-twisted, she would shepherd whatever bill emerged through both houses of the state legislature and to Brown's desk. Finally, she would work to write regulations to implement the law. At some level, Bird must have realized that taking a lead role in implementing such a landmark agenda was bound to make her powerful enemies.

In fact, agribusiness leaders had expressed stunned outrage when Brown announced her appointment; the position of agriculture secretary had historically gone to a farmer no matter which party was in power. Eugene Chappie, an agribusiness supporter and Republican assembly member, undoubtedly summed up the attitude many growers held about Bird when he claimed that she "didn't know the difference between a cucumber and a kumquat. She didn't know what a labor contractor was. She was just totally out of her element."[21]

Bird's seemingly flippant attitude in her first published interview seemed designed to irritate growers further. The reporter took note of the fact that she was the first woman to hold a cabinet position in California and asked if she had any experience or "special interest in agrarian matters." Bird replied, "No, I really hadn't. I did work at Stanford University, but I take it that's not the right kind of farm" (Stanford was sometimes affectionately dubbed "the farm"). Growers might have been alarmed, but few others paid much attention at this point, since Bird was not yet deemed interesting enough to garner much media attention.[22]

Bird's first task before starting work was to get her bearings in Sacramento. She had worked briefly in California's capital in the early 1960s, as a Ford Foundation fellow, but she had been only a temporary resident. In 1975 she was an important member of the Brown administration. At that point, California's capital was still a decade away from explosive growth. Later, suburbs would surround the city, marching relentlessly outward until no plot of land seemed safe from development, but when Rose Bird took up residency, Sacramento still had a somewhat rural ambience.

Driving east from the San Francisco Bay Area, motorists passed through nearly fifty miles of flat farmland—fields of alfalfa and wheat, herds of dairy cows, stands of walnut and almond trees, and acres of tomatoes and rice. A dozen miles from Sacramento, the city's skyline emerged like a shimmering mirage. California's capital sits at the junction of two major rivers—the Sacramento and the American—at the northern end of the San Joaquin Valley. The region bakes with heat in summer and wears a shroud of heavy fog in winter.

The surrounding areas may have been rural, but Sacramento's primary industry was government. State employees and those tangentially connected to politics—lawyers, public relations experts, lobbyists, analysts, journalists—composed a tight-knit coterie, virtually all men. One writer dubbed Sacramento's 1970s ambience a "locker-room political culture."[23] The men gathered for long lunches and after hours at downtown bars and restaurants such as Frank Fats and Poseys. One watering hole entertained its male clientele with a huge fish tank featuring a woman swimming inside. In this environment, women remained in the lowest-level political jobs where they mostly were seen and not heard. In 1975, for example, only three women served in the eighty-member state assembly and none in the forty-member state senate. The next year, Rose Ann Vuich, a Democrat from California's rural Central Valley, became the first woman elected to the senate. She kept a bell on her desk and each time a colleague began a speech with the word "Gentlemen," she rang it.[24]

Vuich's pointedly humorous approach to gender slights differed significantly from the way Bird approached such matters, which was generally to put her head down and work harder. As secretary of agriculture, however, Bird faced challenges far more difficult than Vuich, who was, after all, equal in stature to her male colleagues. Bird oversaw the work of hundreds of employees, many accomplished men not used to taking directions from a woman.

Male cabinet secretaries and department heads could follow the example of Jerry Brown, who defused tensions and smoothed over political disagreements at numerous and sometimes raucous late-night drinking sessions. Brown may have been an ascetic, living minimally in a spare downtown apartment, sleeping on the floor on a box spring and mattress with sheets and blankets borrowed from Napa State Hospital, and driving a battered Plymouth, but as he recalled much later, he spent many nights—and early mornings—closing down Sacramento bars with his contemporaries.[25] Bird would not have been welcomed at such gatherings, even if she had sought to participate. Instead, after a long day at work, she went home to her small apartment. Many weekends, she drove home to Palo Alto, where she had purchased a small home.

When she needed advice, she turned to old friends and acquaintances—Gordon Winton, for example. She had worked for Winton as a Ford Foundation fellow. He had left the state legislature by 1975 and worked as a lobbyist; Bird met him occasionally for lunch, where she "asked questions about procedure and dealing with the legislature." Winton had carried farm bills as a lawmaker and proved to be an invaluable source of information. Bird acknowledged to Winton and others that she initially felt overwhelmed by the immense scope of her responsibilities. "I'm trying to get a handle on all the different departments," she said in one early interview. James Stearns, her predecessor, sympathized with her predicament. He described Bird as "pleasant, intelligent, very much interested but overawed at the magnitude of state government. Not intimidated, but overawed."[26]

Many, if not most, cabinet secretaries would have looked to established politicians for advice on hiring assistants, but Bird was not part of the political elite, not comfortable in the role of supplicant, and (as soon became apparent) suspicious of strangers. Thus she reached back to Santa Clara and Stanford to recruit her former intern and law student, Stephen Buehl, as her chief aide.

Over the years, Buehl came to be ubiquitous, ever on duty as Bird's gatekeeper and protector. If one wanted to meet with Bird, he or she first had to go through Buehl, who then sat nearby in meetings, silently taking notes on every conversation. Bird never explained why she required Buehl's hovering presence, but it soon came to irritate her colleagues, who viewed it as evidence of her untrusting and controlling nature.[27]

Growers who feared that Bird would advance a progressive agenda favoring farmworkers did not have long to wait. Less than three months after taking office, she announced a ban on the short-handled hoe. Used primarily for weeding and thinning crops, the hoe's handle was only slightly longer than a ruler. It forced workers to bend from the waist, facing downward as they walked between rows. After a decade or so using the hoe, many workers could not stand up straight and suffered from spinal injuries. Among those who had worked with it was Cesar Chavez, who estimated that perhaps half of all farmworkers in California had used the hoe.[28] Farm labor advocates had long targeted the use of the hoe as excessively cruel, and many growers had abandoned the practice. But producers of beets and lettuce said they needed the shorter implements. Additionally, some growers argued that their workers used long-handled hoes as leaning posts, making it look to onlookers as if they were working when they actually were resting.

In the early 1970s, attorneys for California Rural Legal Assistance, an antipoverty group, petitioned the California Industrial Safety Board to outlaw use of the short-handled hoe, but the board refused to do so. CRLA took its case to the state supreme court and was awaiting action when Jerry Brown appointed Bird agriculture secretary. The safety board fell within her jurisdiction, and she prevailed on its members to reconsider. They agreed, declaring the use of the hoe to be "a violation of safety" regulations.[29]

Bird admitted to journalists that "there may be some additional costs" involved in eliminating the use of the hoe, but she was decidedly unsympathetic. Costs, she declared, were "insignificant in comparison to the suffering to be prevented." CRLA attorneys later acknowledged Bird's contribution to their cause. "A strong supporter of workers' rights," she "worked assiduously to pave the bureaucratic road toward a formal ban," one CRLA leader said.[30]

The effort to craft a farm labor bill proved much more daunting. Brown assembled a team that included Bird, several other top aides, and Democratic assemblyman Howard Berman, as well as other lawmakers. Brown tasked Bird with meeting all the affected groups to determine whether such a bill was even feasible, given the level of acrimony among the parties. She drove around California, interviewing farmworkers, growers, and Teamsters representatives. She met with legislators and attorneys at sessions where participants brainstormed how to craft a law that gave all parties enough to keep them involved in the process.

Key to any deal, Bird soon realized, was crafting a compromise on the secondary boycott, which had led markets in states outside California and even other countries to stop buying grapes, lettuce, and wine from targeted growers. Gallo, one of California's largest winemakers, had been hit particularly hard. Farmers wanted legislation to replicate the National Labor Relations Act, enacted in the 1930s, which forbade secondary boycotts. Without them, farmers believed they could "negotiate with the union [on] terms more favorable to the employer."

UFWA leaders viewed secondary boycotts as crucial to the union's ability to compel growers to bargain honestly, and they wanted union elections to be held at the peak of harvest, when more workers would be available to vote on representation. In spite of backing from the Brown administration, Chavez—who by the mid-1970s had emerged as the face and voice of the farmworker movement nationally—was a reluctant participant in the legislative process. He feared losing the grassroots "social movement aspect of the UFWA and getting bogged down in ... a lawyer's game that threatened to sap the power the movement had worked so hard to build."[31]

The Teamsters were also reluctant participants, believing that the deck would be stacked against them, since Brown and Bird seemed to so obviously favor Chavez and the UFWA. Despite the seemingly insurmountable obstacles, in late April 1975 Bird told the governor she believed a deal was possible and that all parties could be convinced to participate. To get to this point, Bird had to promise the Teamsters, who had contracts with more than four hundred farmers, covering fifty thousand workers, that any legislation would not automatically invalidate their agreements. Existing contracts would remain in place until new worker elections, she promised. By May, all parties had begun intense negotiations.

Negotiating sessions often took place late at night and early in the morning. LeRoy Chatfield, an ally of Cesar Chavez, remembered weeks of "three or four meetings going on at the same time. These things took place at 2 or 3 in the morning and went on for hours and hours and hours." At one meeting "there must have been 30, 40 people there sitting on chairs, on couches, on the floor." Brown hosted some meetings, either at his home in Laurel Canyon, north of Los Angeles, or in his sparsely furnished Sacramento apartment. Bird carefully wrote down ideas and suggestions in "neat spiral binders" and then moved among the various groups, trying to find consensus. When final agreement came, participants felt like they had "been through the ringer.... It was a dramatic, historical moment," Chatfield later said.[32]

By spring 1975, Bird was no longer "overawed." Any reticence or concerns over her ability to handle such a sprawling agency had disappeared. "I remember being in a meeting one time and she flounced in," recalled legislative counsel Bion Gregory. She wore what appeared to be "a pair of . . . Chinese pajamas. They had the mandarin collar and very loose fitting . . . baggy trousers and her hair was pulled back and tied with a piece of yarn. I mean yarn, just a plain old yellow piece of yarn. She pontificated on something and then left and somebody made a comment like, 'Well at least with Rose . . . you get the pure unvarnished, not truth because everybody's truth is just a little bit different, but pure unvarnished opinion.'"[33]

Some of Brown's aides were grateful to Bird for her directness. The governor disliked meetings and "linear thinking," and he frequently wandered off topic, became easily distracted, and engaged in meandering discussions. Bird "had . . . a sort of Yankee panache that could shut down debate with a few well-chosen words," said a colleague. Once, Brown and some aides were conducting a spirited conversation about a political demonstration scheduled to take place at the state capitol. "The issue was whether providing toilets would make the demonstrators so comfortable" they would refuse to leave.

"The debate had gone on for an hour, when Bird walked in. 'People have to go to the bathroom, give them toilets,' she said. That was it, end of discussion."[34] She also stood up to Brown on financial matters. Early on, a budget shortfall led the governor to suggest postponing state employee raises. "Rose singlehandedly threw a fit," said Marty Morgenstern, who headed the office of employee relations. "She . . . made a speech that it was unethical, that state employees weren't a bunch of fat-cat bureaucrats, but little people."[35]

Like other cabinet members, Bird often became frustrated with Brown's haphazard approach to governing, which she viewed as "a technique of keeping everyone around you off base because people around you don't know what you're going to do. You have control over almost uncontrollable situations because everyone else is thrown off base. . . . Initially I was told to do everything through the governor, but I could never get an answer and finally came to the understanding that he wanted you to make your own decisions." At one point, she decided to respond in kind. When Brown contacted her—usually days or weeks after she first contacted him—she "made it a point to be less available to him just to let him know it's a two-way street."[36]

The "genius" of Brown's system had to do with the issue of accountability, Bird said. "If you do something wrong then it is your fault. After some period of time, increasingly I found I couldn't work within the system as an organized person who is predictable. . . . If you're looking for positive reinforcement, go work for someone else."[37]

Her take-charge approach did not sit well with everyone. Farmers long used to deference from politicians and their aides resented what they viewed as Bird's brusque manner, directness, and impatience with dithering. Grower and state assemblyman Eugene Chappie undoubtedly spoke for many agribusiness interests when he accused Bird "and her people" of using "state vehicles to transport Chavez and his terrorists around." When growers tried to argue with her, she dismissed their concerns, Chappie said. "You absolutely could not get her to sit down and reason and listen to the laments of the ag[riculture] community. She just had her mind made up and that was that."[38]

Even people who liked Bird and agreed with her politics sometimes found her difficult to deal with. Some Brown staff members took to calling her "the nun" for her ascetic lifestyle and no-nonsense persona. Donald Burns, another Brown cabinet member, told a reporter that "whenever she disagreed about something, she would personalize the disagreement. There would be the suggestion, and sometimes it was pretty explicit, that if you disagreed with her you were selling out."[39]

J. Anthony Kline, another Brown administration official who later became an appellate judge, said, "There is somewhat of a stiff-necked quality about Rose. She could be a bit self-righteous and was sometimes unduly suspicious of the motives of others. She tended to see people as either for her or against her, and I think she thought that many more people were against her than actually were." Over time, however, "her suspicions did generate animosities and thus became in some sense a self-fulfilling prophesy."[40]

Bird tamped down her brusqueness and suspicious nature during intense negotiations over the farm labor bill, however. In early May, she appeared before a state senate committee to announce that a deal had been reached. "It's impossible," declared Republican state senator Lou Cusanovich. Bird assured him it was not and that proposed legislation would be forthcoming. A spokesman for the Central California Farmers Association spoke admiringly about the agreement. "The governor's bill is a hell of a lot better than we expected him to propose." Nonetheless, farmers still objected "to the boycott issue," which they hoped would be resolved in their favor by the legislature.[41]

The bill was introduced during an "extraordinary" legislative session in May 1975, which allowed the governor to "fast-track" it. This meant the provisions of what came to be called the Agriculture Labor Relations Act (ALRA) would go into effect immediately after passage, rather than the following January. Since September was "peak harvest" time, farmworkers could almost immediately participate in elections to determine representation. Democratic state senator John Dunlap was designated to carry SB813, which was introduced first in the state senate before moving on to the state assembly. "I was merely the author of it, in the sense that I was the person whom the governor requested to carry it," Dunlap said much later. The bill "was actually drafted under the direction of Rose Bird."[42]

Initially Bird told lawmakers she would accept no changes to the settlement she and other members of Brown's team had negotiated, a declaration that caused head-shaking amazement among veteran legislators not accustomed to taking orders from a political novice, a woman no less, who was not yet forty years old. "I was afraid the whole thing would unravel," she said much later, expressing some chagrin at the recollection of her brashness. However, the insistence on no changes actually came from Brown himself. Ultimately, Bird and Brown had to accept several amendments as the legislation went through several committees before going to the floor for final votes in both chambers. Late in May, after defeating an effort to exempt farmworkers whose religious affiliations forbade union participation, lawmakers in both houses passed the bill by lopsided margins.[43]

In early June, Brown signed the ALRA. It mandated secret ballot elections, with petitions filed when 50 percent of workers agreed they wanted to be represented by a union. Elections were to be held within seven days after certification of petitions and during peak harvest time, when more farmworkers were available to vote. All parties needed to bargain in good faith or face claims of unfair labor practices. Much of the act seemed to favor the UFWA, but Bird and lawmakers managed to finesse the secondary boycott issue. The ALRA allowed the practice but only by unions certified via elections to represent workers.

Unions that lost elections could not organize secondary boycotts against businesses purchasing products from growers whose workers had voted against that particular union. And they could not organize secondary boycotts against farms whose workers voted not to join a union at all, a choice mandated by the ALRA. The new law gave Teamsters something as well: it was limited specifically to agricultural laborers.

Teamsters had feared the legislation would also sweep in construction workers and machinists who worked on farms.

The legislation also set up a five-member Agriculture Labor Relations Board (ALRB) to oversee elections and handle complaints of unfair labor practices. Immediately after passage, Bird gave an interview to the *New York Times*. She allowed a bit of pride to seep into her comments. "Traditionally, farm labor has been organized from the top down. . . . We wanted to change that. We wanted to give farm workers themselves the power. We wanted secret ballot elections to encourage democratization among farm workers." She called secret ballot elections a "key institution in American life." By giving farmworkers this right, "we overcome the question of legitimacy which has plagued farm union organizations here."[44]

In July Brown named five men to the new ALRB, at salaries of $42,500 annually. Four were attorneys. They included Joseph Grodin, a close friend of Justice Mathew Tobriner. Bird and Grodin were not acquainted at this point, but within a decade their professional fates would become inextricably entwined. Brown appointed Roger Mahony, a Catholic bishop from Fresno, chair of the newly formed board. Bird proclaimed all of the men "fair minded people who are willing to work up to 20 hours a day to make the law an effective one. It's going to take that kind of hard work and dedication." Within eighteen months, Bird would have reason to see Mahony in a different light. Brown also named Walter Kintz, an attorney from the National Labor Relations Board in Washington DC, as temporary executive director of the ALRB. Bird immediately went to work with Kintz to craft regulations implementing the new law.

The final language of SB813 stated: "In enacting this legislation, the people of the State of California seek to ensure peace in the agriculture fields by guaranteeing justice for all agriculture workers and stability in labor relations."[45] The hoped-for peace never materialized. The law took effect on August 28, 1975, and immediately hit major speed bumps. Both Teamsters and UFWA representatives swarmed into the fields to sign up workers. The ALRB was deluged with demands for elections. By the end of the first month, the board had hired ninety-one employees to handle the workload—"a great deal more than anticipated," Kintz said.

In addition to arranging elections, the ALRB also had to handle an onslaught of complaints of unfair labor practices. Within five months of its creation, the ALRB had overseen 400 elections; the UFWA prevailed in 195, Teamsters in 120. No union won a majority in the rest. After seven months, ALRB had run through its entire budget for the year.

The legislature eventually agreed to provide more money, but any goodwill the participants had developed during the negotiation process quickly vanished. Brown said the problems suggested "the limits of government." By 1976 his attention had shifted elsewhere, and he declared his intention to run for president of the United States. He won a few primaries, but his campaign soon fizzled out and he turned his attention back to California, though not to farmworker issues.[46]

Bird's attention shifted to other matters as well. Her months of intense focus on farmworker legislation had kept her largely aloof from subordinates, and some employees soon began to chafe under what they viewed as her controlling management style. Brown had appointed department heads, yet they usually had to go through Bird to get to the governor, even though they aimed to further his agenda. Luther "Tim" Wallace, an economist at UC Berkeley, headed the state Food and Agriculture Department.

Wallace eagerly took on the task of implementing one of Brown's pet projects: placing consumers and regular citizens on the boards of professional organizations, including the California bar association and grower groups designed to market farm products. The governor believed that professionals often positioned themselves as "superior" to ordinary citizens, and Brown wanted to bring them down a notch. In an interview, Wallace told one reporter that Brown sought "qualified, concerned citizens" to "help shape the policies" of agriculture marketing boards.[47]

Bird also believed strongly in citizen membership on professional boards and may not have appreciated Wallace's taking on the role of spokesman for the issue. Wallace may have headed the Agriculture Department, but she headed the overall agency, and thus she was Wallace's boss. She soon tightened control over messaging, and Wallace ultimately resigned.[48]

The resignation fueled debate over what some inside government began dubbing Bird's "turf consciousness" and unwillingness to delegate. Not everyone agreed, however. Don Vial headed the Industrial Relations Department. He helped Bird in her campaign to end grower use of the short-handled hoe and stood next to her as she publicly announced its elimination. Vial became a valuable ally and maintained a friendship with Bird for years after both had left the Agriculture and Services Agency.[49] But disagreement with others persisted.

Bird also experienced problems with heads of other departments not under her control. Brown had appointed Preble Stolz, Bird's former law professor at Berkeley, as head of the Office of Planning and Research, and he assigned Stolz and Bird to work together on projects involving land policy. They tussled over a variety of issues. At one point, Bird sent Stolz a plastic stop sign—hinting none too subtly that he needed to back off. She said it was a joke, but "I didn't think it was very funny," Stolz said later. At the time such tiffs seemed minor, but some would come back to haunt her.[50]

Bird's difficulties with colleagues did not affect her relationship with Jerry Brown, though she still often expressed frustration at his reluctance to make decisions. By late 1975, she was widely considered his most influential cabinet member. When President Gerald Ford visited Sacramento in September 1975, Bird sat in on meetings. Some Brown acolytes attributed her status to her willingness to tell the governor when, as one observer put it, "something was a load of crap." Brown obviously respected Bird's counsel. In March 1976 he asked her to participate when he interviewed Adriana Gianturco for the job of California's transportation director.

Bird "had a real track record of accomplishment," Gianturco said much later. "She was somebody whose judgment about things the governor trusted." Gianturco, like Bird, was a self-acknowledged "take-charge individual." Also like Bird, she soon discovered that not everyone in state government appreciated this trait in female bosses.[51]

By spring 1976, Bird had begun receiving wider attention. In April a reporter for *California Journal*, a monthly magazine focused on state government and politics, contacted her. Would she be willing to sit down for an interview? Bird agreed. At exactly the appointed moment, she crossed the lobby of the Agriculture Department to greet the reporter. "Do you want coffee?" she asked. This was quickly followed by the information that she herself chose not to drink tea, coffee, or alcoholic beverages. To this point Bird had been willing, even eager, to meet with reporters for stories focused on her efforts as part of a larger group doing important work.

She was taken aback to discover, however, that this particular article would feature her alone. She had thought, she told the interviewer, that the story would include all of the cabinet secretaries. "Oh, no, I don't want a story [just] on me. I'm not worth a story," she insisted. Then the woman known for being blunt proceeded to lecture the reporter: "People in politics should be written about for their accomplishments, not personalities." She said that she had spent the weeks following the ALRA's passage working ten- and twelve-hour days developing relationships with department heads, though she left out details of conflicts and disagreements. She hoped to use her position to advocate for an end to "useless boards," she said, and to streamline government. And she had an idea for how to finance elections through income taxes.[52]

The *California Journal* was the first publication to experience what many others would soon learn: Rose Bird was a frustrating interview subject. She was willing to talk about herself, but only in an extremely limited way and in general terms. However, her choice of revelations could be interesting. She said, for example, that she did her own shopping: "You should keep up with the price of butter." Left unasked or answered was why a relatively anonymous bureaucrat—at least to many readers of the *California Journal*—would believe she should not do her own shopping.

She also revealed that two months earlier, in February 1976, at the age of thirty-nine, she had undergone a modified radical mastectomy on her right breast. She had spent little time recuperating, returning to work less than two weeks after the operation. She decided to forgo chemotherapy or radiation and to attack her cancer via a strictly vegetarian diet and large doses of vitamin C. Her willingness to reveal this information seems particularly surprising given her extreme reticence in personal matters. Additionally, in the 1970s, only a few individuals—actor and activist Shirley Temple Black and First Lady Betty Ford, for example—talked publicly about breast cancer.[53]

Since Bird originally had planned to be a journalist, her refusal to at least appear friendly and accessible to interviewers seems surprising, particularly because her early heroes had been reporters who relentlessly pursued their subjects and specialized in speaking truth to power. Such reporters probed for weaknesses but could be at least somewhat defanged with flattery, the appearance of accessibility, and a casual, approachable demeanor.

Brown knew how the system worked and reveled in it. He "eats journalists for breakfast," declared one aide. "He knows the game. And in a funny way he's more here when he's on national TV than when he's in the room." These were not qualities Bird possessed. She refused to play the game or to humanize herself via anecdotes or friendly banter. Instead, she often came across as humorless, defensive, or preachy, intimating that any personal questions represented an inappropriate breach of her privacy. In response, writers felt no obligation to present her in a flattering light, though most stories did reflect her complexity as a smart, dedicated woman who struggled to do the right thing but also was intense, suspicious, and exceedingly controlling.[54]

The *California Journal*, for example, revealed that Bird insisted that everyone on her staff call her "Rose," that she loved to bring baked goods from home to share with her employees, and that she occasionally socialized with her aides on weekends, attending movies and roller-skating through her Sacramento neighborhood. But she was also "deliberately analytical and likes to be in control. She lacks Brown's ability to tolerate dissent." Ironically, Brown was in fact not much better at handling dissent, but he was a much savvier interview subject. The writer also noted that Bird kept a tight rein on staff and was ill at ease with new people. She quoted an acquaintance of Bird's who said she was "not comfortable with unknown quantities." Bird agreed that "it's useful in my position to have people you know and trust." Few were women, however. Of nine department heads hired by Bird, only one appointment went to a woman.[55]

Nonetheless, feminists across the country viewed Bird as an example of a successful woman who lived and worked according to her own terms. They promoted her as a candidate for even higher office. For example, when Democrat Jimmy Carter won the presidency in November 1976, Bird was frequently cited as a potential cabinet choice. *Ms.* magazine suggested her for U.S. agriculture secretary. Other *Ms.* suggestions included Colorado congresswoman Patricia Schroeder as defense secretary; Julia Montgomery Walsh, a member of the board of directors for a brokerage firm, as labor secretary; and Columbia University law professor Ruth Bader Ginsburg for the U.S. Supreme Court. Carter did not take any of *Ms.*'s suggestions, though he did appoint three women to his cabinet: Juanita Morris Kreps as commerce secretary, Patricia Roberts Harris as secretary of health and human services, and California judge Shirley Hufstedler as secretary of education.[56]

Shortly after Carter's inauguration in January 1977, feminists cheered the news that Rose Bird might be headed for a new and even more prestigious job. Donald Wright, chief justice of the California Supreme Court, had announced his retirement; rumor had it that Brown intended to name Bird as Wright's replacement. She had just turned forty and had never been a judge, though neither had three other prominent California jurists: the late U.S. Supreme Court chief justice Earl Warren and two former California Supreme Court chief justices—Roger Traynor and Phil Gibson.

Brown's friends and aides urged him to forestall controversy by naming Bird an associate justice and elevating Justice Stanley Mosk to chief justice. Mosk had been appointed to the court by Pat Brown and had long yearned for the top job. Nonetheless, on February 12, 1977, Brown announced Bird as his choice for chief justice, a job that paid $66,839 annually. Her years in his cabinet "writing legislation, seeing it through the Legislature and carrying out its intent" gave her a "real world kind of experience that will be valuable in making the judgments a Supreme Court Justice must make," Brown told reporters. Asked why he had settled on someone with no judicial experience and a reputation as "difficult" for a job that was high profile and demanded collegiality, the governor reminded interviewers of his intention "to shake things up. I look at appointments as a way to get some new blood into the system," he said. Putting a woman atop one of the nation's most prominent courts most definitely qualified on that score.[57]

Appointments Secretary Carlotta Mellon believed "there were a couple of reasons" Brown chose to appoint Bird to the top court job. "One, I think he had an extremely high regard for [her] personally, for her scholarship, for her judicial temperament, for her knowledge, and for her mind.... I also think it was partly, 'if I am going to do it, why don't I do it all the way?'... I think he was surprised as many of us were with the reaction."[58]

Bird said she was stunned but "deeply honored" by the nomination. "The California Supreme Court is considered the most outstanding supreme court in the United States." She added that she saw the court as "collegial rather than hierarchical." She would just be one of seven justices—equal to her colleagues but not above them, she added. Bird would not be the first woman in the country to sit as chief justice of a state supreme court, however. Lorna Lockwood served two stints heading the Arizona Supreme Court, beginning in 1965. Susie Sharp of North Carolina became an associate justice of that state's high court in 1962 and chief justice in 1974.[59]

Brown also announced the appointment of the California high court's first African American justice, Wiley Manuel, to replace retiring justice Raymond Sullivan. Manuel had been a longtime legal advisor to Republican attorney general Evelle Younger and was said to be "stunned" by the appointment. Brown had named Manuel to the state appeals court just a year earlier. Before either could become justices, however, they would have to win approval from the Commission on Judicial Appointments. California utilized a system wherein nominees appeared before the commission, composed of the state's chief justice, the attorney general, and the presiding appeals court judge.[60]

Bird's nomination drew national attention. *Newsweek* lauded her ability to cut "to the core of an issue" and noted that, as chief judicial officer of California, she would be in charge of 264 courts and 1,160 judges.[61] The *New York Times* noted her reputation as "an outstanding appellate lawyer who has demonstrated a flair for writing legislation." In a telephone interview with the *Times*, Bird said, "My role model was my mother, who had to work hard all her life while raising a family." Two reporters asked Bird whether she considered herself a feminist, a natural question considering the pathbreaking nature of her appointment. Bird told the *New York Times* that she did "not consider herself a feminist, although she hopes her success will encourage other women."[62]

She tried to finesse the issue with the *San Francisco Chronicle*. "I don't know quite what you mean by a feminist," she said. "My great hope is that if I am able to serve, I would do a good job and in that sense, help in the implementation of getting others to look at what have been traditional male roles—professional roles." For a woman who prided herself on being direct, Bird's phrasing seems uncharacteristically cautious, and it reflected a sophisticated understanding of how freighted the term "feminism" was in 1977, a decade after the emergence of women's rights as a mass movement dedicated to eradicating gender discrimination.[63]

The women's movement had achieved many gains in the late 1960s and 1970s, including employment protections, the right to credit, equal treatment in high school and college sports, rape shield laws, and abortion rights. But their achievements had fueled a backlash from individuals and groups who believed that changes were occurring too fast or that changes on some issues—like abortion—should not be occurring at all. For conservative critics, Bird's nomination served as a reminder, recognized or not, of feminism's relentless push for women's equality. Bird wanted to be viewed as an individual, not as a representative of the larger "group called women." But in accepting the nomination as California's chief justice, she was stepping into uncharted territory.[64]

The California Supreme Court had long been viewed as an "activist" body, as *Newsweek* phrased it, willing to take on "cases in areas of changing social conditions." Some of them involved gender. Two months before Bird's appointment, for example, justices determined that an unmarried "woman who had been living with a man for six years could pursue financial claims against her former lover as if they had had a [marriage] contract." Few people were willing to acknowledge it, but at least at the beginning, much of the reaction to Rose Bird had to do with how people felt about a woman willing to speak truth to power no matter what the consequences. Whether Bird called herself a "feminist" was entirely irrelevant.[65]

The Most Innovative Judiciary 3

In 1948 Sylvester Davis and Andrea Perez, both in their late twenties, drove to the County Administration Building in downtown Los Angeles to take out a marriage license. The clerk asked the couple to wait while he talked to his supervisor. A few minutes later, he returned and informed them that, regretfully, he could not issue the license, since Davis was African American and Perez was Caucasian. California laws, like those in other states at the time, explicitly forbade "marriages of white persons with Negroes, Mongolians, members of the Malay race, or mulattoes."[1]

Davis and Perez filed suit, arguing that the Catholic Church, of which both partners were members, had no objection to the marriage, so why should the state stand in the way? In October 1948 the California Supreme Court agreed. Writing for the majority in the case called *Perez v. Sharp*, Associate Justice Roger Traynor declared: "Since the right to marry is the right to join in marriage with the person of one's choice, a statute that prohibits an individual from marrying a member of a race other than his own restricts the scope of his choice." Constitutional guarantees of equal protection mandated that laws could not be based on "arbitrary classifications of groups or races," Traynor added.

Associate Justice Jesse Carter went even further, declaring it his "considered opinion that the statutes here involved are the product of ignorance, prejudice and intolerance." Two months later Davis and

Perez exchanged vows. It took nearly two more decades before the U.S. Supreme Court, in the case *Loving v. Virginia*, eliminated the ban on interracial marriages nationally.[2]

The court that Rose Bird hoped to join had long been widely recognized as the nation's most pioneering and prestigious state judicial institution, a reputation built over a thirty-year period. Beginning in the 1940s, the seven-member court broke new ground in a variety of areas, including admissibility of evidence, strict liability, abortion, and the death penalty. Its justices enjoyed international reputations. Chief among them was Traynor, whom the *New York Times* once dubbed "one of the greatest judicial talents never to have sat on the United States Supreme Court." In fact, Traynor's arrival on the court in 1940 heralded the court's rise to national prominence, a situation that might seem somewhat ironic, given the circumstances of his appointment.[3]

Democratic governor Culbert Olson had originally nominated University of California, Berkeley law professor Max Radin to the court, but Radin failed to win confirmation because of what critics deemed his "extreme leftist" views.[4] Traynor, also a professor at Berkeley, specializing in tax law, was Olson's second choice. He easily won confirmation, despite the fact that he had never been a judge. It is hard to imagine Radin as more liberal than Traynor, who within a decade of his arrival had penned several monumentally significant and progressive decisions in civil rights cases.[5]

Traynor was a product of New Deal jurisprudence, which, as one scholar noted, "allowed the expansion of government regulatory powers over the economy while creating a new civil liberties jurisprudence." Traynor himself once explained his judicial philosophy as one in which judges should "descend to the everyday business of life to make ... decisions." Seven years after *Perez v. Sharp*, for example, Traynor wrote a majority opinion that limited the tactics police could use to collect evidence in criminal cases.[6]

Charles H. Cahan was a high-rolling Los Angeles bookmaker. Los Angeles police chief William Parker had declared that he wanted "this son of a bitch in jail" and instructed his officers to use every means necessary to ensure Cahan's arrest and conviction. They happily obliged, breaking into two houses and installing wiretapping machinery. For more than a month, they secretly recorded conversations from listening posts set up in neighborhood garages. At Cahan's trial, officers proudly testified about their actions. Prosecutors won a conviction, but Cahan's lawyers appealed, citing the U.S. Constitution's guarantee of protection against unreasonable searches and seizures.[7]

In April 1955 the state supreme court overturned Cahan's conviction. Traynor's blistering opinion excoriated police tactics. "That officers of the law would break into and enter a home, secrete such a device . . . and listen to the conversations of the occupants for more than a month would be almost incredible if not admitted," he wrote. Such actions represented "flagrant, deliberate and persistent violations of the Fourth Amendment's fundamental right to privacy." It would be another six years before the U.S. Supreme Court reached the same conclusion in the case *Mapp v. Ohio*.[8]

Between 1944 and 1962, the court "sparked a nationwide revolution in product liability law." One case involved a customer injured by a power lathe. Not content to simply rule for the plaintiff, Associate Justice Mathew Tobriner went further, attributing "the consumer's powerlessness" to "a larger 'economic imbalance' that gave big business an unprecedented control over people's lives."[9]

In 1964 Governor Pat Brown elevated Traynor from associate to chief justice and named California attorney general Stanley Mosk to replace Traynor. The court continued on its precedent-setting path. In 1965 it decreed in *Dorado v. California* that defendants had to be advised of their right to counsel at the time of arrest. The case involved Robert Dorado, a prisoner condemned to death for murdering a fellow inmate. At trial he claimed that police coerced him to confess and that he had not been notified of his right to an attorney. The U.S. Supreme Court expanded this doctrine nationally the following year in the case *Miranda v. Arizona*.[10]

In 1969 the California court waded into the murky and turbulent waters of abortion politics with *People v. Belous*, when it overturned the conviction of a doctor who had referred a patient for an abortion in defiance of state law. The decision, written by Associate Justice Raymond Peters, declared that women had a "fundamental right . . . to choose" whether to bear children. The state could regulate the procedure only when it had a "compelling interest" in doing so, he added.[11] The ruling pertained to a single individual, but the *Washington University Law Review* predicted it would have far-reaching consequences, since it "strongly implie[d] that prohibitive abortion laws are per se an impermissible exercise of the state's police powers." Four years later, the U.S. Supreme Court demonstrated the accuracy of that prediction with *Roe v. Wade*, which made abortion legal nationally.[12]

Traynor left the court in 1970. Republican governor Ronald Reagan named Donald Wright, a superior court judge, to replace Traynor as chief justice. If Reagan thought Wright would move the court in a different direction, he was soon sorely disappointed. In February 1972, in the case *People v. Anderson*, Wright wrote the decision eliminating capital punishment in California for a lopsided six-to-one majority. He cited the U.S. Constitution's Eighth Amendment proscription against cruel *and* unusual punishment, and the California Constitution's ban on cruel *or* unusual punishment.

Wright declared that capital punishment "degrades and dehumanizes all who participate in its processes. It is unnecessary to any legitimate goal of the state and is incompatible with the dignity of man and the judicial process." He insisted the ruling was not "grounded in sympathy for those who would commit crimes of violence, but in concern for the society that diminishes itself whenever it takes the life of one of its members." Four months later the U.S. Supreme Court eliminated the death penalty nationally.[13]

Finally, in 1976, the year before Rose Bird's appointment, California justices ruled that partners who lived together without marrying and then went their separate ways had the same rights to financial remuneration as married couples. The case involved actor Lee Marvin and his former lover Michelle Triola and added a new word to the lexicon: "palimony."[14]

Thus, when Rose Bird peered into the future and pondered what her tenure atop the court might look like, she had a thirty-year record of precedent-setting decisions in her sights, as well as recognition of the court's national reputation. The *Wall Street Journal*, for example, had called California's highest tribunal "perhaps the most innovative of the state judiciaries, setting precedents in areas of criminal justice, civil liberties, racial integration and civil procedure that heavily influence other states and the federal bench."[15] And it sometimes chose "to extend the constitutional protections beyond those required by the federal court," something for which Bird herself had argued as a deputy public defender in Santa Clara County.

Legal scholars were particularly enamored of the court. University of Chicago law professor Harry Kalven singled out Roger Traynor for special praise, calling him "a law professor's judge. His opinions are concise; he raises all the issues; his writing is lucid and to the point. His citations are knowledgeable, economical and literate."[16]

Bird undoubtedly knew that the court also had its critics, most of whom were not members of the media elite, law professors, or legal scholars but were conservative politicians and ordinary people critical of what they viewed as judicial "overreach" and excessive activism. These critics complained about many of the majority's rulings, claiming that justices "coddled" criminals and ignored citizen concerns about crime, social instability, and "immoral" behavior. In fact, justices kept desk drawers full of letters from people who wrote missives such as this one: "You are a bunch of stupid idiots." At various points, critics angrily challenged individual justices.[17]

One conservative grassroots group, the California Republican Assembly, called for Traynor's ouster, claiming that he and his fellow justices had "illegally usurped the powers of the Legislature." And critics accused Associate Justice Tobriner, a labor lawyer before his 1962 judicial appointment, of being a naïf and dupe of leftists, even communists. After the Cahan decision in 1955, Los Angeles police chief William Parker condemned the entire court, charging that justices aimed to hamstring police while encouraging the illicit actions of hardened criminals.[18]

In 1965, shortly after the Dorado decision, former Republican governor Goodwin Knight publicly branded the court's liberal majority elitist, declaring them to be "men whose records prove they have had so little actual experience in the practical side of our law enforcement that they are truly living in ivory towers of hair-splitting legal gymnastics." Knight singled out justices by name. Traynor was a man with "no record of ever having practiced private law.... From college he went to the classroom as a professor and stayed until he was appointed to the Supreme Court."

Knight criticized Associate Justice Paul Peek for having only four years of courtroom experience before joining the court, while Raymond Peters had "only practiced law for three years." Knight had to admit that Tobriner had had "some experience in private practice of law"—nearly three decades' worth—but Tobriner also had a "very liberal political record." Justices in general "should remember they are officers of the court, not sociologists or probation officers," Knight added.[19]

But overall, few ordinary citizens paid attention to what seemed to be minor political disagreements or to the court in general at this point. In fact, if put on the spot most people would be hard-pressed to summon the name of even a single state high court justice. Most members of the public had little idea of how the court operated or how it might differ from the U.S. Supreme Court, whose rulings throughout the 1950s and 1960s had drawn far more debate and controversy.[20]

This lack of attention meant that California Supreme Court justices could go about their work largely free of concern about political consequences, even though consequences were possible. State high court justices, unlike their federal counterparts—all men at this point on both courts—did not have lifetime appointments. Following nomination by the governor, they had to be confirmed by the three-person Commission on Judicial Appointments. They appeared on statewide ballots the first general election following their confirmations, again the year that their predecessors' terms would have ended had they remained on the court, and thereafter at twelve-year intervals.

No one had ever been removed from office, though special interest groups occasionally tried to facilitate such campaigns. Agriculture interests, for example, briefly targeted Justice Phil Gibson in 1940. Opponents cited his youth, his inexperience, and the possibility that an individual so biased in favor of workers might remain on the court for decades. Gibson paid little attention to the criticism and stayed for a quarter century, ending his career as chief justice in 1964.[21]

The court had faced intense opposition after a 1966 decision nullifying Proposition 14, a ballot initiative designed to allow landlords and home owners to discriminate on the basis of race when they rented or sold homes. The ballot measure had overturned the Rumford Fair Housing Act, enacted by the legislature in 1963, which had deemed such discrimination illegal. "In conservatives' eyes," wrote Lisa McGirr, "open housing laws compromised absolute property rights in favor of civil rights and social justice, a compromise they were not willing to make."[22]

After the court, in a five-to-two decision, declared Proposition 14 unconstitutional, opponents erected billboards along Southern California highways calling for the ouster of four justices seeking confirmation on the November ballot. But they raised virtually no money, and all four justices won voter confirmation, though by slightly lower margins than usual. The campaign exhausted Paul Peek, however, and he left the court the following year.[23]

A 1971 ruling that suggested California's method of financing K–12 education was unconstitutional also garnered strong criticism in some quarters. The state had long used property taxes as the primary funding source for schools, but a lawsuit filed in 1968 argued that this approach privileged students in wealthier districts over the less affluent. A trial court judge in Los Angeles initially dismissed the case, but the state supreme court overruled him and ordered the case to trial. If the facts alleged were true, justices said, they amounted to a violation of the Fourteenth Amendment's equal protection guarantee. This ruling set off a lengthy set of judicial decisions that ultimately led California to adopt statewide funding for schools.[24]

Given the number and variety of cases that angered special interest groups, what accounted for the inability of critics to gain traction against justices, even when their decisions seemed to go against public sentiment? Part of the explanation hinges on longstanding deference toward the judiciary as an institution. To most members of the public, the court seemed mysterious and unreachable; justices were seen as sitting on an exalted perch, high above mere mortals. Such men held impressive credentials and were extremely learned and accomplished.

In his critique of the court, Knight had reinforced this elite status even as he mischaracterized the legal backgrounds of three justices. It was true that Roger Traynor had not been a judge before Culbert Olson appointed him to the court in 1940, and that he had spent his career as a law professor at UC Berkeley's Boalt Hall, teaching classes on taxation. But judicial experience was not a prerequisite for appointment to the high court. One only had to have passed the state bar and have ten years of professional experience in the field of law.

Traynor's work as a professor definitely qualified on that score, as did his work in government. As a consultant for the state Board of Equalization in the 1930s, he created much of California's modern tax system. And during that same period he worked with the U.S. Treasury Department to draft the Revenue Act of 1938. He also served as deputy attorney general under Republican attorney general—later governor—Earl Warren in the late 1930s.[25]

Paul Peek had only practiced law for six years before Pat Brown appointed him in 1962. But he had worked in all three branches of state government—in fact he remains the only justice to have done so. Peek had been a state assembly member and served briefly as assembly speaker. He had also worked in the executive branch, as secretary of state. Raymond Peters had been presiding judge of the court of appeals in San Francisco before arriving at the court in 1940. He also had created and directed a number of community law programs in and around San Francisco.

Knight did not mischaracterize Mathew Tobriner's professional history. In fact, Tobriner had spent thirty years representing workers and unions before Pat Brown—one of Tobriner's oldest and closest friends—appointed him to the court in 1962. And Tobriner was proudly and unabashedly liberal. He "forcefully advocated" the position that "the court should be an instrument of social change."[26] In 1963 he authored a decision overturning an earlier ruling that had deemed Henry Miller's novel *Tropic of Cancer* to be obscene. Set in bohemian Paris in the 1920s and

1930s, it offered explicit depictions of sexual encounters. "The creations which yesterday were the detested and obscene become the classics of today," Tobriner wrote.[27]

Tobriner also was an extremely affable man who apparently never met a person he disliked, "believed deeply in the inherent goodness in everyone," and preferred to be called "Matt" rather than "Justice Tobriner." He was also self-effacing to a fault. Once when a young lawyer asked Tobriner's advice on the best route to a seat on the state supreme court, Tobriner responded: "Go to high school with someone who plans to become governor." His personality, therefore, made him a difficult target even for those who disagreed with his political views and judicial rulings.[28]

Despite occasional grumbling, politicians in general backed away from direct confrontations over judicial decisions and challenges to judges themselves. One reason: California politics during the first two-thirds of the twentieth century was much less partisan than it later became. Legislators from both parties frequently crossed the aisle to socialize with each other. Additionally, parties themselves tended to be relatively weak, due in part to practices such as cross-filing.[29]

Cross-filing allowed candidates to run in primary elections for both parties, without listing their own party registrations. If they won both primaries—as both Earl Warren and Pat Brown did—they did not have to run in subsequent general elections. The practice tended to sideline candidates for statewide office who possessed more extreme agendas, since, to prevail, these individuals had to appeal to a wider electoral base. However, candidates running for local offices could be more partisan. Orange County and the San Gabriel Valley just east of Los Angeles, for example, tended to elect very conservative candidates, while the San Francisco Bay Area usually elected strongly liberal politicians.[30]

Critics also may have been stymied by the justices' willingness to defend their decisions in speeches and media interviews. In 1954 Chief Justice Phil Gibson told a reporter that "we bend over backward to be as certain as men can be that, great or small, all who come before us receive rightful judgments." Two years later, in a speech before a gathering of American Legionnaires, Associate Justice Jesse Carter branded

Los Angeles police chief Parker "immature" and lacking in judgment for criticizing civil libertarian rulings. Before the Cahan decision, Carter told the audience, police "could break into a home or automobile and use any evidence thus obtained in the trial of a person charged with a crime."[31]

He defended the deliberative process, noting that debates over legal rulings are "not like a prayer meeting where everyone is expected to nod 'amen,' it is more like a battleground where opposing philosophies meet in hand-to-hand combat." And Mathew Tobriner told another audience that "it is the duty of the judiciary to safeguard the rights of individuals." Justices "must be the sentinels to keep this country true to itself and to its ideals."[32]

Justices also willingly took on their critics in cases where they clearly discarded popular sentiment. For example, more than 4.5 million voters had backed Proposition 14, but that did not mean it was constitutional, Roger Traynor said. "Californians might suddenly take a notion to start coining their own money, but no matter how large a majority such an attractive proposition commanded at the polls, it would have to be ruled out on constitutional grounds."

And after writing the majority opinion striking down the death penalty in 1972, Chief Justice Donald Wright told reporters he was "disturbed by attacks which go beyond the merits of the issues and challenge the court's right and even the compulsion imposed upon it to examine and reexamine legislation in the light of prevailing constitutional tests." These explanations did not quell criticism, but they made it difficult for opponents to garner enough public support to oust justices or coerce the court into changing direction.[33]

As she awaited confirmation as chief justice then, Rose Bird might have been excused if she envisioned many years, even decades, of presiding over an esteemed court that continued to issue pioneering rulings in a variety of areas. She had come of age and attended law school during a period when, as many rulings illustrated, "constitutional law should be a vehicle for social change." She felt confident that her own sentiments dovetailed nicely with those of her antecedents and many of her soon-to-be—fingers crossed—colleagues. Critics might target specific rulings, but justices themselves had generally proven adept at defusing opposition; there was no indication they could not continue doing so for the foreseeable future.[34]

But whispers of change were in the wind in early 1977 that might impede Bird's ability to lead the court with the same degree of success her predecessors had enjoyed. Cross-filing had ended by the 1960s, enabling more "extreme" candidates to make inroads politically. And high court rulings such as the 1966 overturning of Proposition 14 enabled conservatives to begin organizing a grassroots movement composed of whites who believed government had "overreached" in its efforts to achieve racial "fairness." The movement quickly gained momentum, particularly in newly built suburbs of Orange and San Diego Counties.

Additionally, a unique set of circumstances had led to thirty years of liberal dominance on the court, even during years when Republican governors presided over the state. Between 1939 and 1977, California had three Democratic and three Republican governors. Republicans served a decade longer than Democrats, largely due to Earl Warren, who won three gubernatorial terms before leaving California for Washington DC in September 1953 to become chief justice of the U.S. Supreme Court.[35]

Yet Democrats had appointed most of the state supreme court justices during this period. Culbert Olson, Democratic governor for a single term from 1939 to 1943, made four judicial appointments, including Phil Gibson and Roger Traynor. Pat Brown served two terms, from 1959 to 1967. He made eight court appointments, including Mathew Tobriner and Stanley Mosk. The three Republican governors—Warren, Goodwin Knight, and Ronald Reagan—had a total of only five appointments. In ten years Warren had only a single supreme court appointment, as did Knight, who served for nearly six years. Reagan had three appointments in eight years. Jerry Brown had not made any judicial appointments prior to Bird and Manuel's nominations, but in two terms he would go on to make seven high court appointments.

And justices appointed by Democrats remained on the court longer than those appointed by Republicans. Phil Gibson, for example, arrived at the court in 1939, became chief justice in 1940, and stayed on until 1964. Roger Traynor stayed for thirty years, from 1940 to 1970. Mathew Tobriner stayed for twenty years. Stanley Mosk had served for thirteen years at the time of Bird's appointment and ultimately would remain on the court for another twenty-four years, becoming the state's longest-serving justice. Only one Republican appointee during this period—Marshall McComb, appointed by Knight—stayed longer than a decade. As a result, the court retained its liberal bent even in periods when Californians elected Republican governors and U.S. senators.[36]

But in 1977 the composition of the court was about to change. Mathew Tobriner was in his seventies. At some point in the near future he would retire, to be replaced by an individual who was an unknown quantity. Tobriner's departure would not present Bird with her most immediate challenge, however. Marshall McComb, appointed by Knight in 1956, was completely senile. During monthly oral arguments on pending cases, he often fell asleep, made nonsensical comments, or got up from the bench and wandered away. During weekly meetings with his fellow justices, he might inject himself into the discussion by intoning: "talk, talk, talk, squawk, squawk, squawk, yak, yak, yak." Or he might phone a friend long distance from the telephone in the chief justice's chambers to talk about the weather. He wore a pair of pig earrings to a meeting, and he urinated in a court bailiff's car.[37]

Despite McComb's impairment—"he was incompetent the whole seven years I was there," said former chief justice Donald Wright—"there was no way of removing him. He was the 'darling' of a great group of individuals in California. . . . I attempted to get him to leave the court, unsuccessfully. I attempted to get his family to use pressure on him, and I was not successful in that."[38] In 1976, at the urging of McComb's fellow justices, the Commission on Judicial Performance launched an investigation into his behavior, but he failed to show up to defend himself. In January 1977, citing "permanent mental disability," the commission recommended his removal. As Bird awaited confirmation, McComb still clung to his job.[39]

The court also contained two justices likely to give Bird problems, each for different reasons. Associate Justice Stanley Mosk was said to be livid at being passed over for chief justice in favor of Bird. Mosk had had a long and distinguished career, beginning in 1939 when he served as executive secretary to Democratic governor Culbert Olson. Before Olson left office in 1943, he named Mosk, then only thirty-one, to the superior court bench in Los Angeles.

In 1958 voters elected Mosk attorney general. Six years later, Pat Brown appointed him to the state supreme court. Known for his wit, Mosk once described the archconservative John Birch Society as composed "primarily of wealthy businessmen, retired military officers and little old ladies in tennis shoes." Asked at one point why he had left the rough-and-tumble world of politics for the staid life of a justice, Mosk said he hated fundraising, particularly "going into a reception, or a public dinner, and looking at everyone with a dollar sign over his head."[40]

Mosk had long hankered for the court's top job and was considered the frontrunner after Chief Justice Donald Wright announced his retirement in January 1977. When Jerry Brown chose Rose Bird instead, Mosk vowed to never again speak to the governor, and he kept his promise. Brown never publicly discussed his reasons for bypassing Mosk in favor of Bird, but he often told friends that he wanted to break down the entrenched "old-boys" network by appointing women and minorities to prominent and high-profile positions. Some observers also believed that Mosk had angered Brown in 1976 by authoring the majority opinion in the affirmative action case *Regents of the University of California v. Bakke*. Brown reportedly decided then that Mosk would never be chief justice.[41]

Allen Bakke was a thirty-five-year-old white man twice rejected by the University of California, Davis medical school. The school had a quota system under which it left a specific number of slots open for minority students, some of whom had lower grades than Bakke. He sued, claiming that the school's affirmative action program violated his Fourteenth Amendment right to equal protection under the law.

Brown and most liberals supported affirmative action, but Mosk agreed with Bakke. Writing for a court majority, Mosk said "the program, as administered by the university, violates the rights of non-minority applicants because it affords preference on the basis of race to persons who, by the university's own standards, are not as qualified for the study of medicine as non-minority applicants denied admission."[42]

Some observers saw different forces at work in Brown's refusal to elevate Mosk, however. *San Francisco Examiner* reporter John Jacobs argued that Brown "had an almost Oedipal need to trash the living symbols of his father's political success." Pat Brown had appointed Mosk, therefore Jerry Brown refused to make him chief justice.[43]

William P. Clark also could prove problematic for Bird, although he had been the only sitting justice to send a congratulatory note following her high court nomination. A fifth-generation Californian, grandson of a sheriff, and owner of a nine-hundred-acre ranch in San Luis Obispo County, Clark was a close friend of Republican governor Ronald Reagan. He had flunked out of both college and law school and also had failed the California bar exam on his first try, but passed it on his second attempt. He briefly practiced law and then left in 1966 to work on Reagan's first gubernatorial campaign. In the late 1960s, Reagan named him to the superior court bench, first in San Luis Obispo and then in Los Angeles. In 1973 he appointed Clark associate justice of the supreme court.[44]

Clark barely won confirmation. Appointees needed two votes from the three-member Commission on Judicial Appointments. Chief Justice Donald Wright reluctantly cast the lone "no" vote. Clark was "not qualified by education, training and experience" to hold such an important job, Wright declared. He acknowledged the potential awkwardness of his decision, since he and Clark would be colleagues. Once on the court, Clark and Wright experienced a period of cool relations; over time, however, their relationship improved somewhat. But they were both men with similar backgrounds and life experiences. Bird could not count on the same level of respect or cooperation. Clark also was a staunch conservative, and Bird also knew he probably would dissent on any liberal court rulings.[45]

Finally, the 1960s and 1970s were transitional decades in state and national politics. The civil rights movement, Vietnam, and Watergate had placed public institutions and politicians under a microscope and challenged the notion that members of the privileged elite should be entitled to any deference or special treatment. Activists, including feminists, argued that the judiciary should reflect society as a whole and demanded the inclusion of ethnic minorities and women.

Conservatives had long railed, with little success, against "activist" judges both nationally and on the state level. The arrival of women and minorities—nonelites—gave them openings to argue that such individuals were "affirmative action hires" and, as such, undeserving of the high-status positions, which they had not earned. The 1966 gubernatorial election of Ronald Reagan infused court critics with optimism.

Soon after taking office, Reagan began targeting "activist" judges and circulating suggestions on how to shake up the judicial selection process. Then, as now, California gave governors the power to select their own judicial candidates, but many other states required chief executives to choose justices from a list of names supplied by a nominating commission composed of judges, lawyers, and members of the public. In some states, appointments also required approval from one or both houses of the legislature.[46]

Reagan wanted to take politics out of the appointment process, he said, and urged California to adopt the commission system. The proposal went nowhere, but the increasing focus on courts had some impact. Historically, voters had paid scant attention to judicial elections; by the 1970s the percentage of people routinely voting "no" on judicial candidates had risen by ten points, from 15 to 25 percent.[47]

Others quickly recognized the implications of this sea change. If people wanted judges held accountable, politicians aimed to please and began to promote the notion that judges needed to concern themselves with the will of the electorate in deciding cases. According to Berkeley law professor Preble Stolz, before the late 1960s and 1970s, both Republican and Democratic leaders defended controversial rulings, believing that the courts were law and justices' decisions deserved support, even if they were personally distasteful. Over time, however, politicians began supporting only decisions with which they—and their constituents—agreed.[48]

Capital punishment was perhaps the issue that gave conservatives their best opening to target so-called activist judges, because it elicited visceral reactions from voters. The February 1972 decision ending the death penalty in California brought significant attention to the state supreme court, if not yet to individual justices. A rising chorus of politicians, pundits, and conservative groups declared that the ruling would release hundreds of vicious murderers to wreak havoc and vengeance on an innocent public.

"The court is setting itself up above the people and their legislators," Reagan noted angrily when he learned of the ruling. "In a time of increasing crime and violence, capital punishment is needed." Public opinion polls taken shortly after abolition showed an immediate bump in death penalty support: more than 70 percent of respondents said they favored it, up from less than 60 percent a few years earlier.[49]

Death penalty opponents countered that the decision commuted the death sentences, not the prison sentences, of condemned prisoners who still would spend the rest of their lives in prison. In their rulings eliminating capital punishment, both the California and U.S. high courts had cited the arbitrary and capricious nature of prosecutions that led to some defendants being sentenced to death while others who had committed far worse crimes received lighter sentences. Neither ruling permanently ended capital punishment. Both required state legislatures to establish specific standards as a condition of reinstating it.[50]

Soon after the high court decisions, pro–death penalty forces in California and elsewhere began unstinting efforts to reinstate capital punishment. They qualified an initiative for the November 1972 ballot; Proposition 17 stated: "The death penalty shall not be deemed to be, or to constitute, the infliction of cruel or unusual punishment." To sell the measure, state senator H. L. Richardson, an ultraconservative Republican, put together a twenty-minute film "laden with shots of bloody victims, Bible quotes and crime statistics." The death penalty, Richardson proclaimed, was "the only thing that protects prison guards from men who are serving life sentences." Voters needed little convincing, approving Proposition 17 by a two-to-one margin.[51]

Before it could be enacted lawmakers had to create specific standards to use in death penalty trials. They wasted no time. George Deukmejian, a Republican state senator from Long Beach, crafted a bill making the death penalty mandatory in murder trials if jurors found even one "aggravating" circumstance. The list of such circumstances included murder for hire, murders committed in the commission of other crimes, and causing a train wreck that resulted in death.[52]

The measure quickly passed both houses of the legislature, and Reagan signed it in December 1972. "It will save lives," he said. Less than four years later, before California could execute anyone, the U.S. Supreme Court again ruled the death penalty unconstitutional, but only in those states—including California—that had enacted mandatory capital punishment laws. States had to give juries some discretion in sentencing, justices said.[53]

In February 1977 Deukmejian introduced new legislation enumerating "aggravating" factors that made defendants eligible for the death penalty but that allowed juries discretion in sentencing. Interviewed on television's *Today Show* that same month, Brown vowed to enforce death penalty laws. "I'll give no blanket pardons," he said. "I will make a judgment in each case viewing the totality of circumstances, trying to be as compassionate as I can, but also mindful of the fact that whatever the law is, my oath of office is to carry it out."[54]

Deukmejian's bill was still working its way through the legislature when Brown nominated Rose Bird to a court beginning to experience heightened scrutiny. Bird had upended decades of tradition during her tenure as agriculture secretary, privileging farmworkers over growers. Before that, she had been a defense attorney. Death sentences were automatically appealed to the state's highest court. Bird's record put pro-capital punishment forces on high alert.

They recognized Brown as a particularly canny politician who could use Bird's sympathy toward society's castoffs to his own advantage. Brown opposed the death penalty. If critics came after him for court rulings overturning death sentences, he could shrug and point out that he was not the one making the decisions. He had no control over supreme court justices. As evidence, he could point to Donald Wright, author of *People v. Anderson*, a ruling that Stanley Mosk deemed "the most courageous opinion I can recall."[55]

Reagan had known Wright only by reputation before appointing him to the state supreme court. Wright was an avuncular man, with a wide circle of friends in the legal profession and beyond. He loved books, music, and art. He had been a judge for twenty years—Earl Warren first appointed him to the municipal court bench in 1950. Introducing Wright to the media, Reagan called him "a man committed to the principle of judicial restraint, who can provide the leadership necessary to restore public confidence in our court system and return it to the highest position of integrity, leadership and respect."[56]

Wright agreed that he believed in "judicial restraint" but disagreed that people had lost confidence in the courts. He was a registered Republican, he told reporters, but not an energetic one. In fact, he had not been active in politics since the Alf Landon presidential campaign of 1936, he joked.

Reagan quickly came to regret selecting Wright, since he turned out to be much less of a team player than the governor had anticipated, his opinion ending the death penalty being one example and his vote against William Clark's confirmation another. Media reports suggested that Reagan had tried to get Wright to retire before his term expired in 1975, since Wright's departure would give Reagan another appointment. Wright later denied this, however. He only met with Reagan once, he said, and the two never talked about the court. He initially intended to stay on the court for only a few years but soon changed his mind. "I did intend to resign, but when I got on the Supreme Court, I found it was such a stimulating life that I had no desire to leave. In fact, I wish I was there now!"[57]

As she awaited confirmation hearings before the Commission on Judicial Appointments in early 1977, therefore, Bird faced many unknowns, but she could be fairly certain on one front: the arrival of the court's first woman justice—and the chief justice to boot—would shake up a judicial establishment that had long been entirely the purview of white men. As a woman, Bird stood unprotected by the cocoon of privilege that had long enveloped her predecessors.

Like many male judges and lawyers, she had attended an elite law school. But her subsequent experience differed in significant ways from theirs. No matter what their political persuasions or backgrounds, male judges had belonged since youth to the proverbial "old boy's club." In this chummy environment, men learned how to compete with one another while also developing professional and personal connections that eased the transition from youth to adulthood and from ambition to accomplishment. The lessons learned along the way were subtle and ingrained in a culture in which white men of a certain class were trained from birth to be society's leaders.

While Bird had struggled to find work after law school, her male colleagues had easily transitioned to academia, prestigious government positions, or private law firms. When they arrived at the court, male justices had decades of professional alliances and friendships to call on. They drank at the same bars and belonged to the same clubs, many of which excluded women and minorities.

Jerry Brown may have been an unconventional governor, but he clearly had benefitted from these same male networks, starting with the friendship between his father and Mathew Tobriner. Pat Brown appointed Tobriner to the court. Soon thereafter Tobriner happily wrote a letter of recommendation for Jerry to Yale Law School and subsequently hired Jerry as his law clerk. When Jerry Brown decided to run for office, Pat Brown enlisted his wide circle of acquaintances and political allies on behalf of his son's candidacy.

Tobriner mentored many other young men as well, including Richard Mosk, the son of Tobriner's colleague Stanley Mosk. The junior Mosk served as Tobriner's law clerk. So did Joseph Grodin, appointed by Jerry Brown to the Agriculture Labor Relations Board. Grodin credited Tobriner for all of his professional success. In the early 1950s, as a law student Grodin worked summers for Tobriner, who also helped Grodin win a Fulbright fellowship to London and then hired Grodin to work in his law firm.

When Pat Brown tapped Tobriner for the supreme court, Tobriner insisted that Grodin take over his law practice. The two men remained close, meeting once a week for lunch for more than twenty years. In the mid-1970s, Tobriner pushed Jerry Brown to name Grodin to the newly formed ALRB and then to appoint Grodin an appeals court justice. Finally, following his own retirement, Tobriner lobbied Brown to give Grodin a seat on the California Supreme Court.[58]

The relationship between justices Phil Gibson and Stanley Mosk offers another example of how the "old boys' network" worked. Mosk grew up in the Midwest and graduated from the University of Chicago, where he started but did not finish law school. He subsequently moved to California and enrolled in Southwestern Law School in Los Angeles. Gibson was then in private practice and also taught at Southwestern. The two men became close friends. Gibson began referring to Mosk as his protégé. "To him it was a flippant remark, but to me it was a badge of honor," Mosk recalled much later.[59]

Both men soon went to work for Governor Olson, Mosk as executive secretary and Gibson as finance director. "We became personal friends as well as associates," said Mosk. Afterward the two men took different career paths, "but our close friendship continued. In our salad days, after some staid bar association functions, we closed many a North Beach [San Francisco] bar while happily musing about law, politics and life generally." In 1964 the relationship came full circle. Gibson's retirement as chief justice gave Pat Brown a court appointment. He elevated Roger Traynor from associate justice to chief justice and appointed Mosk to fill Traynor's seat.[60]

A 1966 newspaper article on Roger Traynor detailed how this life of male privilege and camaraderie translated to the personal arena as well. Describing Traynor as "a gentle dynamo with a quiet voice and a roaring laugh," the reporter also noted that despite Traynor's heavy court workload, he "still finds time to take in a concert, putter about the garden, reread *Franny and Zooey*, write for the law reviews, play with his six grandchildren, attend judicial conferences, and shoot the breeze with old friends from the bench, the bar and law schools."[61]

This, then, was the insider's "club" that Bird—"a born outsider"—sought to join. In fact, all of the justices had long stayed at the male-only Sutter Club when they held oral arguments in Sacramento twice a year. "It was full of legislators, lobbyists and members of the governor's staff," former chief justice Wright recalled. "You'd see them every day. They'd be over to your table to speak to you, invite you to stop by and have a drink or something. They would be very friendly." With Bird's arrival, the ritual would change. She, or possibly all of the justices, would have to find another place to stay during the court's Sacramento sojourns.[62]

Bird knew how to toss a football and had played on office softball teams. She had gone up against male attorneys in court and had negotiated a landmark farm labor bill in the state Agriculture and Services Department. However, all of her accomplishments had come with the help of male mentors, and she had been subordinate to all of them. Now, professionally she would catapult over all but one of her mentors and stand shoulder-to-shoulder with Brown as head of a massive state court system filled with men who had known each other for years, who understood the subtleties and nuances of politics, and who took their privileges for granted as they walked easily through the corridors of power.

4   *Becoming Chief Justice*

It was a chilly morning in San Francisco, March 7, 1977, when the Commission on Judicial Appointments convened a hearing to determine whether Rose Elizabeth Bird and Wiley Manuel would become, respectively, the first woman and the first African American to sit on the California Supreme Court. Ordinarily, the chief justice chaired such hearings, but California had no sitting chief justice, so Associate Justice Mathew Tobriner assumed that role. Attorney General Evelle Younger and presiding state appeals court justice Parker Wood, both Republicans, were the other two commission members.

The setting was impressive: the massive Beaux Arts–style state building that served as headquarters for the state supreme court. The hearing took place inside the same wood-paneled room with its coffered ceiling where justices met four times a year to determine the outcome of cases that shaped the lives of millions of ordinary citizens. The San Francisco courtroom was one of three used by justices, who also heard oral arguments in Sacramento and Los Angeles. For this occasion, commissioners sat in the justices' comfortable, high-backed chairs, behind a heavy, polished wood bench, facing the overflow audience gathered to witness the proceedings.

Manuel's confirmation came first. It was an easy affair. Members of the public had been asked to send comments on both judicial appointments to the commission. All the respondents praised Manuel's legal acumen, pro bono work, and "judicial" temperament, and the California bar association board of governors, with little debate, had deemed him "qualified." Manuel made only a brief appearance at the hearing and was asked only one question: "Have you written on the subject of racial discrimination?" Manuel said he had not and noted that administrative law had been his particular area of expertise. Minutes later, he won a unanimous thumbs-up verdict from commissioners.[1]

Bird, however, was another story. Her road to the hearing had been rocky, and it was unclear on that Monday morning whether she would win confirmation. Trouble had emerged even before Jerry Brown announced her as his choice for chief justice. He had tried to gauge sentiment for the nomination, asking commissioners whether he could count on their support.[2]

Tobriner responded with enthusiasm, but Wood said he planned to reject her; she had no judicial experience. That left only Evelle Younger, whose role was complicated by the fact that he planned to challenge Brown for governor in 1978. He promised to be objective, rather than looking at Bird as a "good" or "bad" appointment, but acknowledged that her lack of experience "troubled" him. Younger faced a no-win situation no matter how he decided. A vote in favor of Bird was certain to antagonize conservatives, but a vote against her was likely to irritate many women.[3]

The governor also had visited former chief justice Donald Wright at his home in Marin County preparatory to making his announcement. Wright had "nothing against Rose Bird as a person at all, or against her being named to the court," he told Brown, "but I did think that it was not a good idea to have an outsider take over who had never had a single day in her entire lifetime in a judicial spot. He listened . . . very patiently. . . . A week later, I guess, he telephoned" to tell Wright that "Rose Bird was such a fine administrator he simply felt he had to appoint her." Wright replied, "Well, you're the governor. You can, of course, do just as you wish."[4]

Brown's effort to finesse the appointment drew sharp criticism. "Normally, governors submit nominations to the commission publicly . . . rather than attempting to win private approval for their nominations before publicly announcing them," noted *Los Angeles Times* reporter William Endicott. He quoted "informed" sources, who revealed that Brown had "made at least two telephone calls" to Parker Wood and "at least one call" to Evelle Younger. Gray Davis, Brown's chief of staff, denied the governor had done anything wrong, but his actions made Bird the subject of internal debate even before Brown announced her appointment.[5]

Problems percolated among members of the court as well. Associate Justice Stanley Mosk still seethed from being passed over for chief justice. He viewed Donald Wright's decision to choose Tobriner as acting chief as an additional slap in the face. Mosk believed Wright's choice of Tobriner hinged on a "glowing speech" Tobriner gave when Wright announced his retirement from the court, though in fact, Tobriner was the longest-serving justice by two years.

Mosk's irritation seems somewhat understandable. Roger Traynor had appointed him acting chief justice when Traynor stepped down in 1970. Thus Mosk had participated as a member of the judicial appointments commission and had approved Wright's nomination as chief justice.[6] And Mosk himself had penned a "glowing" testimonial on Wright for a law review, in which he noted that "the grandest hopes of the bench and bar of California were fulfilled by the distinguished judicial service of Don Wright. . . . He has been a great guy to work with, to play with, to plan with, to discuss issues with, even to argue with."[7] Wright was saddened by Mosk's attitude but denied that Tobriner's speech had anything to do with his decision. Tobriner had assumed that his seniority entitled him to the position, and Wright did not have the heart to inform him otherwise, he said later.[8]

Mosk's resentment led him to approach fellow justice William Clark with a plan to convince a majority of their colleagues to mount what could be considered a coup, voting to replace Tobriner with Mosk, who was the second-longest-serving justice. The plan went nowhere, and Tobriner remained acting chief.

Mosk's motives, other than authentic resentment, are unknown. The appointments commission is a powerful body, determining the fates of all judicial nominees at the appellate level, not just those selected for the state's highest court. It is possible that Mosk hoped to use the temporary position to derail Bird's nomination. As acting chief justice, he—rather than the more sympathetic Tobriner—would sit on the commission, enabling him to vote against Bird, thereby handing a defeat to both Bird and Brown. No matter what his motive, Mosk's clumsy attempt to oust Tobriner presaged trouble, since it essentially guaranteed tense relations between the two men when they returned to focusing on supreme court business.[9]

Bird's nomination had been greeted with both enthusiasm and dismay. Democrats expressed strong support. State finance director Roy Bell praised Bird's "very analytical mind" and her administrative capabilities. Democratic assembly speaker Leo T. McCarthy called her "precise, straightforward, and well-informed. She talks usually in a common-sense, straightforward manner." Her former boss Santa Clara public defender Sheldon Portman said Bird "impressed me as being an outstanding lawyer, and I anticipate she will be an outstanding chief justice."[10] Anthony Amsterdam, Bird's former Stanford colleague and a death penalty expert, called her "a crackerjack lawyer. She comes at problems with a human compassion and sensitivity."[11]

The 1,150-member California Attorneys for Criminal Justice also happily backed Bird. "I have the greatest respect for her and I know she'll be an outstanding chief justice," said Louis Katz, president of the statewide group of defense attorneys. Bird had been a founding member of CACJ, Katz told reporters, and had worked diligently during her years as a deputy public defender to represent the rights of the underprivileged.

A few organizations offered tepid statements. The California Peace Officers Association and the California District Attorneys Association said they would not fight the appointment, though Bird was not their first choice for chief justice.[12]

But the appointment drew opposition as well. Much of it centered on Bird's lack of judicial experience and the belief that she would be "soft" on crime. When reporters sought out former chief justice Donald Wright for comment, he dissembled, as he had done with Brown. He had no concerns about Bird's qualifications, he said, but added: "This is the first time, at least since the turn of the century that the chief justice would be a person with no experience on the bench."[13]

Pete Wilson, Republican mayor of San Diego, said that Brown might have appointed any of the "many men and women of experience and demonstrated judicial skill and temperament" in the legal community. Los Angeles police chief Edward Davis also took note of Bird's lack of judicial experience and voiced concern that she would "show little regard for the public who must suffer the depredations of the lawless." Both Wilson and Davis planned to challenge Younger for the 1978 Republican gubernatorial nomination, so their remarks could be viewed at least partly through the lens of politics. Davis warned that the attorney general's vote on Bird "could play a major role" in the June 1978 Republican primary.[14]

So did Earl W. Huntting, a representative of the five-thousand-member Oakland-based Citizens for Law and Order, who said, "We certainly will not support Younger in the primary [election] if he votes for Bird." He sent Younger a letter containing a not-so-veiled warning. "We've supported you all the way because you have been a strong attorney general on law and order. We expect you not to make political deals on this appointment. We do not need a young lawyer as Chief Justice to change the rules." In total, Younger and his fellow commissioners received nearly a thousand letters, both for and against Bird. The large number of letters using the terms "left-winger," "liberal," or "sympathetic to criminals" suggested a coordinated effort by conservative groups across the state.[15]

Some Republican lawmakers saw Bird's nomination as a way to revisit her role in crafting the Agriculture Labor Relations Act (ALRA). They circulated a letter, signed by nineteen of twenty-three assembly Republicans and seven of fourteen senate Republicans, urging Younger to vote "no." "This hard-line 'social reform' approach could add an entirely new dimension to the court's constitutional function of interpreting the law," the letter noted. They, too, raised the specter of inexperience, which they said might lead to her "inability to resist the strong temptation to lead the court toward increased activism."[16]

People following the Rose Bird saga could be forgiven for thinking that the notion of "judicial experience" had long been an important factor in state supreme court confirmation procedures. In fact it had not been an issue. When critics brought up the topic of experience, Peter J. Belton, long-time staff attorney for the court, recalled muttering to himself: "What about [Phil] Gibson and [Roger] Traynor?" Both men had sailed through confirmation hearings, despite never having been judges, though both initially had been appointed as associate justices. Both also had been in their forties, and Gibson served only a year before Governor Culbert Olson elevated him to chief.[17]

The constant clamor over experience led one constitutional scholar to cite studies debunking it as a predictor of judicial success. Nearly half of all U.S. Supreme Court justices lacked any judicial experience before joining the nation's highest tribunal, Nathan Lewin wrote in an essay. Among them were Felix Frankfurter, Louis Brandeis, and Earl Warren.[18]

But critics knew what they were doing: crafting a narrative designed to pressure Younger to vote "no" on Bird. The letters, opinion pieces, and media interviews were aimed at creating at least the image of a statewide groundswell of opposition to Bird's nomination. Once created, critics also understood that such narratives would be difficult to dislodge or debunk. Thus Bird, if confirmed, would enter office with an already ingrained negative public image: she had no experience, and she would be a liberal, activist judge. Soon a third story line would join the other two: Rose Bird was "difficult." Even Bird partisans might have agreed with this characterization.

The *Los Angeles Times* fed this narrative in a short article announcing the resignation of state food and agriculture director Tim Wallace. Wallace had refused to explain his reasons for resigning, but others filled in the blanks. "It's been rumored for a long time that Tim was going to resign because he was unhappy working under Rose Bird," Clark Biggs, press spokesman for the California Farm Bureau Federation, told a reporter.[19] Bird refused to comment, but J. Anthony Kline, who had worked with her in Brown's cabinet, later offered his own assessment. "Rose didn't have the ability to exert leadership over people who . . . were very jealous of their own prerogatives."[20]

Ordinarily, resignations of political appointees were hardly newsworthy. Several unhappy Brown employees had left their jobs during his first term, including Jim Lorenz, head of the state Employment Development Department, who later wrote a book highly critical of the governor. But journalists needed stories; Wallace's resignation gave them something to write about, and it offered Bird's opponents another opportunity to question her leadership abilities.

Fred Heringer, president of the California Farm Bureau, referenced Wallace's resignation when he criticized Bird's nomination. "She hasn't really been a good administrator because she has lost some key people," he said. Don Curlee, a prominent table grape grower, said he was "hard-pressed" to see what "qualifications and abilities" made Bird an appropriate candidate for chief justice.

Her work as agriculture secretary raised "a rather serious question as to whether she can maintain an objective attitude." And Jack Pandol, member of the state Food and Agriculture Board, said he was "extremely disappointed" with Bird's nomination. He charged Bird with heading a "politburo" that pushed through the Agriculture Labor Relations Act. She might be a good attorney, he added, but that did not qualify her to be a judge.[21]

Agriculture interests undoubtedly believed they could gain more traction by focusing on the ALRA, but some observers thought their real beef with Bird had to do with her decision to ban the short-handled hoe. The ALRA had been Brown's crusade, but the ban seemed to reflect Bird's stubborn refusal to be swayed when confronted with issues she cared about.[22]

Farmers also needed to continue flexing their muscles, to remind politicians—including Jerry Brown—how much power they still wielded. He clearly understood. Shortly after nominating Bird, he reconfigured the Agriculture and Services Agency, removing the Food and Agriculture Department from the larger entity and elevating the department to cabinet status. He named a farmer to head the newly constituted and much more powerful entity.[23]

The most damning criticism of Bird came from an entirely unexpected source: Roger Mahony, Catholic bishop of Fresno. Brown had named

Mahony to the Agriculture Labor Relations Board (ALRB) just after the ALRA became law, and Mahony worked with Bird to implement the legislation. At the time, Bird lauded the appointment and called Mahony "fair-minded." But eighteen months later, in a "confidential" letter to members of the judicial appointments commission, he offered a far less charitable description of Bird.

She possessed, he wrote, "questionable emotional stability" and "a vindictive approach to dealing with all persons under her authority. I experienced personally her vindictiveness on many occasions.... She has a personal temperament which enables her to lash out at people who do not agree with her. Her normal approach is to become vindictive, then to transfer her feelings to a long phase of non-communication."[24]

The letter had a somewhat circuitous history. Hearing rumors that Brown intended to appoint Bird to the court, Mahony first contacted the governor to voice his opposition. When that strategy failed, he contacted Mathew Tobriner, "whom he knew slightly and respected greatly." Tobriner told Mahony he planned to vote for Bird but suggested that Mahony write a letter to the commission explaining his position. It would remain confidential, he assured Mahony. But Evelle Younger refused—"in fairness to Rose Bird," he said—to keep its contents secret.

In his own letter, published on the editorial page of the *Los Angeles Times*, Younger justified his decision to make Mahony's missive public. "Without the total letter being available to Miss Bird and the public, everyone would be justified in believing that a confidential, unanswered letter might in some way influence our decision." He also used his media platform to criticize both Pete Wilson and Edward Davis. "I pray that should either of them assume the awesome responsibilities of the governorship, they too might find it wise to withhold judgment until all of the evidence is in."[25]

Bird said she was stunned by Mahony's action. She had enjoyed a cordial relationship with the bishop, she said, or at least she thought she had. She refused to discuss the letter, other than to note her surprise that Mahony was "so emotional about it. He never said anything to me personally about it."[26] Brown also expressed surprise; Mahony had always spoken highly of Bird. Other members of the ALRB quickly distanced themselves from Mahony's comments. Joseph Grodin dubbed the allegations "outrageous." Bird "seemed to be a capable and efficient administrator."

Grodin recalled meeting with her on a handful of occasions. At one point they disagreed about a legal matter, but the disagreement was settled amicably, Grodin said. He later acknowledged, however, that "Rose was capable of being quite stubborn," with a style that could be "at times hackle-raising."[27] Gerald Brown, who succeeded Mahony as chair of the ALRB, praised Bird for her "keen intellect" and "her helpful and cooperative" approach to farm labor issues. He denied that Bird ever tried "to interfere in ALRB decisions."[28]

Dick Johnson had been a growers' association representative before joining the ALRB. He called Bird's "integrity beyond reproach, she is neither emotionally unstable nor vindictive. Her high degree of personal integrity is well-known and her intellect certainly qualifies her for the Supreme Court." Harry Delizonna, general counsel for the ALRB, said he had "heard Roger was going to write a letter to Younger, but I refused to believe he would do such a thing. The remarks he made about Rose Bird are just not her by any stretch of the imagination. Perhaps women are supposed to be overcome by emotion more easily than men and that is where Roger got this idea from, but I can tell you she is a tough, highly intelligent person."[29]

The contents of Mahony's letter surprised even some of his Catholic colleagues. They included Monsignor George Higgins, secretary for research of the United States Catholic Conference. Before learning of the missive, Higgins had written a congratulatory note to Bird declaring: "I have also heard our mutual friend Bishop Mahony speak of you in the highest terms on more than one occasion." Mahony never divulged his reasons for writing to the commission. "It was written with the understanding that it was for [the commissioners'] eyes alone and neither they nor I would release it to the press," he told reporters at the time, and he subsequently refused all requests for interviews on the subject.[30]

Some sources suggested that Bird and Mahony first crossed swords soon after his appointment as chair of the ALRB, when she brought outside consultants, including some from the Washington DC–based National Labor Relations Board, to Sacramento to help craft regulations for the new agency. She also was extremely frugal, and the ALRB quickly began spending copious amounts of money to hire staff, oversee union elections, and handle claims of unfair labor practices. The ALRB did not come under her jurisdiction; nonetheless, she would have been vocal in her disapproval. Mahony may have resented what he considered interference in his work.[31]

Additionally, both Bird and Mahony had strong personalities and were known for forcefully articulating their own points of view. He may have been "tall, lanky and affable," as one journalist described him, but he was also outspoken and quick to anger if treated with less deference than he believed was his due. He demonstrated the latter trait early in his tenure as chair of the ALRB.

Mahony had been close to Cesar Chavez and marched alongside him and other UFW organizers. From the beginning, Teamsters protested the composition of the ALRB as too partisan in favor of Chavez and the UFW. At one point Teamsters representatives became so angry that they picketed the ALRB headquarters in Sacramento and confronted Mahony, among others. He dubbed them "terrorists." As he told one journalist, "We have absolutely no intention of allowing any terrorist group to interfere with the operations of this board."[32] He also was intolerant of dissent. At one point, he ordered parishes in Stockton, California, to stop hosting speakers "without his express permission."[33]

Bird may have challenged Mahony on his seeming partisanship and urged him to be more equitable. At least that is how one pro-Bird source saw it. Her interest was in farmworkers, not in which union represented them. "Here were these guys [on the ALRB] running around with UFW buttons on, checking in with Cesar Chavez at every opportunity, searching for ways to help the cause, and Rose Bird, who really didn't have any authority over them, was worried that an agency with such an obvious bias would never survive." Her "discomfort with the board soured her relationship" with Mahony.[34] As Don Vial, a Bird partisan and director of the Department of Industrial Relations, noted: "She was not a wheeler-dealer, she was not going to play games—you knew she would never sell short her principles just to get something together. Her objective—the linch-pin of the bill she drafted—was to ensure the integrity of the election process for the workers."

No matter what Mahony's motivation, the letter had a long shelf life. Months later, famed *Los Angeles Times* cartoonist Paul Conrad proffered his own rendition of the kerfuffle with a drawing depicting the bishop "sitting at his desk. In front of him was a bud vase containing a single rose. Looking inspired, the bishop wrote the words: 'A rose is a rose is a DIRTY BIRD.'"[35]

The most important consequence of Mahony's letter was the reinforcement of Bird's image as prickly and intolerant of other people's ideas and opinions. But it also served as a reminder of her gender. None of the adjectives he and other critics used to describe her could be literally construed as gender-specific. Most anyone working in a large bureaucracy, or any job for that matter, might use such terms to describe any number of bosses, coworkers, and subordinates, male and female. The words seem freighted, however, when describing a powerful woman preparing to ascend to professional heights no female had yet attained in California.

Gender had obviously played a prominent role in her appointment and in fueling intense public interest in the nomination. Brown may have praised her administrative abilities, but he chose her almost certainly because of her gender. He might have appointed another woman with more experience—Mildred Lillie, for example. Governor Earl Warren had first appointed Lillie to the municipal court bench in 1947. At the time of Bird's nomination, she sat on California's Second District Court of Appeal. Lillie had very nearly become the first woman on the U.S. Supreme Court. Richard Nixon had planned to name her in 1971—even though she was a Democrat—but the all-male judiciary committee of the American Bar Association had rated her "unqualified." At sixty-two, Lillie was a generation older than Brown, however, and he undoubtedly wanted someone his own age and whom he knew personally.[36]

ALRB counsel Harry Delizonna had alluded to the gender component of Mahony's criticism when he offered this sarcastic observation: "Perhaps women are supposed to be overcome for emotion more easily than men." In fact, Delizonna also was known for being a difficult and demanding boss. Rather than "vindictive," however, the phrasing most often used to describe his approach was "a combative management style."[37]

Barbara Jean Johnson, president of California Women Lawyers, also took aim at what she viewed as sexist comments, blasting the "absolutely unprecedented double-standard" involved in evaluating Bird's appointment. "It is unprecedented that a candidate has been attacked by non-lawyer groups to the extent that she has been." In fact, her gender "should be a plus factor in considering the appointment," Johnson said. "The [current] justices are woefully lacking in knowledge and background of sex-based discrimination law."[38]

It is difficult, forty years after the fact, to understand the level of rancor surrounding Rose Bird's nomination. Few of her critics knew her personally or had any professional association with her; they relied on secondhand and even thirdhand information. Yet the level of antipathy was unprecedented. Johnson's reference to "sex-based discrimination law" offers a possible window into the mindset of at least some of Bird's opponents. Before the 1960s and 1970s, few people could have envisioned the existence of such a term, let alone the notion that women would somehow use the court system to successfully push an equal rights agenda. Bird's nomination could not have failed to remind observers of the women's movement, fueling concern that she might use her position to further advance a feminist agenda.

Additionally, the act of judging is replete with rituals designed to demonstrate power and prestige, "from the 'all rise,' to the wearing of the robes, to the physical layout and design of the courtroom where judges sit above the parties before them." Rose Bird's elevation to chief justice literally and physically placed her above everyone in the courtroom, except for her fellow justices. And she occupied the middle seat. This was a symbol of female power that few could miss.[39]

No one in authority directly raised the issue of gender when talking about how Bird might administer the court, but the experiences of other women in the judiciary suggest it was on the minds of many, if not most, establishment men in the 1970s. Shirley Abrahamson had been appointed to the Minnesota Supreme Court in 1976. During her confirmation hearing one questioner mused: "Do you think women judges will make a difference in the administration of justice?" Abrahamson directly confronted the issue: "What does my being a woman specially bring to the bench? It brings me and my background. All my life experiences—including being a woman—affect me and influence me."[40]

Responses from ordinary Californians reflected concern over Bird's gender. One letter writer strongly urged a "no" vote: "Don't do it Mr. Younger. Please don't do it! If you do, the average guy like myself is going to lose again." Another may have spoken for many men when he wrote to commissioners: "As a woman she has the natural sensitiveness tipical [sic] of her sex. She lacks the maturity needed to sit in judgment in a court where critical cases at every level of criminal and civil jurisdiction are to be decided. There is no reason for senamentalism [sic] in the courts."[41]

But other factors drove critics as well. Chief among them was antipathy toward the governor and his openly expressed contempt for traditional politics and authority figures. These included judges, whom Brown frequently characterized as pretentious and overpaid. But supreme court confirmations—no matter who was governor, or his general popularity—historically drew yawns, not hundreds of letters to the Commission on Judicial Appointments. In fact, Manuel's nomination, by comparison, drew little public interest and few letters, though he also had been appointed by Brown.

And no controversy had arisen over Ronald Reagan's appointment of William P. Clark almost exactly four years earlier. Clark had been only a year older than Bird at the time of his appointment. Despite his failure to graduate from either college or law school, the state bar association found "nothing that disqualified" Clark from serving. Few people wrote letters to the commission. Evelle Younger and Parker Wood had both served on the judicial appointments commission during the 1973 hearings, and both voted to confirm Clark without comment.

Only Chief Justice Donald Wright had voted against him. Years later,

Wright explained that "Bill Clark had a miserable academic record. He had flunked out of Stanford. He went for six quarters and only barely got four quarters of credit. . . . Then he joined the service, and when he came back to Loyola Law School nights, he flunked out of the place. Finally, he studied for the bar while working for a lawyer."[42]

Both Manuel and Clark had been appointed as associate justices, however. The "chief" part of the title undoubtedly fueled much of the vociferous reaction against Rose Bird. As *Newsweek* phrased it, the "position has perhaps more influence than any other state judge in the U.S." This was not an entirely accurate characterization. When it comes to choosing and deciding cases, the chief has only one vote.[43] The chief justice's job is as much administrative as judicial, and this is where a good portion of the power lies.

Much of the opposition to Bird from people within the court system undoubtedly centered on the realization, as administrative appeals court justice Marc Poche put it, "that the governor could take someone with no experience—a woman no less—and thrust her on top of the heap, so that she would be setting rules for judges who had put in long years on the bench growing barnacles on their butts; that caused deep-seated resentment." Ken Maddy, a longtime Republican lawmaker, described the "tradition" whereby "old-time experienced lawyers become judges and you waited your turn and if you were established enough you became a judge; Jerry overwhelmingly turned it upside down overnight."[44]

Debate continued unabated as Bird's confirmation hearing neared. Younger asked her to submit what some called a "job application" and what he called a "questionnaire." It consisted of fourteen questions. Among them: whether she would "attempt to nullify" death penalty laws via "judicial legislation"; she said she would not do so. Younger's query hinted at critics' concerns that Bird might push the court to circumvent or challenge laws passed by state legislators. He also asked Bird "how she viewed the U.S. Constitution in relation to the state Constitution."[45]

Bird's supporters slammed this line of questioning, but Younger explained that he asked the same questions of all candidates for judicial positions. Meanwhile, her opponents held to the fervent hope that her responses on the "application" would prove so damning Brown would be forced to withdraw the nomination.

Just days before the hearing, the California bar association deemed Bird "qualified" to become chief justice. The decision came only after a fierce, daylong debate, acknowledged President Ralph Gampell, an ally of Bird and of Brown. Nonetheless, the endorsement meant she had passed a crucial test, since bar recommendations ordinarily received "considerable weight" in the confirmation process. Gampell told reporters that he "deplored the fact that politics have been injected into the nomination of Ms. Bird." He particularly abhorred the pressure on Evelle Younger. "It is said . . . that he would be in political trouble if he votes a certain way. I would hope the decision should be confined only to Ms. Bird's qualifications, without regard to the political consequences of a vote one way or another."[46]

By the time her confirmation hearing got under way on the afternoon of March 7, most anyone paying attention to California state politics knew the name Rose Bird and understood that she was a highly controversial figure, whether or not they could explain exactly why this might be so. Sixty-five witnesses had signed up to testify both for and against the nomination. Bird's seventy-two-year-old mother, Anne, sat in the front row, the only family member in attendance. She never spoke to reporters, but they must have wondered how she felt about all of the negativity directed at her daughter. All but two of the first twenty-four witnesses supported the appointment.

Former chief justice Phil Gibson went first. He told commissioners he had met Bird for the first time the previous week, when the two held a lengthy conversation. He came away impressed. Younger wanted to know, however, whether Gibson understood just how important Bird's appointment might be. At the age of forty, she might remain atop the court for thirty years. Gibson was amused, since this same argument had been used against him decades earlier. "Every appointment is important," Gibson responded. "I think she is eminently qualified. Without any hesitation I say so."

Tobriner asked Gibson how much judicial experience he had possessed before his appointment to the court in 1940. "None," Gibson replied.[47] Bird later offered a humorous anecdote about her first meeting with Gibson. "I think he set some sort of precedent when he said goodbye to me that day. I am sure it was the first time one chief justice ever referred to another as 'darlin.'"[48]

San Jose mayor Janet Gray Hayes also strongly endorsed Bird and took aim at what she deemed the "sublimated sex discrimination" behind much of the opposition. "Attacks on women in high office as being emotional and unreliable are the most blatant sex discrimination. I know from personal experience that's what they mean." State bar president Ralph Gampell also spoke in favor of Bird, as did Justice David Zenoff of the Nevada Supreme Court, for whom Bird had worked as a law clerk.[49]

Two witnesses opposing the nomination sat on the board of the California bar association, and both disputed the public account of how Bird came to be deemed "qualified." The reported bar vote had been twelve in favor, three opposed, with five members abstaining. As Fresno attorney Oliver Jamison and Los Angeles attorney Joseph Cummins described it, however, this account omitted crucial details. Only fifteen of the twenty-one voting board members were attorneys; the other six were public members appointed by Jerry Brown. "No more than six attorney members actually supported the nomination," Jamison told commissioners. He implied that the other six "yes" votes had come from public members under pressure from Brown.[50]

Gampell insisted, however, that "there was no undue influence brought on any member by any person." And he offered further details on the "qualified" vote. One person voting "not qualified" said he did not have enough information about Bird, as did three of the five abstainers. Two abstainers offered no reasons for not voting.

The bar association conflict over Bird in some ways can be seen as an effort to get back at Brown for what members viewed as his effort to diminish their stature. Brown believed the state bar to be a particularly insular organization, serving "primarily the private self-interest of lawyers."[51] Lawmakers agreed and passed legislation requiring the addition of public representatives. The public members joined the board of governors in 1976, but a year later some professionals, including Cummins, still refused to accept the new order. He complained that public members "strayed from matters that affect lawyers." Public members shot back. One compared the practice of having only lawyers set policy for lawyers to "having wolves watch the sheep."[52]

Bird herself testified for slightly more than half an hour in the room where she hoped to preside over oral arguments. She sat at the circular end of a horseshoe-shaped table and faced the three commissioners. Onlookers, including reporters and photographers, pressed in on three sides. She spoke slowly and in a low voice as she narrated a chronology of her legal career—clerking for the Nevada Supreme Court, trial and appellate court work for Santa Clara County, teaching at Stanford, crafting the farm bill.

Subsequent questions hinted at how each commissioner viewed Bird. Parker Wood, who had already announced his intention to vote against Bird's appointment, asked her to discuss a letter from nineteen Santa Clara prosecutors opposing her nomination. She had been "an ardent and dedicated defender of indigent criminals," the prosecutors claimed, "but she had little sympathy for their victims."[53] Bird insisted that she understood the difference between an advocate, which had been her role as deputy public defender, and a judge, adding, "I would only indicate that the senior deputies in the district attorney's office did not sign the letter. Most of the people I had dealings with did not sign." Tobriner leapt to her defense: "How many deputy district attorneys did Santa Clara County have?" he asked. Approximately eighty, Bird replied.[54]

Younger prodded Bird on the notion of judicial responsibility versus political philosophy. She responded: "If you are asking that if a statute was passed that was in conformity with the U.S. and California Constitutions, would I strike it down based on my personal conviction—my answer is no." But she refused to discuss any potential cases or possible rulings. It would violate the canon of judicial ethics, she insisted. Asked about her relationship with former employee Tim Wallace, she said she and Wallace had a "difference of opinion on policy matters. Overall, our relationship was cordial." She refused to say more. No one asked about Mahony's letter.[55]

By late afternoon Monday, with forty witnesses yet to testify, Tobriner gaveled the hearing's first session to a close. When it resumed on Friday, March 11, the room again was packed. Bird was not in attendance; instead, she watched the proceedings from a separate room, via television. First to testify were several opponents of the nomination. Los Angeles attorney Daren T. Johnson termed Brown's choice of Bird "appalling." The governor had passed over far more experienced and able candidates, he argued. Johnson wanted observers to understand, however, that his criticism had nothing whatsoever to do with gender. "I would be happy if the seven justices were all women, if I could say they were qualified," he said. "The lady is not qualified for one basic reason—the complete lack and absence of any judicial experience." He compared Bird's appointment to expecting a person without flying experience to take the controls of a passenger plane.[56]

Several prosecutors told commissioners they suspected Bird had an anti–law enforcement bias. Thomas Hanford, a Santa Clara County deputy district attorney who had prosecuted some of the defendants that Bird represented in court, proffered a serious accusation. Hanford claimed that Bird attempted in one case "to perpetuate a fraud on the court" by telling the "judge that an agreement had been made to reduce charges against her client" when this, in fact, was not true. Hanford had been "tied up in another courtroom" when he learned of the claim, he said. He rushed back to deny the existence of an agreement. Could there have been a misunderstanding? commissioners asked. "No," he replied.[57]

Hanford's testimony was offset, however, by two prominent Bird supporters: Justice Herbert Ashby of the California Second District Court of Appeal (an appointee of Ronald Reagan and colleague of appointments commissioner Parker Wood) and James Geary, Santa Clara County sheriff. Both denied that Bird had ever engaged in questionable behavior as an attorney.

After two days of testimony, a clear picture had emerged. Bird's partisans believed her to be extraordinarily competent, legally brilliant, and eminently qualified to assume the role of chief justice. Her critics, on the other hand, viewed her as dangerously inexperienced, adamantly procriminal, and possibly borderline either incompetent or venal in her practice of law.

At 2:50 on Friday afternoon, Evelle Younger announced that he had heard enough. Twenty-four witnesses remained, but they were unlikely to add any new information. Younger said he was ready to vote. Tobriner and Wood quickly followed suit. After weeks of agonizing indecision, Younger said he had decided to support Bird's appointment. The final vote was two to one.[58]

Bird's partisans erupted in cheers and applause, but Younger had a sober message. "I do so reluctantly," he said, "because I believe there are many California judges better qualified by training and experience to assume this high office. It is the governor's opinion, not mine, that is significant. The law does not require that he appoint ... the best-qualified person. My limited responsibility requires only that I determine if Rose Bird is qualified. . . . The record clearly indicates that Rose Bird is intelligent and industrious. She was a good student and a good instructor." Criticism "concerning her allegedly vindictive nature and her inability to get along with others has been overcome by overwhelming evidence to the contrary," Younger said. "In my opinion, there has been no substantial question raised concerning her honesty or integrity."

Speaking as much to his political base as to the media and the audience gathered in the court chambers, Younger noted that many Bird critics had challenged what they dubbed her "liberal" or "left-wing" sentiments. "Assuming, without deciding, that she is, in fact, extremely liberal," he said, "that is not a legal disqualification. A former deputy public defender is no less qualified to be a judge than is a deputy district attorney."

Bird met with the press immediately after the confirmation. "I am deeply honored," she said. "I hope to dedicate my professional life to honoring fairness and justice." She thanked her supporters, particularly "the women's groups." She was now willing to acknowledge what her appointment meant for other women. "The most important thing was the breakthrough of having a woman at the head of the judiciary. Beyond that, I want to be judged as an individual."[59]

Asked about the bruising road to confirmation, she responded cautiously. "I think the process demands openness and a great deal of discussion. I think it's probably healthy for our political system." In a jab at her critics, however, she declared that she understood the "real difference" between the adversarial role of an attorney arguing a case in court and a judge, whose role is to be an impartial arbiter. "I see that very clearly in my mind. What you have seen today is that the adversary system goes too far."[60]

She also wanted her critics to know that she did care about crime victims. "I have an elderly mother," she said. "I have concern about her being able to walk safely on the streets. No one is in favor of the citizen being ripped off."[61] Asked for his response, Brown said he was "very relieved. When you plow new ground, of course there are those who are fearful." Republican gubernatorial hopeful Pete Wilson dubbed the appointment "political cronyism."[62]

Fifteen days after her confirmation, in the renovated B. F. Hastings Building where in the 1850s the first generation of California Supreme Court justices had held court alongside Sacramento's bustling waterfront, Rose Bird took the oath of office as chief justice and as the first female justice. It was in the same building in 1854 that justices had declared the Chinese to be members of "a race of people that nature has deemed inferior, and who are incapable of progress or intellectual development beyond a certain point."[63]

Bird's installation was a happier occasion. Guests included newly minted justice Wiley Manuel, as well as associate justices Mathew Tobriner and Frank Richardson. Conspicuous in their absence were Stanley Mosk and William Clark. No one expected the ailing Marshall McComb to be present, and he was not. Anne, again, was the only family member in attendance. Beneath her judicial robe, Bird wore a black pantsuit; a yellow ribbon bobby-pinned atop her French twist added a touch of color. Ever frugal, Bird had purchased a used robe for the occasion, leading a few pundits to refer to her as "second-hand Rose."[64]

Controversy accompanied even this celebration. Traditionally, the chief justice administered the oath of office to incoming colleagues. In the absence of a chief, the senior presiding justice did the honors. Tobriner had sworn in Wiley Manuel at a private ceremony in San Francisco two days before Bird's swearing-in. But Jerry Brown had insisted on personally administering the oath to Bird. "This is a ceremony that very fittingly takes place in the first week of spring," Brown said in introductory remarks. "It's a renewal of an institution. It's a time of celebration, of investiture." He praised Bird as a person "of insight and of wisdom" and predicted, more accurately than he could have known, that her appointment "would be remembered as an act of lasting significance."[65]

Critics depicted the governor's usurpation of Tobriner's role as just another effort to thumb his nose at tradition and to draw attention to himself. And it linked Brown and Bird together in the public's mind as young, arrogant, and willing—even eager—to flout the rules. She tried to explain that Brown had forced her into a corner. What should she have done, she asked, decline his request and disrespect the governor who had appointed her? However, she acknowledged later that Brown's action had sent the wrong message and created the wrong image, that of "an outsider being brought in by [another] outsider."[66]

One moment of levity came when Bird lost her place as she took the oath of office and had to start all over again. She was overcome by laughter. "I never could take directions from the governor," she joked. In an impromptu speech following the ceremony she praised California's judicial system as "the finest in the nation." But she expressed concern "that even our own system, as well as others across the country, is becoming more and more removed from the people who bring their disputes before the court."[67]

She added: "The individual rights of the accused must be balanced against the individual rights of those who suffer a loss at the hands of law violators. A major part of the role of the criminal courts is to ensure that a proper balance is always maintained so that individual freedom can flourish within the ordered structure of the community." Depending on one's point of view, Bird's remarks either reflected a courageous commitment to humanizing the judiciary or evidence that she was, in fact, highly partisan and possessed of an agenda she intended to pursue as chief justice. At a reception following the investiture, California Women Lawyers president Barbara Johnson lauded Bird as a "role model for girls and young women to emulate, and concrete evidence that the highest goal is attainable."[68]

As she prepared to assume her historic role atop the nation's preeminent court, Bird could be forgiven for hoping controversy was behind her and that the court could resume its work free of debate or conflict. It was not to be. She had little time to savor her accomplishment. Critics would continue to follow her every move with a vigilance bordering on obsession, ready to pounce at the slightest misstep.

California judges had long labored in relative obscurity. No more. Henceforth, critics would make sure that every Californian of voting age knew about the state supreme court—now dubbed "the Bird Court"— and the woman who sat in the middle seat. She would, in fact, soon become the main target in a larger campaign by conservatives to reshape the judiciary, and society in general, along more "traditional" lines.

Rose Bird had come a long way via hard work, smarts, timing, and assistance from a few well-placed mentors. Now she would be entirely on her own. If she wanted evidence of that, it was not long in coming. A week after her investiture, Wiley Manuel phoned. Would she like to ride with him to a luncheon their colleagues had arranged to welcome them to the court? Bird was stunned. She had not been invited to the luncheon.[69]

5 *Hail to the Chief*

Rose Bird wove in and out of San Francisco traffic before easing her Dodge Dart to the curb in a loading zone. As the car sat idling, an aide jumped out, clutching a newspaper classified ad section. He entered a phone booth, closed the door, and made a call. His boss was looking for an apartment to rent during the work week; he wanted to know if the advertised unit was still available. He returned to the car to inform Bird that the owner wanted references before showing the place. She laughed, then quipped: "They let anyone on the court these days."

It was April 1977 and Bird had been on the job for two weeks. She had agreed to let *Los Angeles Times* reporter Betty Liddick accompany her as she went about her daily tasks; as the writer noted, her subject was "uneasy," "guarded," and extraordinarily reluctant to talk about herself. "If I was dull before, I'm boring now," Bird insisted. Explaining her reticence, she referenced her tenure as agriculture secretary. "I guess it was partly a result of seeing what I thought was a misplaced value in political life—trying to find out as much as you could about the person, almost to the extent of what kind of bed they slept in, details of that sort that really have no relevance to what kind of job they do in terms of governing the state."[1]

Asked how the controversy over her appointment had affected her, Bird said: "I suppose as an individual when you're personally attacked, it's not easy, but it's a part of political and public life. If you let yourself become hurt every time it happens, you're going to be bruised all the time." She added: "I think the question involving prior judicial experience was a legitimate one and probably healthy to have discussed out in the open. Some of the other parts of it I could have avoided."[2]

Overnight, and to her dismay, Rose Bird had become an extraordinarily sought-after interview subject. From the moment she became chief justice, journalists began to telephone her office, and the calls "came in incessantly thereafter."[3] Despite her reluctance to divulge personal information, *Times* readers could glean some interesting information about California's new chief justice.

For example, Bird drove a Dodge Dart; previous chief justices had utilized the services of drivers and limousines. She chose to sell the court's limousine. "It didn't fit; I couldn't see myself in it," she told reporter Liddick. Besides, she did not believe taxpayers should foot the bill for state employees' personal luxuries.[4] At the same time, Bird did utilize the services of an assistant to conduct personal business—she paid him out of her own funds when he was not working on court issues. In fact, an aide accompanied her at virtually all times, essentially enabling her to shield herself from uncomfortable situations. Most often the aide was Stephen Buehl, who moved with Bird from the Agriculture and Services Agency to the supreme court. Readers, therefore, might have come away with a mixed view of the new chief justice: frugal and principled but also possessing a sense of entitlement.[5]

The latter trait might seem almost a given for a chief justice; certainly many, if not most, of her predecessors had believed themselves entitled to special attention and conveniences—hence the use of a court limousine and driver.[6] But few people had cared about a long line of middle-aged white men who seemed blandly indistinguishable from one another. Bird was a different story, and it remained unclear in spring 1977 how many people both on and off the court felt inclined to cater to a woman who, according to some, had not earned her title.

How Bird expected to be treated and how she reacted to the way others chose to treat her would help determine her success as California's first woman chief justice. Her introduction to the court did not bode well for the future. Associate Justice Stanley Mosk still seethed from being passed over as chief justice, and he let Bird know immediately where he stood. "I certainly cannot blame you for being here," he told her by way of welcome, "but I blame Jerry Brown for putting you here." Mosk later admitted that she "never let me forget that statement."[7]

He refused to let go of his anger, taking umbrage at every comment and action that he found irritating or offensive. For example, justices' offices spanned the fourth floor of the court building in San Francisco. Once Bird made an offhand comment about leaving work so late that her colleagues' chambers had all been dark. She knew this because the office doors featured windows above transoms. Mosk interpreted the remark as criticism of his work habits, so he hired a carpenter to cover his window with wood, making it impossible for Bird to know if he was inside. Bird explained that she had meant nothing by the comment, but Mosk remained resentful and unconvinced.[8]

Of the other five justices, only Mathew Tobriner and Wiley Manuel befriended Bird in her early days as chief justice. William Clark and Frank Richardson, both Reagan appointees, largely ignored her. Marshall McComb was a nonfactor; in May 1977 the Commission on Judicial Performance forced his resignation, due to advanced senility. Governor Brown soon appointed Bird's law school professor Frank Newman to replace McComb, but Newman did not join the court for several months.

Whether they were inclined to support her or not, all of Bird's colleagues expressed dismay at her unilateral decision to sell the court limousine, and at another decision to trade the luxurious accommodations where judges stayed during conferences for cheaper alternatives. Both moves may have saved the taxpayers money, but to her colleagues, the court's image was at stake, along with the prestige of its members.

Relationships with her fellow justices would not entirely define Bird's tenure on the court, however. As law professor Preble Stolz phrased it, "Some great judges in history were ... despised by the bar and hated by at least some of their colleagues."[9] Two of these were mid-twentieth-century U.S. Supreme Court justices—William O. Douglas and Warren Burger.

Associate Justice Douglas had been appointed by President Franklin D. Roosevelt. He was a strong civil libertarian who liked "people" in the abstract but was rude and dismissive to his colleagues and almost everyone else.

Richard Nixon had appointed Burger as Earl Warren's replacement in 1969. "In his seventeen years as chief, Burger . . . managed to alienate all of his colleagues," wrote Jeffrey Toobin. One associate justice, Potter Stewart, became so incensed that he "responded eagerly to an approach from author Bob Woodward . . . letting the journalist know that he would cooperate with an extended investigation of the Burger court."[10]

As in every bureaucracy, the staff held the key to smooth operations, and many employees of the California Supreme Court awaited Bird's arrival with trepidation. Former chief justice Donald Wright had wandered the halls in his stocking feet, dropping into offices unannounced for friendly chats. Bird's no-nonsense reputation made such an approach seem unlikely. Her first actions did not allay fears. As one writer put it, somewhat acerbically, she "did not have the good grace, as an outsider, to settle in slowly."[11]

Instead, she hit the ground running, sending in a "transition team"— four hand-picked young attorneys, all men—to analyze all aspects of the court. No prior chief justice had ever utilized the services of a transition team or conducted what employees widely viewed as an investigation. Within days, her brusque manner and take-charge attitude had alienated many staffers. She later explained that she had only two weeks after her confirmation to transition from the Agriculture and Services Agency to the court, giving her little time for niceties or leisurely conversations. She had to learn an entirely new bureaucracy from the ground up. The range of her duties must have seemed staggering even to a workaholic.

Chief justices oversee the budget for the statewide court system and lobby the state legislature and the governor—sometimes unsuccessfully—to provide adequate funds. They are responsible for staffing at the supreme court, including secretaries, clerks, bailiffs, and attorneys. They appoint judges to sit on courts at all levels when individual courtrooms are overloaded with cases or when judges are ill or on vacation. They appoint judicial members of the state Judicial Council, the policymaking arm of the California court system, and they serve as ex officio chairs of the council. Together with other justices, they appoint lawyer members of the Commission on Judicial Performance, the entity responsible for investigating complaints about judges' conduct.

The chief justice also presides over weekly conference sessions where justices discuss petitions seeking court hearings and decide which ones to accept or decline, assigns individual justices to write opinions, and presides over monthly oral arguments. Finally, the chief participates in the writing of opinions and oversees the issuance of press releases to announce important rulings. As California's first female chief justice, Bird also fielded and accepted dozens of invitations to speak to women's groups and to legal organizations. Even critics had to admit that she was extraordinarily adept at public speaking—witty, charming, and engaging.[12]

Prior to Bird's appointment, many administrative tasks at the supreme court had been handled by court administrative officer Ralph Kleps, who had arrived in 1961. Over the subsequent sixteen years he took on more and more responsibility, largely because Bird's two immediate predecessors had little interest in that side of the job. Roger Traynor disliked administration, explained staff attorney Peter Belton. He "was a scholar and wanted to stay in his chambers writing landmark opinions." Wright tolerated administration but prized collegiality above nearly all other traits and thus was unwilling to confront Kleps or to downgrade his responsibilities.[13]

Kleps believed that Bird, as an inexperienced newcomer, would rely on him even more than her predecessors. Shortly before her swearing in, he contacted her. He had written a booklet about the supreme court's administration that she might find informative, he said. Then he handed her a set of papers granting him administrative authority. Her predecessors had relied on him, Kleps said, and it would make her job easier. Bird refused. "I don't do things blindly," she said later. She needed to understand her responsibilities before delegating tasks to someone else, she told Kleps. Meanwhile, he was to answer to her. Also, she needed him to authorize funds for her to hire the members of her transition team.[14]

Stunned, Kleps felt as though he "had been run over with a bulldozer." He saw himself as kind and thoughtful and Bird as ungrateful. She saw it differently. Over the years, Kleps had created what she viewed as a dangerous "shadow court." Others quietly shared this perception. As the court's administrator, wrote one observer, "he, rather than the chief justice controlled the staff and often the policies of the California judicial system." Bird also found Kleps's attitude toward her condescending and patronizing.[15]

Six weeks after Bird's arrival, Kleps tendered his resignation. He was sixty-two and had hoped to remain on the job until retirement. Instead, he took his talents to the legal newspaper *Los Angeles Daily Journal*, writing columns on various aspects of the court's operation. The paper was read avidly by judges and lawyers. Kleps also wrote for law journals. Until his death five years later, he took every possible opportunity to criticize Bird, either explicitly or implicitly.

In a *Hastings Constitutional Law Quarterly* essay, for example, he offered a paean to Donald Wright, who had handled his job "with competence, courage, and candor. His prior service at all levels of the California court system, his management experiences in the military service and in California's largest trial court and his willingness to delegate duties to his associates and to his staff all contributed to a golden era of court administration in California."[16] Virtually anyone paying attention understood Kleps's real intention—to diminish Bird in comparison to Wright. She had, as it turned out, made a powerful enemy.

To replace Kleps, Bird chose California bar president Ralph Gampell, a longtime acquaintance who had testified for her at the confirmation hearing. This decision irritated even colleagues who were inclined to support her. The hiring of such an important person needed to be a team effort with all of the justices participating, they declared.[17]

Bird soon managed to anger others. Each associate justice had on staff attorneys who researched case files, crafted memos for conference and calendar hearings, and sometimes helped to draft opinions. Bird criticized the work of a few staff attorneys and suggested that some justices relied too much on them. She determined that some staff work should be handled by law clerks rotating on and off the job on a yearly basis.[18]

Most surprising to those who knew Bird was her decision to transfer female secretaries who had worked exclusively for previous chief justices to the general secretarial pool—a demotion. One observer dubbed the last decision "an act of breathtaking insensitivity." Such an action also seemed totally out of character for the daughter of a factory worker, who had long championed lower-paid employees and had authored a landmark labor relations bill benefitting farmworkers.[19]

In fact, at the same time she was demoting secretaries, Bird gave speeches urging feminists to concentrate as much effort on nonprofessional and blue-collar women as they did on highly paid professionals. "The true challenge is to ensure that the women's movement is a grassroots movement . . . for all women, not just those advancing to the highly paid, most clearly visible white collar positions at the top," she told attendees at a conference of Southern California Woman and the Law in April 1977.[20]

In retrospect, Bird's confrontation with Kleps seems inevitable. She faced a no-win situation no matter how she responded to him. If she catered to his ego and allowed him to continue administering the court, he would never respect her; on the other hand, treating him as just another employee while encouraging him to remain on the job would enable him to undermine her. And questioning staff attorneys might have irritated them, but it does not seem that unusual. The secretaries, however, had no real power. Perhaps she believed they had gotten too comfortable and that others deserved the same opportunities. Whatever her reasons, her action revealed what critics had previously characterized as tone-deafness in dealing with other people. It also altered the personal dynamics of the court. Wrote Stolz, "The chief justice had been a protector; she was now a threat."[21]

Within weeks of her arrival, court personnel had learned to tread lightly when Bird was around. Her actions also fired up the office gossip mill. Court staff criticized her personal appearance—the pantsuits, hair bows, French twist and curls framing her face, and lack of makeup. It is hard to imagine such comments aimed at any of her male predecessors, whether or not they were friendly or sympathetic. Some complaints bore a wistful cast, harkening back to the "good old days." She filled her chambers with plants, hung photos of flowers on the walls, and played classical music on her office stereo. She replaced the curtains on her chamber windows with more energy-efficient blinds and moved the conference table where justices held their meetings. The table had stood in the same spot for decades. As Bird later recalled, her decision to move it "nearly caused a riot." Mosk prevailed on her to put it back in its original location.[22]

She also allowed friends and staff to use her chambers, challenging longstanding etiquette practices. She invited one friend, an appellate judge who lived in Ventura, to use her Los Angeles chambers whenever he heard cases in that city. The judge, Richard Abbe, took her up on the offer. "You know, I have this sneaking suspicion that Richard is sleeping in my chambers," Bird told another friend. She was right. "He took a sleeping bag. He'd get up early in the morning and go running," then take a sponge bath in the chief's bathroom, the mutual friend acknowledged.[23]

Bird's aides often ate their lunches in her San Francisco chambers. One court employee nearly became unhinged when he saw the aides sprawled across the chairs, spilling food and dropping crumbs on the carpet. "The staff has always considered [the chief justice's] chambers as a sanctuary deserving of the highest respect," court bailiff Frank Ludlow told one writer. Employees even took issue with the coffee cup she kept on her desk. It bore the word "Ms.," a term utilized by women who considered themselves feminists.[24]

Gossip inevitably focused on Bird's extreme personal reticence. As one observer noted, she "found direct communication . . . and confrontation over issues personally painful, and she tended to withdraw and to limit her contacts to known friends and formal events that kept her distant."[25] These traits enabled critics to label her "paranoid." For example, soon after arriving at the court, she changed the locks on her chamber door. As she later explained it, she was working late on one Saturday night when she heard a key turn in the lock. She looked up to see an appellate judge, who seemed surprised at finding her still at work. Without explaining how he had a key, or why he needed access to the chief justice's chambers, he backed out of the room. Rattled by the notion that anyone could gain access to a room containing legal case files and private correspondence, she hired a locksmith.[26]

Bird's tendency to rely almost exclusively on her own staff also became a consistent topic of conversation. Virtually everyone remarked on the constant presence of Stephen Buehl and other aides. To meet with Bird, court personnel—including fellow justices—had to phone for appointments and then wait up to several days for a response. During meetings, Buehl remained nearby, taking copious notes.

The contrast between Bird and Wright was too dramatic not to beg comparison. Wright had treated court personnel like "family." She held them at arm's length. He trusted everyone; she seemed to trust no one—at least no one she did not know personally. Staff attorney Peter Belton had been at the court since 1960, and in the late 1970s he worked for Mosk. He offered a relatively sympathetic appraisal of Bird's early troubles: Brown should have appointed her an associate justice. He "did her no favors" by appointing her chief justice. Mosk "was the natural choice," Belton said, and he never let her forget it.[27]

Additionally, she "must have been intimidated and she responded by circling the wagons." Even her old mentor Gordon Winton weighed in. "Mosk's hostility set the stage for Bird's defensiveness and isolation," he said. "[Mosk] wanted it very badly and he ... I think, it's my opinion that he always resented Rose Bird because he didn't get it." Mosk's anger and her sense of herself as an "outsider" caused her to be defensive and to go into the job with "a little bit of a chip on her shoulder."[28]

Over time, Bird settled into the court routine, though she still remained guarded. Clearly sensitive about her public image, she granted a few interviews to reporters whom she perceived as friendly. *California Journal* editor and writer Ed Salzman had known Bird since her years at Berkeley. In a May 1977 article, Salzman tried to humanize her via revelations that she brought a brown-bag lunch to work every day and often ate alone in the cafeteria. Each Monday morning, Bird battled traffic on the Bayshore

Freeway, "just like other commuters traveling between San Francisco and Palo Alto." And she wore "the garb of middle class America (at least for women), the pantsuit, to work every day."

Still, she could not resist making comments that seemed designed to irritate members of the judicial establishment. People felt alienated from the judiciary, she told Salzman, because "prestige and priority are placed upon those courts . . . with the least direct contact with people and their problems."[29]

The arrival in summer 1977 of her old friend and law professor Frank Newman to replace the senile Marshall McComb lessened her sense of isolation somewhat. She had pressed Brown to appoint Newman as an associate justice, though he was an unlikely candidate for the court. Newman was sixty years old and had spent virtually his entire career as a law professor, a job he cherished because it allowed him to travel widely and spend time in the leisurely research and study of constitutional issues. At one point Pat Brown had selected Newman to serve on a committee to revise the state constitution, but Newman's passion was international law and the protection of human rights.[30]

Normally, the chief justice swore in new colleagues; in fact Bird had been criticized for allowing Brown to administer her oath of office, rather than acting chief justice Tobriner. No one challenged Newman, however, when he asked a close friend to do the honors. Bird was happy to have him on the court. The support of Tobriner, Newman, and, to a lesser extent, Manuel helped to offset the antagonism of Mosk and (by this point) Clark. Ideologically they may have been miles apart, but from the moment of Bird's arrival, Mosk seemed to gravitate toward Clark as a possible ally in his campaign to thwart the new chief justice.

She tried to defuse tensions by bringing cookies and cakes to work for justices to share during Wednesday conference sessions, believing, she said, that "when you break bread together . . . you can remain personally cordial."[31] But difficulties remained, and they extended to the process of deciding cases. She was direct in dealings with others, while her male colleagues tended to be indirect and subtle to the point of passive-aggressiveness. In conferences discussing cases, for example, they often danced around disagreements. "It was like a minuet," she told one friend. "A justice would say, 'what a wonderfully crafted memo you have done.'... And he would go on for five minutes like that. I had trouble keeping the votes straight because I didn't realize the person doing this basically disagreed with the entire memo."[32]

Several months after arriving on the court Bird suffered a recurrence of cancer; the removal of her right breast a year earlier had not ended the threat, and doctors removed a small malignant tumor from her left breast. This second bout with cancer led her to focus on survival and reflect on her life. She became obsessive about the kinds of foods she ate, more focused on what she hoped to accomplish in her remaining time on Earth, and even less inclined to tailor her personality to the needs and desires of other people.[33]

She also became freer about confronting issues such as gender discrimination. On one occasion, she used a speech before the Chancery Club of Los Angeles—a social organization for lawyers—to chide members for their refusal to admit women. She put her remarks in the form of a rhyme:

> You're a microcosm, in my humble estimation,
> Of our society's dilemma when dealing with discrimination.
> Women members, it's been said, you simply do not take
> Unless, of course, they've been hired to jump out of a cake.[34]

One constant hung over Bird and other members of the court during her first months on the job: the looming November 1978 election when she and three colleagues would go before California voters. Justices did not run against opponents; rather they faced straight up or down votes. Their names appeared on the ballot accompanied by the words "yes" and "no." A "yes" vote for Bird meant she would remain in office at least until her next confirmation election in November 1986. A "no" vote meant she would leave the court in January 1979.

No justice had ever been rejected by the state's electorate, but no justice had ever drawn so much attention or controversy. Voters knew little about her at this point, so they would cast their ballots largely on the basis of her judicial opinions. She presided over her first oral arguments on April 4, 1977, less than two weeks after taking office. Justices heard arguments ten times each year in sessions alternating among court facilities in San Francisco, Los Angeles, and Sacramento. The sessions lasted three to four days, and members of the public could attend; in fact, this was the only part of the court's work open to public view. Ordinarily, such sessions drew few people besides attorneys, but Bird's arrival fueled significantly enhanced interest.

The part of justices' work that the public did not see began weeks before oral arguments with hundreds of petitions arriving at the court's San Francisco headquarters, covering both civil and criminal matters appealed from lower courts. In the late 1970s the court received up to four thousand petitions each year. The court clerk assigned them in "mechanical rotation" to the six associate justices to ensure that each had essentially the same workload. The chief justice did not participate in this initial phase of the process. Staff attorneys researched the facts and relevant case law in each petition and wrote three- to five-page conference memos listing the pertinent issues. These became the basis of weekly sessions held each Wednesday in the chief justice's chambers.

During this day-long meeting, justices discussed as many as sixty or seventy petitions, separated into "A" and "B" piles, with the latter generally viewed as nonstarters. If four of the seven justices voted in favor of hearing a case, the chief justice assigned one colleague to prepare it for oral argument. Records, which sometimes ran a hundred pages or more, were sent over from the jurisdictional court to the relevant justice, who then assigned a staff attorney to prepare a "calendar" memo setting forth the facts, analyzing the arguments, and offering recommendations. These averaged anywhere from twenty to fifty pages in length and sometimes ran even longer.

Less than 10 percent of petitions made it past the initial part of the process. The chosen few had to meet specific criteria: they had to raise important questions of law, cover issues that impacted many people or institutions, or reflect conflicting views among appellate courts that needed to be resolved. Larger legal issues had to be at stake, "not questions of justice between individuals," according to staff attorney Peter Belton. Sometimes the court let appellate decisions stand even if justices disagreed with the findings, if they believed the lower court had used the correct legal reasoning to reach its conclusion.[35] Death penalty cases did not follow this pattern. Death verdicts went to the supreme court on automatic appeal, along with a few other types of cases, such as those involving the constitutionality of ballot measures.[36]

Preparing for oral arguments could be a daunting experience for justices and their staffs. Scott Sugarman, a former student of Bird's who served as her research attorney for a period, recalled driving from the East Coast to San Francisco in April 1977 to begin work at the court. He arrived the Thursday before her first oral arguments. Shortly after he greeted Bird, she pointed to a "three-foot-high stack of documents sitting on her desk. Could I, she asked softly, review all those cases and discuss them with her Sunday afternoon?" Sugarman suggested an alternative, discussing the cases each day before oral arguments, and Bird agreed.[37]

Arguments began each day at 9 a.m. and ended at 4 p.m. Each side had a half hour to present its case; the justices, like their federal counterparts, peppered attorneys with questions throughout. At the end of each session, and sometimes during lunch breaks, justices gathered in the chief's chambers to take tentative votes. If the majority agreed with the points made in a justice's calendar memo, and with the attorneys' arguments, the chief justice assigned that justice to write the opinion. If the majority disagreed, the chief assigned the opinion to a justice on the "no" side of the argument.[38]

Writing opinions represented the final stage of the process, but it was not always a straightforward proposition. Justices sometimes added comments in response to colleagues or changed their minds and switched sides altogether. In the latter case, the decision had to be reassigned. Final rulings could take months, even years. "I spend more than half my time here just deciding what to decide," Mathew Tobriner once said. The paperwork involved in the process often proved daunting. "I don't know what to do with all of this paper," was a recurring lament among justices.[39]

Neither Bird nor Manuel asked many questions during their first session, and neither participated in writing opinions that emerged from that initial gathering. Bird's first lead opinion appeared five months later, in September 1977. Retail giant Sears sought court approval to videotape the reenactment of an accident in which a customer severed four fingers while using a radial arm saw. The plaintiff objected. Lower courts had sided with Sears, but Bird, writing for a unanimous court, sided with the customer.[40] She wrote for a unanimous court as well in December 1977, in a case involving a Madera family whose farm sat downwind from a sewage plant that gave off a noxious odor. Justices determined that the town, which had authorized the plant, owed the family compensation.[41]

Most of her early writing leaned toward caution, but her sympathy for women left to fend for themselves after divorce emerged in another unanimous decision in January 1978. The case involved a woman whose former husband sought to cut off spousal support. Married twenty years, the plaintiff had not worked while raising children. "A wife who has spent her married years as a homemaker and mother may, despite her best efforts, find it impossible to reenter the job market," Bird wrote. Maintaining spousal support represented "ordinary common sense, decency and simple justice."[42]

Altogether, Bird wrote lead opinions in sixteen cases between September 1977 and November 1978, most of only "middling importance," according to one court watcher. Mosk may have harbored personal resentment, but he signed on to all of her opinions. All but three, in fact, came on unanimous votes, including one in which justices determined that a man who had accidentally killed his wife could still inherit her property. Three of the thirteen unanimous decisions featured concurrences from one or more of Bird's colleagues, agreeing with the outcome but taking issue with minor legal points.[43]

Two cases were decided by 5–2 votes and another by a 6–1 vote. All of the dissents came from the two Reagan appointees—William Clark and Frank Richardson. Bird concurred or dissented in fourteen additional cases and signed on to decisions without comment in dozens more. In one, Mosk determined that police had to have "reasonable suspicion" before stopping an individual for questioning. Bird concurred but dubbed the term "reasonable suspicion" too vague to be useful.

By spring 1978 it was becoming clear that the antipathy revealed at Bird's confirmation hearing had not dissipated; it had in fact coalesced into several efforts aimed at defeating her in November. Conservatives, shut out of many statewide offices before the emergence of Reagan in the midsixties, had crafted—mostly in Southern California—a grassroots strategy that elected candidates for school boards and city councils. From this beginning, politicians moved on to higher-profile offices.[44] Republican state senator H. L. Richardson was among the most successful of this brand. Richardson represented the San Gabriel Valley in eastern Los Angeles County. He was ultraconservative, a founder of the group Gun Owners of America, and a member of the virulently anticommunist and conspiracy-obsessed John Birch Society. He also headed the Law and Order Campaign Committee, devoted to toughening death penalty laws.

A year before Bird's appointment, Richardson had helped pioneer a new and game-changing form of political fundraising—the direct mailer—in which campaign organizers searched out specific individuals and issues, fueled public support or opposition, and then used emotional pitches to raise money. Donor names were complied on mailing lists, which could be used over several campaign cycles, as organizers repeatedly went back to the same contributors and added new names to the lists. Richardson also made his lists available, for a price, to other campaign fundraisers. He named his company Computer Caging Corporation.

By 1977 the Law and Order Campaign Committee had raised $800,000 for a ballot initiative toughening capital punishment laws. In early 1978 Richardson claimed to have sixty-five thousand names on his mailing list. In June he announced that he intended to raise an additional $1 million to defeat two of three Jerry Brown appointees—Rose Bird and Frank Newman. Within a few weeks, however, he announced his decision to focus entirely on Bird. Agriculture interests announced their own campaign against the chief justice. Led by Mary Nimmo, the daughter of Justice William Clark's friend Robert Nimmo, they called their group

"No on Bird." The executive committee of the Republican Party also declared its opposition to Bird but operated mostly behind the scenes.[45]

Bird's partisans cried "sexism," just as they had at her confirmation hearing. What else could explain a level of antipathy that seemed so utterly unwarranted? A political campaign targeting a single justice was unprecedented. None of her lead or concurring opinions had been particularly liberal, at least no more so than those of her colleagues. As one writer noted, "In the 15 months she has been [chief justice], she has taken part in so few controversial decisions that it is difficult to tell what direction, if any, she will try to lead the court."[46] As evidence of sexism, Bird's supporters could point to Rosalie Wahl, the first woman appointed to the Minnesota Supreme Court in 1977, who was also facing conservative opposition in her bid to retain her office. Wahl's opponents charged her with being "soft" on rape and drug trafficking. Despite the opposition, Wahl retained her seat.[47]

Richardson loudly proclaimed Bird to be "anti–death penalty," but capital punishment was in flux in California in 1978, and she had not participated in any death penalty cases to date. Writer Ed Salzman reinforced the notion of sexism in an August 1978 *California Journal* article positing that "the deciding element" in her confirmation or rejection might be "how the public feels about a woman holding possibly the most important public office in the state."[48]

But the reasons conservatives continued to target Bird were more complicated than simple sexism, just as they had been in her confirmation hearing. Agriculture interests still smarted over her role in crafting the Agriculture Labor Relations Act and in banning the short-handled hoe. Republican politicians saw Bird as a stand-in for Brown, who had proved a canny and elusive opponent, thwarting them at every turn. Going into the fall election, Brown appeared likely to sweep to a second term in a lopsided match with Attorney General Evelle Younger. Business interests also viewed the Bird court with alarm. Virtually every business-oriented case since her arrival had gone against them.[49]

As an example, they could point to *Mellencamp v. Bank of America.* Cynthia Mellencamp bought a home in Riverside County in 1975 and assumed the sellers' loan, at 8 percent interest. Bank of America held the mortgage and refused to approve the loan assumption, citing a law that required new homebuyers to take out loans at prevailing interest rates. In 1975 the prevailing rate was 9.25 percent. Mellencamp refused to renegotiate the loan, so the bank returned her first payment and filed a notice of default. She sued, and the case eventually ended up in the state supreme court.

In August 1978 the justices sided with Mellencamp. The decision, written by Wiley Manuel and signed by Bird and four other justices, overturned the law, which had been in effect since the Depression. It could not "be enforced ... unless the lender [could] demonstrate that enforcement is reasonably necessary to protect against impairment to its security or the risk of default," justices wrote. Bankers were enraged. Manuel may have written it, but Bird sat atop a court that clearly seemed to be no friend of theirs.[50]

Perhaps the most significant reason for targeting Bird was her perceived vulnerability. Her bruising confirmation battle had exposed weaknesses. She had a brittle personality, had bruised egos on her way up, and had angered some colleagues and staff during her months on the court. Gender played at least some role in her vulnerability. Opponents denied it was a factor, but it had been a subtext at her confirmation hearing, and the arrival of a woman to the court brought significantly increased public interest, both in her and in the institution. As legal scholar Laurence Tribe saw it, Bird's "liberal inclinations, her personal style, and her gender seemed too threatening a combination even for California."[51]

Conservatives saw Bird's perceived vulnerability as a major opportunity to begin unraveling a court system they had long viewed as "the last bastion of liberalism."[52] The year 1978 must have seemed particularly promising, since three of the seven justices were newcomers with little experience either in the judiciary or in the bruising world of politics. Manuel and Newman, however, were somewhat problematic in this regard, since Manuel had been a judge before his appointment (though only for a year), and Newman had been a law dean. Bird, an inexperienced woman, represented a win-win situation, particularly for H. L. Richardson.

His branch of the Republican Party had long been marginalized by the mainstream, turned off by what moderates viewed as his "extremism." But Richardson tapped into the zeitgeist. He knew how to capitalize on the growing resentment of white, working-class voters toward liberals and feminists who strove for racial and gender equality at a time when many white men felt devalued in a rapidly changing society. By focusing on a single individual rather than a faceless bureaucracy, Richardson and other anti-Bird forces hoped to gain traction with such voters and others. They carefully combed through legal cases for this purpose.

People v. Caudillo and Proposition 13 seemed most promising. The former dealt with violent crime and the latter with taxes. The facts of *Caudillo* were horrifying. Daniel Caudillo had kidnapped a young woman from an elevator in Los Angeles, took her to her apartment, and sexually assaulted her for two hours. As he left, he stole sixty dollars from her wallet. The trial judge, calling the case "one of the most horrible" he had seen, and citing the "great bodily injury" suffered by the victim, added a four-year "enhancement" to Caudillo's three-year sentence. Caudillo's attorney appealed, arguing that the enhanced sentence was illegal, since the state legislature had not included rape under the "bodily injury" umbrella. Appellate judges agreed with the trial judge. Caudillo's attorney then appealed to the California Supreme Court.

In early 1977, before Bird's arrival, the supreme court had accepted the case. She was on hand for oral arguments, which took place that summer, and she assigned the lead opinion to Bernard Jefferson, an appeals court judge sitting on the high court temporarily, since Newman had not yet taken his seat as associate justice. Observers wondered at her decision to give the case to Jefferson, rather than to a permanent member of the court, but none of the justices appearing on the November 1978 ballot may have been willing to write the lead opinion on such a potentially explosive case. As it turned out, the court felt obliged to agree with Caudillo, and justices overturned the sentence enhancement. The ruling was released in June 1978. None of the justices evinced any sympathy for the defendant, but according to Jefferson, the state legislature had tied their hands by establishing specific criteria for "great bodily harm," and under current law, rape did not qualify.[53]

Five justices signed the opinion. "It is apparent to us [that] the Legislature intended the term 'great bodily injury' to refer to substantial or significant injury in addition to that which must be present in every case of rape," Jefferson wrote. Bird signed the majority opinion but wrote a lengthy concurrence. "I have given this case considerable thought," she wrote, "and find I am compelled to sign the opinion . . . since the legislative history of Penal Code section 461 indicates that the Legislature intended that rape per se could not be deemed 'great bodily injury.'

"Personal repugnance toward these crimes cannot be a legitimate basis for rewriting the statute as it was adopted by the Legislature. It is precisely because emotions are so easily called into play in such situations that extra precaution must be taken so that this court follows the legislative intent and not our own predilections or beliefs." She urged the legislature to revisit rape laws, which lawmakers did within months of the decision.[54]

Immediate and intense reaction ensued. The magazine *New West* carried a story that featured noted feminists attacking the ruling. Attorney Gloria Allred labeled it "abominable." She said: "I would expect Rose Bird to take a feminist point of view," but, she added, "I shouldn't say there's any sense of betrayal over the Caudillo case."[55]

Without the enhancement, Caudillo's sentence had to be recomputed and reduced, which meant he could be released from prison within a few months. "Next May that rapist could be on the streets again because Rose Bird and the Supreme Court reversed an appellate court decision," declared H. L. Richardson.[56] In fact, Caudillo was set for release in fall 1978, but numerous legal challenges kept him in prison until the early 1980s.[57]

Proposition 13 dealt with property taxes. Rapidly rising home values in the 1970s fueled rising property taxes as well, since taxes were based on home values. Many older people who had lived in their homes for decades had no idea how much they might owe in taxes from year to year. Proposition 13 on the June 1978 primary ballot rolled back assessed values to 1975 levels, capped taxes at 1 percent of assessed value, and limited annual increases thereafter to 2 percent of assessed value. Property could only be reassessed when owners sold; then the new owners paid taxes based on the full market value at the time of purchase.

The initiative, which had been crafted as an amendment to the California Constitution, was backed by 62 percent of voters. Thus it could not be revised by the state legislature. Immediately after passage local government agencies, facing significantly lower revenues, petitioned the state supreme court, seeking a decision on its constitutionality. Richardson strongly backed Proposition 13, which, he knew, placed Bird and her court in a tight spot. If they declared it constitutional, conservatives had won a major battle. If not, justices faced voters' wrath and possible rejection at the polls. Richardson happily declared Proposition 13 "more than a bonus. It's the $64,000 payoff."[58]

As the summer of 1978 wore on, politicians on both sides of the aisle pondered the court's eventual decision on Proposition 13 and its potential impact on Bird. National magazines carried stories about the "tax revolt" in California. Tom Wicker of the *New York Times* called the measure "a massive rejection of liberal government as it had developed in the post–New Deal Era." "Even under the best of circumstances, this did not promise to be a good year for Rose Bird," wrote a *Los Angeles Times* reporter. "So she needed Proposition 13 like she needed a bad headache." One Brown aide acknowledged that Proposition 13 added a "troubling dimension to the efforts against her, but I don't think Richardson's threat is as serious as it purports to be." But some private polls showed her losing.[59]

In late September the court issued its ruling: Proposition 13 was constitutional. Reagan appointee Frank Richardson authored the decision, which he carefully presented as a narrow reading of the initiative, focused only on its constitutionality, not on its merits or lack thereof. Justices had been asked to rule on seven different issues, including constitutionality, conformance to the single-subject requirement for initiatives, vagueness, and compatibility with equal protection laws.

Bird agreed with the majority on all but one issue—equal protection.

"By pegging some assessments to the value of property at its date of purchase [after 1978] and other assessments to the value of property as of March 1, 1975," she wrote, Proposition 13 "creates an irrational tax world where people living in homes of identical value pay different property taxes."[60]

Brown had campaigned against the initiative before the June election; when it passed, he did an about face. Asked if he thought Bird's dissent would hurt her, Brown did not mention her by name. Instead he said: "I think we have a very excellent court. I think the court is doing a good job. . . . They didn't go into whether Proposition 13 made sense. I don't think the effects . . . will be felt for several years." But opponents seized on Bird's dissent as further evidence that she was out of step with the mainstream. She refused to take the bait. "I don't think people would want me to come to this court and vote just the way [H. L.] Richardson wants me to vote. If we fold at whatever the whim of the moment is, we set a bad example for the rest of the judicial system."[61]

The court's Proposition 13 decision seemed to take much of the air out of Richardson's sails. He had to admit that his $1 million goal was unattainable, but he plowed ahead with his anti-Bird effort and announced he was lowering his fundraising goal to $600,000. He also debuted a dramatic television ad that leaned heavily on the *Caudillo* ruling. It showed a young woman entering an elevator and then emerging, sobbing, with her clothes torn and disheveled. Bird partisans unleashed a torrent of complaints and prevailed on television networks throughout the state to ban the advertisement.[62]

But Richardson's inflammatory approach backfired even without the protests. The agriculture-oriented "No on Bird" group quickly distanced itself from him. Meanwhile, Bird's backers ramped up activity as they began to seriously consider the possibility that she might be defeated. Part of their concern lay in her unwillingness to directly challenge her critics, aside from giving a few speeches bemoaning the influence of "a small group of extremists in this state fighting to ensure ideological domination" of the judiciary.[63]

Several groups and individuals worked for her confirmation, but their efforts were not exactly organized, and not all of them shared the same agenda. Women's groups composed much of the membership of Californians for Chief Justice Bird; trial attorneys led both Californians for the Court and Californians for an Independent Judiciary. Hollywood personalities also backed her retention but were not affiliated with any group.[64]

In early October 1978, Tom Houston, who had worked for Bird at the Agriculture and Services Agency and still worked in state government, took a leave of absence and moved from Sacramento to Los Angeles to pull together a coordinated pro-Bird effort that included all of the independent efforts. He reached out to journalists across the country, likening the anti-Bird effort to a witch hunt. He placed H. L. Richardson's "extremism" front and center. And he pushed Bird to make "unpublicized visits to the editorial boards of many of the state's major newspapers" seeking their endorsements.[65]

Within days, money and endorsements began pouring in. The *Sacramento Bee* opined that the contrast between H. L. Richardson "and the dignified silence and honorable records of Rose Bird and the other three justices on the ballot is striking." The *Los Angeles Times*' full-page endorsement was particularly strong. It read: "Rose Bird is under intense and intemperate attacks by powerful interests."[66]

Since she refused to campaign, others "must rebut the false and even hysterical charges against the first woman ever to serve on the California Supreme Court, and the fact that she is a woman animates much of the opposition to her. . . . There are proper grounds for deposing a judge: incompetence, a demonstrable bias that contravenes the law, dishonesty or lack of judicial temperament. None of those grounds apply to Bird."[67]

Bird's supporters also prodded her to lighten up in interviews, to reveal something—anything—about herself that might humanize her to readers or viewers, but she refused to cooperate. "I have no interest in that whatsoever," she said, for perhaps the hundredth time. "I'm not willing to exploit myself for a job. I don't believe in government by public relations. I don't put out press releases. I'm not a flamboyant person. I suppose if I was smart politically," she added, "I'd . . . get into [San

Francisco reporter] Herb Caen's column that I was eating at Vanessi's [restaurant] with some tall, dark, handsome stranger."[68]

By late October, polls showed Bird winning confirmation but barely. On November 2, five days before the election, H. L. Richardson admitted he had only managed to raise $200,000. Half had gone to mailings sent to five hundred thousand California voters, and the rest had been spent on advertisements. With no resulting bump in anti-Bird sentiment, he seemed resigned to defeat. So did the "No on Bird" campaign, which had raised less than $45,000.[69]

More challenges lay ahead for the Bird camp, however, and they came from an unexpected source. It seemed that Stanley Mosk might vote against her, according to one news account. This information came via a letter leaked to the press by an unnamed source, noting that the California Trial Lawyers Association (CTLA) had named Mosk Appellate Justice of the Year but that he had refused to accept the honor. The group's support for Bird had allegedly played a prominent role in his refusal.

"I am very unhappy with your association getting involved in politics this year," the letter quoted Mosk. "He said we had no business getting involved in the Rose Bird campaign or coming out in support of her without knowing all the facts," a CTLA spokesman said. The organization gave its award to Wiley Manuel instead. Reached for comment, Mosk denied he had linked his refusal to Bird's election, though he admitted objecting to the group's involvement in politics. "I wrote no letter to CTLA and did not authorize anyone to write on my behalf," Mosk said. "I did not indicate to CTLA or to any other group how I intend to vote on any issue."[70]

Three days before the election, Bird agreed to give an interview to KQED, San Francisco's public television station. She blamed her opposition on "special interests" and on her gender. Special interests, she declared, might view the judiciary as an easier target than the legislative or executive branches of government. And "when you're the first of either your race or your sex . . . in any position, two things really apply to you and that is that you are under a microscope and you are allowed no margin of error."[71]

As Election Day dawned, Bird's supporters crossed their fingers and dared to hope. Then they opened their newspapers. On the front page of the *Los Angeles Times* was a story on yet another court case, *People v. Tanner*. It suggested that the court had postponed ruling on California's "use a gun—go to prison" law until after the election. The reporters cited unnamed sources, who claimed that justices had decided to overturn the law but feared that releasing their decision before the election might cost Bird and possibly the two other Brown appointees on the ballot.

The article, by *Times* reporters William Endicott and Robert Fairbanks, read:

> The California Supreme Court has decided to overturn a 1976 law that required prison terms for persons who use a gun during a violent crime, but has not made the decision public, well-placed court sources said Monday.
>
> The decision in People vs. Tanner is certain to anger law enforcement officials around the state.
>
> The court sources said the decision was reached on a 4–3 vote, with Chief Justice Rose Elizabeth Bird, whose name goes before voters today, among the majority.
>
> The sources said that the announcement of the decision is being delayed by Associate Justice Mathew O. Tobriner, who has been one of Ms. Bird's strong supporters against a well-organized campaign to win voter disapproval of her appointment to the court.

Endicott and Fairbanks had tried to contact Bird for the story, but she was "unavailable," they wrote. They did reach Mathew Tobriner, who told the reporters that his judicial oath of office forbade discussion of any case under consideration. "I can say nothing, absolutely zero, zero, zero." Two other unnamed justices had been more forthcoming, at least according to the reporters. Both had "confirmed that individual decisions were signed some time ago by all members of the Court. The justices could not explain why the outcome had not been announced."[72]

Bird issued a statement late that afternoon: "There are no completed cases before this court where release has been delayed for political reasons or for any other reasons extraneous to the decision-making process. . . . It is a curious coincidence that this story appears on the morning of the day when the voters are going to the polls. Those involved in the campaign against me, knowing full well that neither Justice Tobriner nor I may properly comment on any pending case, seek to exploit the fact that we honor that ethical standard."[73]

The story came too late to affect the outcome. In the end, Bird won voter confirmation but by the smallest margin of any supreme court justice in California history. Slightly less than 52 percent of voters agreed that she should remain in office, a far lower percentage than her three colleagues on the ballot. Analysts suggested that partisanship, antipathy toward the courts in general, and hostility toward Jerry Brown had cost Bird votes.

But voters had more strongly supported the other justices; it appeared to be Bird, rather than the court in general, that large numbers of voters disliked. Meanwhile, Brown had won reelection by a margin of twenty points. Most voters clearly approved of him. A more likely scenario is that the incessant drumbeat of attention and negativity from a variety of sources had fueled voter antipathy toward Bird.[74]

Virtually no one except close observers of the judiciary noted in the election's immediate aftermath that the "unnamed sources" in the *Times* article had come from inside the court itself. This information gave the story more credibility than it otherwise might have had. But who at the court might have given "inside" information to reporters? No one but staff attorneys and justices knew the status of pending cases.

Newspaper reporters ordinarily did not seek out comments from staff, though they might have done so in this case. None of the justices on the ballot was a likely source, since revealing such inflammatory information might blow back on all of them, not just Bird. Tobriner was a decidedly unlikely source, since the story tagged him for holding up the "use a gun" case. That left only two likely sources: Mosk and Clark—Bird's nemesis and the colleague he saw as most simpatico, at least when it involved the chief justice.

With the election over, Tobriner and Bird might have chosen to ignore the *Times* story and return to work. Bird would be secure in the knowledge that she had another eight years before facing the electorate for a second time. Mosk's continuing enmity, irritating though it might be, held few negative implications for her professional stature or tenure. Journalists would move on to other news, and the *Times* article would be forgotten. Justices would release their "use a gun" decision to a flurry of attention. This, too, would fade away.

But neither Tobriner nor Bird let the matter drop. Tobriner had earned a stellar reputation during his sixteen years on the court. Now it was in danger of being tarnished, perhaps fatally. Bird had tolerated criticism about her personality, her lack of experience, and her "liberal" proclivities. The *Times* story had publicly impugned her integrity. A boundary had been crossed. Tobriner asked all of his colleagues to sign a letter verifying that he had not held up the "use a gun" decision. Without telling any of her colleagues, Bird sat down to write her own letter to the Commission on Judicial Performance, asking for an investigation into the *Times'* allegations.

She believed such an investigation would clear the air and absolve her and Tobriner of blame. Instead it unleashed an unprecedented series of events that pulled back the curtain on a court riddled with pettiness and intrigue. For decades, the California Supreme Court had enjoyed a unique status, deemed politically off-limits by all but a few archconservatives; now it was fair game.

6 *Disorder in the Court*

On Thanksgiving weekend 1978, Associate Justice Frank Newman was vacationing in Carmel, California, when he received a phone call from Chief Justice Rose Bird. More than two weeks had passed since the November election, and Bird was still smarting over the *Los Angeles Times* article, as well as subsequent newspaper accounts that implied the court had held up its ruling on *People v. Tanner*.

If true, such an action could be construed as judicial misconduct. As he described the conversation years later, Newman recalled telling Bird that "I certainly don't think any letter should be sent until we meet on Monday." Bird told him she had already sent the letter. Newman replied: "I think it's a terrible judgment that you've decided all by yourself without consulting us."[1]

Bird never explained her reasons for acting without input from her colleagues, but they are not difficult to discern. She believed strongly that Stanley Mosk and William Clark were the two unnamed court sources behind the stories. Both undoubtedly would refuse to sign on to an investigation aimed at revealing their participation in an action that also might be construed as judicial misconduct. She also knew that her critics outside of the court were likely to keep hammering on its handling of specific cases and hoped that an investigation would put the issue to rest. It is also not difficult to imagine that Bird, angry over what she viewed as continued efforts to sabotage her, thought that publicly outing the press leakers might embarrass them and discourage future such endeavors. Finally, others—including the California Chamber of Commerce—had begun asking for an investigation, and she undoubtedly wanted the inquiry to happen on her own terms.

Whatever her motives, she got far more than she bargained for. Rather than silencing critics, the ensuing investigation placed the judiciary under a microscope and provided the public with a close-up view of how the court went about its work. The picture was not a pretty one. The hearings revealed justices not as ethereal and impartial beings but as ordinary people—petty, hypersensitive, and backstabbing. Critics of the judiciary may have cheered this development, but many others did not, and they blamed California's first female chief justice for tarnishing the court's reputation.[2]

On the surface, *People v. Tanner* seemed too ordinary a case to fuel accusations and heated rhetoric. In January 1976 twenty-seven-year-old Tanner held up an East Palo Alto 7-Eleven. Police captured him a short time later on the street outside the store and confiscated his gun—a .22-caliber pistol—and forty-one dollars he had taken from the cash register. Tanner went to trial, and a jury convicted him of robbery. Under a law enacted less than a year earlier, dubbed "use a gun—go to prison," anyone using a firearm in the commission of a felony had to serve prison time. Tanner had used a gun, thus he had to be sentenced to prison—end of story.[3]

But the case was not exactly as it seemed. Tanner's "robbery" had been staged. He worked for a company that provided security to convenience stores, and his job was to "shoplift" items to determine how much attention clerks actually paid to customers. The East Palo Alto 7-Eleven had recently terminated its contract with the security firm, so Tanner decided to fake a crime to convince store owners to reinstate the contract. His gun contained no bullets; Tanner alerted the cashier, asked him to call police, and then casually waited for them to arrive.

Everyone involved in the trial agreed on one thing: pulling such a stunt was incredibly stupid—but what to do? Tanner had no criminal record; he had even served honorably in the military. Yet under the "use a gun" law, he had to be sentenced to prison. The judge, who called the case "very, very bizarre," decided to strike the gun charge, enabling him, he believed, to sentence Tanner to a year in San Mateo County Jail, a psychiatric examination, and five years' probation.[4]

California attorney general Evelle Younger was irate. He appealed the lenient sentence, and an appellate court agreed that the judge had acted illegally; under the law, Tanner had to go to prison. Tanner's attorney appealed to the California Supreme Court, which heard the case in February 1978. Tanner then became one of dozens of cases circulating among the justices. The average time from argument to final ruling in the late 1970s was seven months, though some cases were decided in as little as two months and others took up to two years. For Bird's opponents, the clock started just after oral arguments ended.

When a ruling was not forthcoming by September 1978, they saw an opportunity to pounce. Nothing else had seemed to stick, so they took a new tack: declaring that the court had decided to hold the decision until after the election to help Bird win confirmation.[5] The *Daily Journal*, a legal newspaper, first raised the prospect of intentional delay in a September article by three prominent members of the law enforcement community, including Ronald Reagan acolyte Edwin Meese III. The article criticized what the writers deemed the court's "pro-defendant" slant. "It is not at all clear what is holding the [Tanner] decision up. . . . [T]here has been a slowdown in the release of important decisions as the November elections draw nearer," the writers charged.[6]

In October Evelle Younger, running for governor on the Republican ticket, added his voice. At one campaign stop he said: "I believe the Brown Court has reached many important decisions which have been written and have only to be released." In a conversation with reporters, Younger went further. "I have suggested certainly that the Court is deliberately withholding the [Tanner] decision until after the election." He later walked back his accusations, but his recanting garnered far less attention than his original allegations.[7]

The fact that Bird's opponents circulated such damning charges might be construed as little more than political posturing. But without exception accusers suggested they already knew the court had decided to ignore the "use a gun" law and refuse to send Tanner to prison. They also seemed to know that Associate Justice Mathew Tobriner had been assigned to write the lead opinion. Both pieces of information suggested that someone inside the court was leaking the information. This would have been virtually unheard of in the pre-Bird era, where judicial rulings remained closely guarded secrets until the date of their release.[8]

As November approached, the drumbeat grew louder. State senator H. L. Richardson contacted *Los Angeles Times* Sacramento bureau chief Robert Fairbanks, suggesting that the paper follow up on the allegations about Tanner. "I wanted the press to pursue it," Richardson explained later, though he admitted he had no evidence the decision had actually been held up. He then telephoned Associate Justice William Clark— who prided himself on being accessible to journalists—and informed him that Fairbanks and his colleague William Endicott planned to do a story about the Tanner case.[9]

At Richardson's suggestion, Fairbanks called Clark and suggested that Clark's colleague Stanley Mosk had already spoken to Endicott. Fairbanks laid out Mosk's purported comments and, after some feints and parrying back and forth, asked Clark if he would have problems seeing the story he had just outlined in print the next day. Clark later said, "I don't think I responded, or if I did it was—I am certain—not a yes or a no, but maybe a chuckle."[10]

It is possible that Clark did not intend to signal agreement with the story angle presented by Endicott and Fairbanks; if so, he never proffered a vigorous denial. But if this account is correct, it invites the question: why would Clark help reporters, even passively, with a story likely to harm at least two of his colleagues and draw negative attention to a court of which he was a member? To that point, he had seemed to bear Bird little of the ill will that had characterized her relationship with Mosk. And Clark had served amicably alongside Tobriner for six years.

But Clark did have strong ideological differences with the court's liberal wing and was almost always on the losing side of decisions. His conservative nature had as much to do with religion as politics. He was a devout Catholic who preferred Latin masses, and his San Luis Obispo County ranch held a chapel—built partly of stones from William Randolph Hearst's "castle" and from European monasteries visited by Clark and his wife, Joan.[11]

Clark also was very close to Ronald Reagan; within a few years he would leave California and follow President Reagan to Washington to take on a variety of advisory roles. *Time* magazine once called Clark the most powerful man in the White House after Reagan. As both governor and president, Reagan had made what he deemed "activist" courts a centerpiece of his agenda. Additionally, Clark's friend Mary Nimmo had led the "No on Bird" campaign, and in fall 1978 Clark himself travelled throughout California, giving speeches that took aim at "the liberal faction of the high court." In one San Diego speech, for example, Clark claimed the court "blazed too many legal trails," making, rather than interpreting, law.[12]

Finally, most of Clark's fellow justices viewed him as a legal lightweight undeserving of his position on the court. Former chief justice Donald Wright recalled him as a nonfactor. "I don't recall ever hearing him express an opinion on much of anything. In fact, it was difficult to get a vote out of him. When we would have discussions after our hearings on cases, and we were making the final vote, Bill's response would usually be, 'Well, I'll have to make more study of that. I don't know.'" Clark seems to have felt little connection to his colleagues; he virtually never went to lunch with them. "Occasionally he would get talked into it following a Wednesday conference, but the rest of us used to all go out to lunch together," Wright said.[13]

The election did not end media focus on *Tanner*, and the stories expanded to include details of justices' personal relationships, information that might have appealed to a segment of the reading public more interested in gossip than in court cases or practices. On November 15 Endicott and Fairbanks mentioned William Clark by name for the first time and suggested that all was not well between Clark and the chief justice. It seemed that Clark had written a sharply worded dissent in *Tanner* specifically mentioning Bird, who believed Clark meant to demean and humiliate her.

"Reportedly, the dissent charges that the chief justice switched legal philosophies between the sentencing case [*Tanner*] and a well-publicized rape decision of last June [*Caudillo*]," the journalists reported. "In both cases, her vote was in favor of criminal defendants."[14] On November 16 Endicott and Fairbanks reported that Tobriner had unsuccessfully tried to get all six of his fellow justices to sign a statement declaring that the court had "done nothing improper. . . . However, at least one justice has refused to sign the statement and has said he will not do so." Clark later admitted being that justice, though he offered varying explanations for his refusal.[15]

On November 23, the day before Bird wrote her letter to the Commission on Judicial Performance, Endicott described the rising tensions and "unprecedented leaks from inside the normally sacrosanct court chambers." Leaked information included details about Tobriner's efforts to get colleagues to sign his statement and "reports from court insiders of justices angrily shouting at one another, some not speaking to others and one describing the atmosphere . . . as Nixon-like." By this time, the story had gone national. Lou Cannon of the *Washington Post* detailed how Bird had angrily demanded that Clark remove the critical reference to her in his *Tanner* dissent.[16]

Clark had not only refused, Cannon wrote, but instead elevated the comment from a footnote to the body of his dissent, giving it even more prominence. Some legal scholars and lawyers viewed Bird's response to Clark as hypersensitive, since judges often used opinions to verbally spar with each other, sometimes viciously. One Stanford law professor recalled U.S. Supreme Court opinions in which justices tossed around such derogatory terms as "intellectual incoherence," "vacuousness," and "blatant willfulness."[17] But it seemed to Bird partisans that Clark had gone out of his way to cause trouble by putting the chief justice on the defensive and forcing her into an attack mode.[18]

If this was Clark's objective, he was astoundingly successful. By Thanksgiving, the situation had become intolerable from Bird's perspective. "It is my firm conviction that in this way the false allegations made against this court and its justices can be fully and completely examined," she wrote in her request for hearings. And she wanted the process made public, to discourage opponents from dubbing the investigation a "whitewash."[19]

Her unilateral action dismayed others besides her colleagues. "You just have to ride out the storm," said one official. "The buck does stop here. . . . That criticism goes along with the job."[20] Or as Harvard law professor Laurence Tribe put it, "Anybody can assert at any time that somebody is up to no good." Tribe later acknowledged, however, that "once Chief Justice Bird's opponents and the court's critics had stirred the public's anger, the politics of the situation made some form of open hearing" inevitable.[21]

A few days after receiving the letter, the commission agreed to initiate an "unprecedented inquiry" into accusations of improprieties involved in the *Tanner* case and others.[22] But its relationship with the court significantly complicated the situation. The legislature had created the commission in 1960 to investigate judges at all levels for alleged malfeasance or incompetence. Normally, investigations focused on individual judges, not an entire court, particularly one to which the commission was inexorably bound. Supreme court justices appointed five members of the nine-member commission.

Before hearings could commence, however, the Judicial Council—the policy-making body of the state judiciary—had to establish a set of guidelines. It too was closely linked to the supreme court, since the chief justice appointed fifteen of the twenty-one council members and chaired the council as well. At the time Bird wrote her letter, all fifteen were appointees of former chief justice Donald Wright. In February 1979 they would step down to be replaced by Bird's appointees.

Critics might be excused for skepticism about an arrangement that basically amounted to the court investigating itself, a circumstance that, as one appellate judge put it, placed the commission "in a politically untenable position." Ordinarily hearings into judicial malfeasance were held behind closed doors. The public only saw the commission's final report, a problematic arrangement under the present circumstances. To forestall any hint of impropriety, the Judicial Council, after a rancorous meeting, decided that the commission, for just this one occasion, would conduct a preliminary investigation, followed by hearings, which would be open to the public.

Those who opposed this move complained of its ramifications for the future. "Once the Commission embarks on a course of public hearings in some cases, it would have difficulty in resisting insistent demands in other cases," wrote one Judicial Council member. Judges under suspicion "would almost be compelled by public opinion to join in the request for public hearings, lest they be suspected of having something to hide." The vote for open hearings meant that the public and media representatives—including television reporters—could drop in on the proceedings at any time and watch state supreme court justices dressed in street clothes testifying about court practices in front of a panel composed partly of other judges. Everyone took great pains to insist the proceeding was not a trial, but the visuals suggested that it was.[23]

To oversee the hearings and act as special counsel, the commission hired Seth Hufstedler, a prominent Los Angeles attorney and the husband of President Carter's education secretary, Shirley Hufstedler. He was a consummate insider and longtime leader in the state's judicial establishment. A Stanford Law School graduate, Hufstedler had served as head of the California bar association, and his legal practice focused on business and commercial law, with clients mostly sent to him by other lawyers. He also had close ties with the state supreme court, having previously served on the Judicial Council.

Soon after his appointment, Hufstedler—who would be paid $100 per hour—announced the mission of the pending hearings: to examine delays in releasing opinions as well as the "unauthorized disclosure of confidential information regarding any of the pending cases prior to the public release of the decision."[24]

Meanwhile, as various groups and individuals began debating the scope and structure of the hearings, in December 1978 the court released its long-awaited *Tanner* decision. As journalists had predicted and now reported, the court overturned the "use a gun" law by a 4–3 majority. At least journalists interpreted the decision that way. And Tobriner had, in fact, written the lead opinion. But Tobriner denied then and later that the ruling had actually nullified "use a gun," since the state legislature had left intact another provision that granted discretion in sentencing to judges. Thus, according to Tobriner, the legislature had not intended to entirely "remove from the trial judge the power . . . to strike a charge that a defendant used a gun and to grant probation when the interests of justice so dictate." If lawmakers had intended to take away all discretion, they would have done so "in clear and unequivocal language," Tobriner wrote. Mosk and Newman joined his opinion.[25]

But three other justices wrote opinions as well, and none of the rulings garnered a majority. Bird concurred that the trial judge did have sentencing discretion but offered a different reason than Tobriner. Legislators had no power to dictate what judges could or could not do in sentencing, she wrote. Such an action "violated the separation of powers provisions of the state Constitution," since the judiciary and legislative branches of government were separate and coequal.

"No one condones using a firearm to secure an illegal end," she added, but the *Tanner* case was the product of "myths" and "slogans." Besides, the judge had not just let Tanner off with probation; he had sentenced Tanner to jail. Tanner had served nine months of his year-long sentence and at the end of 1978 was working for a computer firm in the San Francisco Bay Area.

Clark wrote a blistering dissent, joined by fellow Reagan appointee Frank Richardson. Tobriner had come to his decision via "convoluted analysis," and he "twisted the meaning of the law" to suit his own ends. Bird, meanwhile, was a hypocrite. Six months earlier in the *Caudillo* rape case, she had "acknowledged that it is the Legislature in which the Constitution vests authority to prescribe criminal penalties." But in *Tanner*, she said the legislature possessed no such power. Manuel wrote a short, separate dissent that seemed extraneous, since he mostly agreed with Clark, arguing that the legislature had intended to bar judges from granting probation to anyone using a gun to commit a crime.[26]

The law's author, George Deukmejian, called the ruling "incomprehensible" and requested a rehearing, since the lead opinion had not garnered support from a majority of justices. Even Governor Brown added his voice to the chorus, saying "he would seek 'whatever necessary' from the Legislature to revive the law." That threat was rendered moot within weeks, when the court announced plans to revisit the *Tanner* decision.[27]

Several months later, bowing to public pressure and without explanation, justices reversed themselves. With Mosk now joining the majority opinion written by Clark, the court decided that judges did not have sentencing discretion after all. But Harold Tanner would remain a free man. Sending him to prison after all this time would be unfair, the court decided. This time it was Associate Justice Newman who wrote the withering dissent: "A shrill, clamorous campaign—inspired and nurtured by experienced, well-financed and posse-like 'hard on crime' advocates—has had a still incalculable but dismal impact on the judicial process in California."[28]

More than six months after Bird's request for hearings, the Commission on Judicial Performance opened the proceedings on June 11, 1979. The setting was the auditorium of San Francisco's sleek, modern Golden Gate University, situated in the Mission District, one of the less opulent sections of the city. No justice made an appearance the first day, but print and television reporters were on hand, as were lawyers, court staff, the public, and eight members of the commission. The ninth member, appellate judge John Racanelli, had recused himself, citing personal friendship with the chief justice.

Bird had authorized $250,000 to cover the cost of the hearings. Five justices had hired attorneys. Bird hired Jerome Falk, a law school classmate and high-profile appellate attorney; Stanley Mosk hired his son, Richard Mosk; Wiley Manuel hired Roger Traynor's son Michael; Frank Richardson hired Richard Johnston; and William Clark said he would rely on staff attorney Richard Morris.[29]

Hufstedler had kept busy in the weeks prior to the opening gavel gathering information via interviews, depositions, and nearly 1,300 pages of court documents. He and three other attorneys interviewed all of the justices, "almost the entire staff of the Court, and many people outside of the Court who seemed to have relevant information." His opening statement consumed sixty-nine pages and took two hours. He promised (or warned) his audience that it would "for the first time ... become acquainted on an intimate basis with its Supreme Court." And he acknowledged that the court was "a powerful institution, but a fragile institution."

He also revealed the state supreme court's staggering caseload—larger than that of the U.S. Supreme Court. During the first six months of 1978, the weekly average number of cases circulating in judges' chambers was 163. And unlike their U.S. Supreme Court counterparts, who started over each year with a new slate of cases, California high court justices carried over cases from one year to the next.[30]

The public portion of the proceedings would take more than a month and feature testimony from four justices and several staff members. Some of the discussions were mind-numbingly arcane, such as lengthy debates over the definition of a "list."

Observers who knew little about how the court operated became accustomed to hearing references to boxes stuffed with case materials being passed back and forth among justices. The boxes remained in an office until a justice had written a preliminary opinion, and then he or she passed them on to a colleague. One reporter began carrying her own "box" to the hearings. It became the object of much merriment among other media representatives.

Little else proved amusing, however. By the time the hearings dragged to a close, some justices owed as much as $40,000 in legal fees. One justice had filed suit to close the hearings, and the longstanding notion of judicial comity and collegiality had been buried beneath an avalanche of bitterness and misunderstandings.[31]

Frank Richardson was the first witness. He had joined the court in 1974 as the third and final appointee of Governor Reagan, who had hoped to avoid a reprise of the rancorous reaction to his appointment of William Clark. The legal community regarded Richardson, formerly an appellate judge in Sacramento, as qualified, quietly competent, and somewhat conservative but not overtly political. His comments hinted at the excruciating toll the accusations had exacted on the court. "I value my colleagues highly," he said. "They are a group of able, hard-working people." He did not believe *Tanner* had been held up for political reasons, he said. "I have never felt in this case or any other that I should push an individual who is working on a case, because ... I have my own faults and they are numerous. This is a sensitive area for a justice."[32]

Tobriner came next. He fiercely rejected the idea that he had treated *Tanner* differently than any other case. Throughout his long career, both as a lawyer whose practice extended back to San Francisco in the 1920s and as an esteemed colleague of four chief justices, no one had ever hinted at any impropriety. Yet at the age of seventy-five, as author of the *Tanner* decision, it was his life's work and reputation that were most on the line.

He alluded to this in his introductory remarks. "After seventeen years on the court that I should be accused of holding a case up, to me was disastrous, was a tragedy; at least in my life."[33] No matter what the outcome, his longstanding friendship with Mosk also lay in tatters. Bird's appointment had been the catalyst. Mosk believed that Tobriner should have voted against her confirmation. Their relationship soured even further when it became obvious that Tobriner viewed himself as a paternal figure, helping Bird navigate her early days as chief justice, rather than letting her sink or swim on her own.

In fact, Tobriner's helpfulness to Bird seemed to lie at the heart of the accusations on the "use a gun" case. "One issue the commission has to look at is the extent to which Justice Tobriner was seeking to protect the Chief Justice," Hufstedler said in his opening remarks. Tobriner denied being Bird's "protector," insisting that he had supported other chief justices, including Roger Traynor and Phil Gibson. But he told commissioners that he believed Bird to be "a person of integrity, a person who was doing an excellent job on the court," and he quickly became angered by the "terrible things" her opponents were doing, "just terrible."[34]

He dismissed the notion that political implications for Bird's election might have held up the *Tanner* case. "Many cases in our court—in fact almost all cases—do have political consequences," he said. And *Tanner* seemed an unlikely candidate for fueling outrage. Several previous legal cases had granted judges sentencing discretion, and since state lawmakers had left one such provision on the books, they must have understood there would be instances where the "use a gun" law did not apply.

Tobriner's first sense of *Tanner*'s electoral significance came on Election Day with the *Los Angeles Times* story, he said. He acknowledged meeting with Bird in her chambers. "We wondered . . . who the [reporters'] sources were."[35] William Clark had been the one to suggest holding *Tanner* until after the election, Tobriner claimed. After Clark wrote the dissent that angered Bird, Tobriner had tried to smooth the waters by asking Clark to delete the critical reference. Clark refused, instead suggesting that if Bird was so worried about the political implications of *Tanner*, she could simply hold up the decision until after the election. The suggestion stunned him, Tobriner said.[36]

Asked whether he had informed other colleagues about the conversation with Clark, Tobriner initially said he had not. "I felt that it would only harm the situation. . . . I didn't want to create any more tension on the court." He later corrected himself, acknowledging that he might have reported the conversation to Bird. From that point, Tobriner added, he tried to distance himself from Clark. He no longer trusted his colleague, particularly after Clark refused to sign his statement exonerating the court from any improprieties in *Tanner* or other cases.[37]

During her five days of testimony, Bird also homed in on Clark. She had known early in her tenure that she would face stiff opposition in her bid for retention; "I never had any doubt about that," she said. By summer 1978 she had grown weary of "nameless, faceless accusers" but did not anticipate that Clark might be affiliated with any of these individuals. Then in early autumn, she began to notice private comments Clark had made to her appearing in the campaign literature of opposition groups.[38]

Bird, like Tobriner, denied that *Tanner* or any other case had been intentionally delayed. The court was juggling dozens of cases during the summer and fall of 1978. Only a single justice had completed work on *Tanner* by Election Day, she said, though she did not specify which one. She had no idea that the case would prove controversial until she began reading newspaper accounts and learned of Clark's decision to include a reference to *Caudillo*, first in a footnote to his *Tanner* dissent, then in the dissent itself.[39]

She believed that Clark, his staff attorney Richard Morris, or both men sought to use the reference to embarrass her. Several times, she said she had decided to "call them on it." Asked what she meant by this term, Bird said she wanted to respond to what she believed to be a continuing effort to demean her in the eyes of the public. She felt justified, she said, because the *Caudillo* and *Tanner* cases dealt with completely different issues, though her explanation might have seemed like splitting hairs to nonlawyers. *Caudillo* dealt with sentencing, she said, while *Tanner* dealt with adjudication, or the determination of punishment.[40]

At some point after learning that the dissent mentioned her by name, Bird sent her staff attorney Scott Sugarman to talk to Morris. If Sugarman did not get a "reasonable" explanation for the pointed comment, Bird instructed him to ask whether the dissent was designed to embarrass her politically.[41] Bird's decision to approach Morris, rather than Clark, followed from her assumption that Morris had actually written the dissent in question.

Rumor had it that Clark seldom, if ever, penned his own opinions—in fact, some in the legal community believed that justices in general leaned heavily on staff attorneys for more than just preliminary work on cases. Bird had lent credence to this notion by openly criticizing the purported practice in her early days as chief justice. Her decision to send Sugarman to talk to Morris can be viewed in some sense as a power play, designed to put Clark and Morris on notice that she knew her esteemed colleague had not authored the opinion that bore his name.

But Clark made a power play of his own, apparently informing his colleagues and staff that Bird personally had demanded that he remove the *Caudillo* reference. In her testimony to the commission, Bird labeled this claim entirely false. She had never asked him to remove the citation; that conversation had taken place between their two staff members, she testified. She admitted being "pretty annoyed" by Clark's allegation.[42]

By October 1978 Clark and Bird were barely on speaking terms. A few days after Evelle Younger's speech accusing the court of holding up

Tanner, Bird and Clark finally met face to face to try to iron out their differences. Bird brought along her chief aide, Stephen Buehl, to take notes, and she relied on the notes for her testimony. Clark offered to drop the *Caudillo* reference if she joined Tobriner's majority opinion, joined his dissent, or simply concurred without comment. She refused, and the conversation degenerated from there, with both justices accusing each other of bad behavior.

"I never asked you to remove anything," Bird said. "No you did not," Clark admitted, "but this really is not important." Bird disagreed: "It's important to me." Clark shifted to the contention that cases had been held up. "I have had calls from the press. I got a call in the last hour." After Bird accused him of giving confidential information to reporters, Clark accused her of being "overly sensitive to the press." Besides, he was often misquoted, he said. When Bird asked if he tried to correct misperceptions and wrong information, Clark replied, "No." If he confronted every journalist over mistakes, he would have time for little else.[43]

Clark had made the same suggestion to Bird that he had made to Tobriner: "Maybe the case should not be gotten out until after November." Bird had replied: "No, it goes out when it's ready to be filed—no earlier and no later." Asked by commissioners whether she viewed Clark's dissent in terms of her election, Bird said she did not. "I didn't know what Justice Clark's or Mr. Morris's motivation was," she said. "I was more concerned about how I was going to keep dealing with Mr. Clark."[44]

Clark also spent five days testifying. Commissioners had been fairly gentle in their treatment of Tobriner and somewhat more probing and skeptical with Bird. Clark proved a frustrating and slippery witness, sometimes drawing incredulous queries. He was friendly and engaging but had a tendency to refer to himself in the third person and to express puzzlement when asked about his actions and motives. For example, he denied trying to embarrass Bird with an explicit reference to *Caudillo* in his *Tanner* dissent. He was simply trying to get her attention, he testified. At least one commissioner reacted with dismay. Did Clark not realize that such an action might embolden Bird's opponents? Not at

1. Rose Elizabeth Bird graduated from Sea Cliff High School in New York in 1954. Her classmates recalled her as serious, intense, and ambitious. Her long list of activities belied her later insistence that she had been a plodder and a grind who stayed home on the weekends to bake bread. Source: North Shore School District, Sea Cliff, New York.

2. Rose Bird was active in many sports during high school. As one of the tallest girls in her class, she excelled at basketball. Sea Cliff may have been virtually all white, but Bird's class held two African American girls, including Valerie Gordon, standing to Bird's right in the back row. Source: North Shore School District, Sea Cliff, New York.

3. After high school, Rose Bird won a full scholarship to Long Island University, where she majored in English and hoped to be a foreign correspondent. After being named the top student in the class of 1958, Bird left New York for Berkeley and graduate school. There she lived in International House and met future governor Jerry Brown. Courtesy of Bancroft Library, University of California, Berkeley.

4. (*opposite*) Rose Bird was a complete unknown when Jerry Brown appointed her to be the first woman in a gubernatorial cabinet in California. As agriculture secretary, she played crucial roles in the passage and implementation of the Agriculture Labor Relations Act. She also gained powerful enemies and a reputation as "difficult." Courtesy of Bancroft Library, University of California, Berkeley.

5. (*above*) The legal establishment was astounded in 1977 when Jerry Brown named Rose Bird chief justice of the storied California Supreme Court. Stanley Mosk believed he should have gotten the job. Front row, left to right: Mathew Tobriner, Bird, and Mosk. Back row, left to right: Wiley Manuel, William Clark, Frank Richardson, and Frank Newman. Courtesy of Bancroft Library, University of California, Berkeley.

6. Before Rose Bird newspapers largely ignored the California Supreme Court, but the period surrounding the 1979 hearings into possible malfeasance unleashed a spate of editorial cartoons focused on justices and their troubled relationships. Courtesy of Steven Greenberg.

7. By 1985 five of seven justices were Jerry Brown appointees. Republican governor George Deukmejian hoped to change those numbers in November 1986, when six justices would appear on the ballot for voter confirmation. The court, front row, left to right: Stanley Mosk, Rose Bird, and Allen Broussard. Back row, left to right: Malcolm Lucas, Cruz Reynoso, Joseph Grodin, and Edward Panelli. Courtesy of Bancroft Library, University of California, Berkeley.

8. Dozens of candidates appeared on the November 1986 ballot, but one—Rose Elizabeth Bird—received most of the attention. To many she seemed more a symbol than a flesh and blood person. Both her opponents and her supporters recognized that ousting a sitting supreme court chief justice would set a precedent for future judicial elections. Courtesy of Bancroft Library, University of California, Berkeley.

first, Clark said, but later he understood the implications. Nonetheless, he could not know why Bird saw his dissent as politically motivated.[45]

Clark also acknowledged talking to other justices and their staffs about his dispute with Bird, and trying to garner their support for including the *Caudillo* reference in his dissent. In his telling, most of his colleagues agreed with him. Clark also complained about perceived snubs from Bird. "My attempts to even get into pleasantries failed." Once, Clark told commissioners, Morris ran into Bird in a courthouse elevator, and she turned the other way. When he "went into her chambers for Wednesday conferences, there was no acknowledgement." Bird also ignored his staff members and failed to give his secretary a promised piece of carpet, Clark said. "It may seem petty now. It seemed awfully important to us all at that time."

At one point, Clark went to Mosk for advice. Mosk suggested he talk to Tobriner, who was not sympathetic. Instead, he suggested that Clark remove the contested citation. It was then, Clark acknowledged, that he had suggested holding the *Tanner* decision until after the election. His motives were entirely pure, he insisted. They were also pure when he made this same suggestion to Bird. At least one commissioner expressed skepticism. "Didn't you realize that if Justice Tobriner or the chief justice were to rise to that bait, they might be stepping into the very trap that [opponents] had [set] earlier?" commissioner Hillel Chodos asked.[46]

Clark denied speaking to friends outside of the court about the internal conflicts in general and about the *Tanner* case in particular. He admitted talking to Edwin Meese in September 1978, just about the time Meese's article alleging the *Tanner* holdup appeared in the *Daily Journal* newspaper, he said, but he insisted that he never discussed the case. Besides, he added, Meese had other friends on the court besides himself.[47]

When the commission moved on to discussing the *Los Angeles Times* story alleging intentional delay, Clark acknowledged having spoken to reporter Robert Fairbanks three times the day before the November 7 election, but he denied that he had confirmed allegations about the *Tanner* holdup. "In hindsight, I can understand that good reporters— and these are good reporters—could interpret what they had heard that day and perhaps report in conscience that justices had confirmed [the information]." He continued, "But I looked upon it, and do now, as being something they felt they were confirming, but it wasn't necessarily so from those they were talking to."[48]

He also admitted speaking on Election Day morning to K. Connie Kang of the *San Francisco Examiner*. Clark recalled Kang phoning him after her editor awakened her to say that he wanted a follow-up to the *Times* story. In Clark's recollection, she asked: "Is it true?" He declined to comment. She asked if he had been one of the justices quoted. "I certainly hope not," he had responded.[49]

For many journalists, revelations of justices' relationships and personalities trumped the nuts-and-bolts testimony about how the court operated in general. The testimony of Bird and Clark gave them more than they could have hoped for in this vein. *Los Angeles Times* reporter Bella Stumbo described the scene "inside the auditorium at Golden Gate University [where] Supreme Court justices and their attorneys and staffs continued . . . to treat each other like liars and backstabbers and possible thieves."[50]

As Lou Cannon of the *Washington Post* saw it, the hearings revealed the California Supreme Court to be "a seething cauldron of fear, suspicion, political hostility and petty jealousy. . . . So far, the investigation . . . has proved much less, and revealed much more, than critics have alleged." And *San Diego Union* reporter Margaret Warner portrayed the hearings as "closer to a family saga novel than a whodunit mystery. . . . Unraveling before the commissioners is a story about loyalty and suspicion, confidence and fear."[51]

Court personnel also kept close tabs on the hearings. "We all brought radios to work and turned [them] on in our offices," Staff attorney Peter J. Belton recalled. "You could walk down the hall and never miss a word."[52] Meanwhile, outside the hearing room, Golden Gate University law students manned the information desk. Having grown up in a jaded and cynical age in the aftermath of Vietnam and Watergate, they had little interest in the "circus" inside, they informed reporters. One wore a T-shirt bearing the words "The Bird is the Word—Drink Wild Turkey."

Another called the hearings "hypocritical," adding: "Most judges are political hacks, that's how they get their jobs in the first place. Courts have been political since Day One, and everybody knows it."[53]

The circus soon folded up its tent. Reporters packed up their notebooks, microphones, and cameras; the law students moved on to other pursuits. Clark's was to be the last testimony open to the public. Subsequently, witnesses would only testify in private. The immediate catalyst was Clark's discussion of a purported conversation between himself and Mosk. According to Clark, Mosk had mentioned visiting Tobriner's chambers before the election to warn Tobriner that "it was obvious cases were being held for filing until after election, and if it were later revealed, [Tobriner] would have to pay the consequences."[54]

So far, Mosk had avoided getting dragged into the morass of accusations playing out before the public. For weeks, Clark, Tobriner, and Bird had been the featured players. Clark's testimony shifted the spotlight to Mosk, who obviously would be asked about the alleged conversation, among other topics, including whether he had divulged confidential information to reporters. From the beginning, Mosk had argued against open hearings as unconstitutional and "devastating" to the future ability of justices to work together "as a collegial body." The day after Clark's revelation, Mosk filed a lawsuit to close the proceedings. Richard Mosk offered assurances "that his father would be happy to appear before the commission privately," but he would not testify in public.[55]

Thus began a tug-of-war that took three months and enveloped three courts, including the state supreme court. After a superior court judge ruled against Mosk and an appellate court ruled for him, the case landed in the lap of the same state supreme court whose members were mired in the hearings. Six justices immediately recused themselves; six appeals court judges replaced them. Only Newman refused to step aside, declaring that he was perfectly capable of deciding the merits of the lawsuit, despite his involvement in it. Eventually, the ad hoc court disqualified Newman and replaced him with another temporary justice. In October the ad hoc high court ruled in favor of Mosk.[56]

By that time, testimony was virtually complete. As commissioners awaited a final verdict on Mosk's suit, the three remaining justices testified behind closed doors. Mosk denied ever warning Tobriner about holding up cases, or telling Clark about any such conversation. Clark was wrong, he said. Besides, "I would not talk to Justice Tobriner that way." Mosk added that he had no knowledge of any case being held up pending the November 1978 election and denied that he had been a source for the *Los Angeles Times*. He spoke twice with William Endicott, he said, but never replied with anything more specific than "no comment."

Mosk said he had been less concerned about *Tanner* than with another case, *Fox v. City of Los Angeles*. It had nothing to do with elections but with "sensitivity." *Fox* focused on a dispute between residents and officials about an illuminated cross erected at City Hall during the Christmas and Easter holidays. Plaintiffs argued that such a display privileged Christianity over other religions. The case had been argued more than a year earlier, and the critics who charged the court with holding up *Tanner* made the same accusation about *Fox*.[57]

Bird had assigned Newman to write the lead opinion, and he was proceeding at an agonizingly slow pace. Since he had been Bird's law school professor at Boalt, she was reluctant to prod him. "I was a good deal younger," she testified. But she had an additional problem, she said. Newman "had very firm views about how we ought to reform the way we write opinions. . . . His view was that we needed to add a more modern style of writing." This approach engendered "natural resistance" in other justices and slowed down the process of completing opinions.[58]

Mosk feared that releasing *Fox* too close to the 1978 Christmas holiday might make justices appear "insensitive" to people's religious beliefs. When he voiced his concern to Bird, she expressed irritation. The decision, she said, "was not going to go out on Christmas Day. It was not going to go out on New Year's Eve. It was not going to go out on New Year's Day. . . . It was going out no sooner and no later than when it was ready." That turned out to be December 15, 1978. In a 5–2 ruling, justices agreed with plaintiffs; the city had to remove the cross.[59]

With Mosk's testimony complete, only Manuel and Newman remained. Manuel's appearance took only two hours. His dissent in

Tanner had been blamed for holding up the opinion; it came at the end, after all the other justices had weighed in. Since it seemed to replicate Clark's dissent, critics of Bird had suggested that either she or Tobriner, perhaps both, had asked Manuel to write a separate dissent to slow the process. Manuel vehemently denied the allegation. The decision was his own, he said.

He disagreed with Tobriner's majority opinion but also with Clark's reference to Bird and *Caudillo*. And he "had strong feelings on the matter. He considered both Bird and Clark to be his friends." He wanted everyone to get along but saw Clark's dissent as "legally inappropriate" and "part of a running series of attacks on the Chief and on the court."[60] The final justice, Newman, offered no new information and claimed that his comments and conversations with colleagues were privileged information.

In early November 1979, exactly a year after the election that had fueled allegations of judicial impropriety, the hearings limped to a close. The commission, having heard testimony for five months, unanimously found insufficient evidence to charge anyone with wrongdoing. But members could not divulge how they had come to this conclusion, since Mosk's successful lawsuit barred them from commenting on any aspect of the investigation or its findings. The final bill for the proceedings: $510,000. Much of the money went to Seth Hufstedler and his law firm. In the end, virtually no one emerged unscathed.[61]

Bird was relieved by the outcome but under no illusion that it would end debate or shift the harsh glare of media and public attention away from the court. In an interview with the *New York Times*, she said that, from the beginning, she had "harbored no illusions that the job would be easy." But she "had no idea it would be the kind of warfare it has been." She blamed gender, her outsider status, and efforts of "right-wing groups to politicize the bench" for the conflict.

"I was a woman being placed at the head of an aristocratic body, a kind of priesthood." She denied allegations that her arrival had fueled a new level of acrimony at the court. Personality clashes had always existed, she said, but justices used to be viewed as "larger than life individuals.

To say the present court is not collegial, that's nonsense. It's no different than it was."[62]

In a speech before the National Association of Women Judges, Bird elaborated on the role gender played in her troubles, or at least her perception of its role. "These are unkind and fearful times," she said. "The anger felt toward minorities and women in our society in general can be seized upon at election time and turned against judges who happen to be minorities or women. They are the least able to protect and defend themselves from criticism and attack." Though progress had been made, "we still have some distance to go before women are fully accepted as partners in the judicial enterprise."[63]

As Bird had predicted, the end of the hearings did not bring an end to the controversy. "Because we weren't able to explain our action . . . I see no reason [why] the public should accept the result [of the investigation]," said commission member Thomas Willoughby. Court critics soon pounced. "We said in the beginning this was going to be a whitewash," said Earl Huntting, president of the Oakland-based Citizens for Law and Order. "And that's just what it turned out to be."[64]

How one came to view the hearings and their outcome seemed directly related to how one viewed Chief Justice Rose Bird. Within four years, two books focused solely on the hearings appeared. The first was authored by Bird's former Boalt Hall law professor Preble Stolz. *Judging Judges: The Investigation of Rose Bird and the California Supreme Court* was published in 1981. Stolz took a stab at objectivity but placed most of the blame on Bird. According to Stolz, "a successful Supreme Court justice must have . . . a genuine respect for the views of others, combined with an instinct for finding the core issue that divides; a capacity to find solutions that accommodate seemingly conflicting principles, a desire to participate in the give-and-take of controversy without accumulating grudges; and finally, the ability to lead and inspire a small bureaucratic team."

Bird possessed few of these traits, felt Stolz. Instead, she was humorless, thin-skinned, and a poor administrator. But the book also featured a foreword by Anthony Lewis, the *New York Times* legal affairs reporter, who took strong exception to Stolz's analysis. He saw Clark as the main culprit.[65] As if to reinforce Stolz's depiction of her as thin-skinned, Bird contacted the book publisher and asked for changes, though it was unclear what alterations she sought. Stolz accused her of trying to "bully and frighten my publisher."[66]

Some observers wondered why Stolz would write such a book. Had Bird somehow antagonized him at Boalt? Stolz claimed not to recall her as a student; perhaps she failed to attend class, he joked. But Stolz had had a short, unhappy stint working as the director of Planning and Research in Jerry Brown's administration, where he crossed paths with Bird. And Brown subsequently rebuffed his efforts to gain a judicial appointment.

In 1983 journalist Betty Medsger's book *Framed: The New Right Attack on Chief Justice Rose Bird and the Courts* covered essentially the same ground but from Bird's perspective. As its title indicates, Medsger saw the controversy over *Tanner* as part of a concerted effort by conservatives to capture the courts by fueling voter outrage about activist "liberal" judges. Clark, according to Medsger, was a pawn in this effort. "California has been the scene of an ominous dress rehearsal," Medsger declared on the first page of her book. "Since 1978 the New Right has been refining its plan to revolutionize the nation's courts by attacking the California courts."

Rose Bird's gender made her an attractive target, Medsger wrote. "The loss of the Chief Justice's chair to Bird probably angered the old boys' network more than any appointment, judicial or otherwise, that Brown made as governor."[67] Medsger's book also featured a preface by writer Richard Reeves, who blamed H. L. Richardson for the mess. "We're not playing patty-cake," Reeves quoted Richardson as saying. "We're talking about the ideological direction of the court, and we've got to grab people's attention with tough talk." Medsger, like Stolz, had a personal connection to Bird. She was married to appellate judge John Racanelli, the commission member who had recused himself.[68]

Most people in California and elsewhere soon forgot about the hearings. By 1983 all but two of the justices caught up in the controversy had retired; only Bird and Mosk remained. They would never exactly be friends, but their enmity had diminished significantly. Both Manuel and Clark retired in 1981. Tobriner and Richardson retired in 1982. Tobriner left the court in January and died just three months later; the hearings had devastated him. The retirements gave Brown four new appointments. All of them were men, though two were minorities. And all had significant judicial experience.

Otto Kaus had been an appellate judge in Los Angeles. He favored lifetime tenure for state high court justices. As he told a reporter, being targeted over judicial rulings was "like having a crocodile in your bathtub." Allen Broussard was the court's second African American. In the 1950s, he had clerked for Associate Justice Raymond Peters and had served for two decades as a judge in Alameda County. Cruz Reynoso became the court's first Latino justice. He had been a civil rights lawyer, director of California Rural Legal Assistance, and an appellate judge. Joseph Grodin, Mathew Tobriner's longtime friend, had been an appellate judge and also held a PhD from the London School of Economics.

Frank Newman waited until 1983 to retire and return to UC Berkeley. Academics better suited his deliberative nature, he said. By that time, George Deukmejian, author of the "use a gun" law, had become governor; Newman's departure gave Deukmejian the first of what would be eight appointments to the state's highest court. Much later, Newman recalled the hearings as "a miserable period of, what was it, ten months?" He blamed the media and special counsel Seth Hufstedler for most of the problems. "The press was so terrible that people felt they had to protect, first themselves, then the court. Not everyone protected the other members." He characterized Hufstedler as a publicity seeker who "dominated the others far too much." The result was "a kangaroo court," Newman said. "It all had a terrible impact."[69]

When the hearings ended, few could have predicted that they would be a game changer. For decades the California Supreme Court had plowed new ground in cases involving civil rights and personal liberties. Conservatives and even some moderates might have groused among themselves, but justices, as Rose Bird acknowledged, had been viewed as "larger than life individuals." No longer. "In a sense, the justices have come down from Olympian heights to mingle with mere mortals," one state official told a reporter.[70] Another writer feared, he said, that the hearings had opened the door to the "emergence of the political judiciary," something that began to play out over the next few months and years.[71]

George Deukmejian was not a firebrand like H. L. Richardson, but he too had made "law and order" the pivotal issue in his long political career. In the early 1960s, as civil libertarians gained traction in the legislature and courts, Deukmejian had railed against criminals and soft-on-crime lawmakers and judges. He had authored the "use a gun" law and death penalty legislation that was still pending when Bird became chief justice. Six years later, the legislation was in place and yet no executions had occurred. Deukmejian thought he knew whom to blame: Bird. She had endured a bruising confirmation, a rocky beginning at the court, and a devastating set of hearings; her real ordeal was just beginning.

7 *The Politics of Death*

In January 1978 twenty-one-year-old Lavell Frierson forced two men into a car outside a seedy motel in Inglewood, California, robbed them of their wallets and wristwatches, and shot both in the back of the head execution style. One man survived and identified Frierson, who was tried, convicted of first-degree murder, and sentenced to death. The case then went on automatic appeal to the state supreme court.

Twenty months after the crime, in September 1979, justices unanimously overturned Frierson's conviction and sentence. His court-appointed lawyer had failed to put on any kind of defense, they agreed. Frierson was also borderline mentally retarded, but this information had not been provided to the jury. He would have to be retried; meanwhile, he would remain in prison.[1]

Frierson's case involved a larger issue, however. The justices had to determine what laws governed his retrial and thus needed to grapple with California's somewhat convoluted death penalty laws. Since 1972, when both the California and U.S. Supreme Courts declared capital punishment to be "cruel and unusual" and thus unconstitutional, laws had been in flux. Twice in the 1970s, state lawmakers wrote new legislation that, they hoped, would conform to federal guidelines.

In 1976 the state supreme court invalidated the first rewritten law;

it failed to give jurors sufficient sentencing discretion—a requirement of the U.S. high court. So the legislature went back at it and, in 1977, enacted a new measure. Authored by state senator George Deukmejian, it listed a series of "special circumstances" that qualified defendants for the "ultimate punishment," and it gave jurors discretion in sentencing. Jerry Brown vetoed the legislation, but lawmakers garnered the two-thirds majority required to override the veto. "I don't believe in the death penalty," Brown said, "but the Legislature has spoken and now it's up to the courts."[2]

For some conservatives, however, the new legislation did not go far enough. They included John V. Briggs, a firebrand Republican state senator from Orange County, carved from the same mold as his colleague H. L. Richardson. Both men had tied their careers to rising public anger toward criminals and strong support for tougher punishments, sentiments reflected in polls revealing a significant increase in pro–death penalty support in the years following its abolition. Briggs planned to run for governor in 1978. To distinguish himself from the field of moderate Republicans, he crafted a measure to appear on the November 1978 ballot. Proposition 7, the "Briggs Initiative," would be "the toughest death penalty law in the country," he said.[3]

Deukmejian's legislation had enumerated eleven "special circumstances." They included murder of a policeman, murder for hire, a second or subsequent murder, and murder committed during the commission of a robbery, kidnapping, rape, burglary, lewd acts on a child, or torture. The "intent" to kill had to be present. The Briggs Initiative added more special circumstances: murder to aid an escape, murder by poisoning, murder as a hate crime, or an "especially heinous" killing. It also toughened penalties for second-degree murder and barred parole for all murderers before they served at least fifteen years.[4]

Accomplices could be charged with murder even if they did not commit the actual crime, and in "direct repudiation" of an earlier California Supreme Court ruling—*People v. Morse*, from 1964—juries could be told that anyone given a life sentence without the possibility of parole might eventually be released from prison. Judges also were required to inform juries that they had to sentence defendants to death if "aggravating" circumstances outweighed "mitigating" circumstances.[5]

Proposition 7 easily garnered enough signatures to qualify for the ballot and passed by a whopping margin—72 percent to 28 percent, reinforcing the notion that California voters wanted murderers punished severely and sooner rather than later. The measure's passage did not help Briggs professionally, however; he dropped out of the race before the June primary. Evelle Younger, the Republican nominee, lost in November to Jerry Brown. Voters might want criminals punished, but they were not yet ready to replace Brown. And voters solidly rejected another Briggs ballot measure, Proposition 6, which would have mandated the firing of gay teachers.[6]

The passage of Briggs's death penalty measure so soon after Deukmejian's placed the state supreme court in a quandary. Did the initiative supersede Deukmejian's legislation? Deukmejian believed that Proposition 7 simply expanded its scope. Most importantly, did either law pass constitutional muster? Justices had to decide these issues in order to "provide guidance" to the hundreds of trial courts across the state facing an influx of capital cases. Frierson had committed his crime before the Briggs Initiative appeared on the ballot, however, so the court had to focus solely on Deukmejian's legislation.[7]

The decision was fraught with peril for all of the justices, who were emerging from nearly a year of turmoil and intense public scrutiny as a result of the Commission on Judicial Performance hearings. But the stakes were highest for Rose Bird. H. L. Richardson and others already had managed to convince a significant number of Californians that she was "soft on crime," "antivictim," and overly sympathetic to murderers. And that was before she ever participated in a death penalty decision. *Frierson* placed her opponents on high alert, but since the decision to overturn Frierson's conviction had been unanimous, criticism was muted on that score. As for the larger issue: the court decided, in a decision written by Frank Richardson and signed by four other justices, that Deukmejian's legislation was constitutional.

The wording hinted at the emotional stress involved in deciding capital cases in an era when voters and politicians closely watched court opinions. Richardson's ruling did not necessarily represent a ringing endorsement. "Since 1972, the sovereign people of this state twice directly and through their elected representatives . . . have mounted a continuous, strong and joint effort to restore the death penalty," Richardson wrote. "If the people and the Legislature are correct in their assumption that the penalty acts as a deterrent, then it is possible that some persons contemplating the commission of capital crimes may be diverted by a clear and unqualified ruling upholding the constitutionality."

Stanley Mosk concurred with Richardson's opinion but only "with the utmost reluctance." Laws might pass constitutional muster, but that did not mean the death penalty was moral or just. "The day will come when all mankind will deem killing to be immoral, whether committed by one individual or many individuals organized into a state," he wrote. And he criticized the U.S. Supreme Court for failing to provide states with adequate guidelines.[8]

Both Bird and Mathew Tobriner dissented from the majority ruling. Others might bow to public pressure, Bird implied, but she would not. The majority decision represented "a rush to judgment," she wrote. "No matter how clamorous the movement of the moment, the right to be free of cruel and unusual punishments, like the other guarantees of the Bill of Rights, 'may not be submitted to a vote.'"[9]

For someone who had faced unrelenting public scrutiny for the better part of three years, Bird's dissent seems excessively confrontational. Supreme court justices seldom talked directly to the public. Their judicial rulings spoke for them, and justices virtually always refused to explain their reasoning or how they achieved the results. In cases involving minor or "unimportant" issues, at least to a wider audience, few people paid attention. But criminal cases were different—particularly death penalty cases. When the court issued its ruling on *Frierson*, no executions had occurred in California for more than a decade. Bird had to know she was walking into a minefield. Every future death penalty opinion of hers would go under a microscope.[10]

The same could be said for her colleagues, but Bird's gender placed her in a different category. Ordinary people seemed to feel they could walk up to her in public and vent about the court and its decisions. And they often used her first name when they did so, rather than her title. It is hard to imagine Stanley Mosk or Mathew Tobriner facing down angry shoppers at the supermarket who called them "Stan" or "Matt," but it happened to Rose Bird with some frequency. Once, an irate woman accosted her as she was paying for groceries. The woman had a friend with an abusive husband, she told Bird. When the friend called police, the officer said he could do nothing, since the "Bird Court" sympathized with criminals.

Such confrontations rattled Bird, though she continued to write assertive opinions in high-profile cases. But they did encourage her to change the way she looked; perhaps fewer people would recognize her if she cut her hair and wore some makeup, she reasoned. "My hairstyle was so distinctive, it sometimes made it difficult when I went out," she told a reporter. So she had it cut to shoulder length and wore it loose and curly. She regretted having to make this concession, but she added, "I have to take [the heat]. Once you accept a position, you can't walk away from it because it is unpleasant or people say mean things."[11]

Occasionally, the "mean things" took on a more ominous cast, and she received death threats. She did not worry about herself, Bird insisted, but about her mother, who lived alone in Palo Alto when Bird worked in San Francisco. At some point, she removed the street address from the front of the house and scratched it off the curb as well. And she hung a sign—"Beware of Dog"—on the gate.[12]

The *Frierson* decision opened the floodgates with regard to capital punishment. The justices still had to rule on the constitutionality of the Briggs Initiative, while they confronted a mounting number of capital appeals. By the end of 1981, trial courts throughout the state had issued ninety-one death sentences. For each, transcripts had to be readied, capital-qualified appellate attorneys hired, appeals filed, and hearings set and reset to fit the schedules of attorneys and judges. As a result, the high court had heard only eleven capital cases, overturning nine death sentences and upholding two: those of Earl Lloyd Jackson and Robert Alton Harris. Bird dissented in both.

Jackson was nineteen when he robbed and murdered two elderly Long Beach widows in late summer 1977. He also raped one of his victims with a wine bottle. His appellate petition included a long list of issues, mostly hinging on trial counsel's inadequate defense and inadmissible evidence. Richardson wrote the 4–3 opinion, released in October 1980. It stated: "Mindful as we are of the extreme gravity for which the defendant stands convicted and the ultimate punishment which has been imposed . . . we conclude that no miscarriage of justice has occurred." Mosk, Tobriner, and Bird dissented. All three used their opinions to revisit Deukmejian's 1977 legislation, which they found lacking. Mosk criticized the trial counsel for failing to present any mitigating evidence during the penalty phase.

Bird's dissent would be used over the following years as evidence of her lack of sympathy for victims and obsession with making sure no one—not even the worst of the worst—ended up in the gas chamber. "Today, this court sends to his death an impoverished, illiterate and possibly retarded 19-year-old black youth," she wrote. "I respectfully submit that it is unconscionable to affirm a conviction." Throwing down the gauntlet to death penalty supporters, she added: "If the death penalty is to be imposed, it must be done under a system that ensures fair and consistent results at the trial level." The 1977 legislation offered "no meaningful standards."[13]

Robert Alton Harris was twenty-five, just out of prison, and looking for a car to use in a robbery in summer 1978 when he spotted two teenagers eating hamburgers in a San Diego supermarket parking lot. He commandeered their car, drove to a deserted area, ordered the boys to run, and then shot both in the back. His appellate attorney argued that pretrial publicity—the father of one teenage victim was the police officer who arrested Harris—should have gotten the trial moved out of San Diego County. William Clark wrote the 4–2 opinion upholding the death sentence. "None of the many contentions raised by the defendant has merit," he wrote. Less than a month later Clark left

California for Washington DC, where he became President Reagan's deputy secretary of state.

In her dissent, Bird made no mention of Harris's impoverished or abusive youth but focused intently on the media's sensational saturation coverage of the case, which lasted for weeks. She also acknowledged the "terrible crimes," which were "exceptionally cold-blooded and senseless." Nonetheless, Harris had been deprived of a fair trial. Media accounts had depicted him as "sewage polluting society." The right to "'a fair trial in a fair tribunal' is a basic component of due process," Bird wrote.[14]

With every passing month, death penalty proponents grew ever more impatient and angry. The court needed to speed up the process and, more importantly, uphold more death sentences. Justices might cite numerous problems having to do with "due process" and other constitutional guarantees, but those were just excuses. "Rose Bird's Court" was purposely slowing down and subverting the legal process. Justices understood the implied threats that underlay the critics' comments. Four justices would be on the November 1982 ballot for voter approval, three of them Brown appointees.[15]

Bird was not on the ballot for reconfirmation that year, but she remained solidly in the forefront of public consciousness. Several individuals had begun recall efforts, with the aim of getting enough signatures to force her to face voters in a special election. Four years after his initial effort to defeat Bird, H. L. Richardson was still actively pursuing her. In early 1982 he announced a recall campaign. "You give me $400,000 and I'll deliver Rose Bird on a platter," he told an audience of conservatives. Three months later, having received only $20,000, he abandoned the effort. "The people of California deserve Rose Bird," Richardson said disgustedly.[16]

Anthony Rackauckas, a deputy district attorney in Orange County, also sought to recall Bird. He became a vociferous critic after prosecuting Maurice Thompson, convicted and condemned for murder during the commission of a robbery. The court, in a decision written by Bird, overturned Thompson's death sentence. Bird claimed that the defendant had not intended to kill, thus no special circumstance existed. Bird "misused her position to advance her liberal beliefs," Rackauckas declared.

He was confident he could raise $500,000, he added; direct mail targeting had gotten so sophisticated by 1982 that "you can even get a list of voters who own pickup trucks." But his effort, like Richardson's, failed.[17]

Marvin Feldman, a private citizen who disliked "activist" judges, also undertook a recall effort. He borrowed on his La Canada home to raise money to recall several jurists, including Bird, but he abandoned the effort after bankers threatened to foreclose. To recoup funds, he wrote and then tried to sell lyrics to a ballad he called "This Is America."[18]

The court and legal experts recognized what was at stake in the mounting opposition. Tobriner took note of groups who "seem to be cranking up a public opinion campaign to force the California Supreme Court to validate the death penalty with threats" implying that "if you don't let a couple of guys get knocked off in the gas chamber, we're going to throw you out of office."[19]

Bird's supporters spoke out on her behalf. Shirley Hufstedler, whose husband, Seth, had chaired the Commission on Judicial Performance hearings, organized a tribute to Bird. In a speech to women's groups, Jerry Brown blamed Bird's troubles on sexism. If she had been a man, "she would be far less controversial," he said.[20] Two ex–chief justices—Phil Gibson and Donald Wright—also weighed in. Bird was doing "a good job," both men insisted, and she did not deserve such ill treatment. Santa Clara law professor Gerald Uelmen noted the "widespread public perception that the decisions of the California Supreme Court have frustrated implementation of the death penalty in California." However, "the issue is much more complex."[21]

Much of the complexity had to do with the Briggs Initiative. More than three years after its passage, justices still had not ruled on its constitutionality. Some factors—confusion on whether intent to kill had to be present, and the ability of judges to tell juries about the possibility for parole—were troubling. All of the justices implicitly understood that finding any aspect of the initiative unconstitutional could unleash a fierce backlash. Nonetheless, in January 1982, in a 6–1 decision, they did just that. The Briggs Initiative's jury instruction represented "a violation of due process," the majority declared.[22]

For pro–death penalty forces, the court's Briggs decision was unfathomable. Most of the measure remained intact, but nonetheless conservatives took to the airwaves and op-ed pages of major newspapers to accuse justices of thumbing their noses at a citizenry that was sick and tired of criminals. The group Citizens for Law and Order urged state legislators to force justices to rule "within a reasonable amount of time" on capital cases or forfeit their pay.

Attorney General George Deukmejian called the ruling "outrageous" and asked the U.S. Supreme Court to overrule the state high court. Families of crime victims added their voices to the mix; where were their rights? They further demonstrated growing clout by promoting a wide-ranging ballot measure mandating tougher treatment of criminals.

Proposition 8, the "Victims' Bill of Rights," appeared on the statewide ballot in June 1982. It restricted the rights of criminals and those suspected of crimes, abolished the "diminished capacity" defense, compelled criminals to provide restitution to victims or their families, and required courts to admit evidence even if doing so violated defendants' rights. It passed, 56 to 44 percent. Backers wondered cynically how the "liberal" court would rule on its constitutionality.[23]

In September 1982 the court reluctantly upheld the "Victims'" measure. The wording of Frank Richardson's majority opinion again made it clear he was responding to intense public pressure, rather than to the measure's merits. "While we might disagree with both the accuracy of the premise and the overall wisdom of the initiative measure . . . it is not our function to pass judgment on the propriety or soundness of Proposition 8," Richardson wrote.[24]

Rose Bird, as she had done in other instances, refused to cater to popular opinion. In a "scathing dissent," she referenced her childhood hero, journalist Elmer Davis, noting that Davis had once remarked "that the republic was not established by cowards, and cowards will not preserve us. His words apply equally well to the Constitution." Stanley Mosk's dissent was nearly as critical: "The Goddess of Justice is wearing a black arm-band today, as she weeps for the Constitution of California."[25]

If justices believed that upholding Proposition 8 might defang critics, the

November 1982 election of George Deukmejian as governor demonstrated the folly of this notion. Deukmejian, the son of Armenian immigrants, began his political career as a state assembly member from Long Beach in the early 1960s and methodically charted a path to power despite having a personality variously described as "dull," "unimaginative," and "plodding." In some ways, these traits made him more effective than H. L. Richardson or John Briggs, because they led his opponents to underestimate him.

Over his two-decade career, Deukmejian had focused almost entirely on one issue: crime. He fervently believed that California courts and politicians for too long had allowed criminals to get away—literally—with murder. Few people outside the Republican establishment paid him much attention until he became state attorney general in 1978. His timing was propitious. Republican politicians in California and beyond had long railed against judicial "activism," and the California judiciary under Bird seemed to have lost its aura of invincibility. Voters demanded more accountability from politicians and judges, hence their strong support for ballot measures such as Proposition 13, dealing with property taxes; the Briggs Initiative; and the Victims' Bill of Rights.

Deukmejian had spent most of his four-year term as attorney general gearing up to run for governor on a platform targeting liberals who "coddled" criminals. These included politicians who ignored small-time scofflaws such as marijuana growers. At one point Deukmejian, wearing a flak vest, accompanied "a posse of armed deputies" in their raid on a Mendocino County marijuana operation.[26]

The death penalty was his major focus, however. As attorney general he sat on the Commission on Judicial Appointments, and he directly asked nominees about their willingness to uphold death sentences. If they failed to give him the answer he sought, he voted against them. In 1981 he voted against two Jerry Brown appointments to the state supreme court—Allen Broussard and Cruz Reynoso.

"It's not business as usual any more as regards the judiciary in California," Deukmejian said. Both Broussard and Reynoso won confirmation anyway, since Bird and presiding state appeals court justice Lester Roth, a Democrat, also sat on the commission. Reynoso became the court's first

Latino justice and Broussard its second African American. Deukmejian also urged voters to oppose Broussard, Reynoso, and a third Brown supreme court appointee, Otto Kaus, on the November 1982 ballot. All three men won voter approval but by much smaller margins than justices historically received. In comments, Bird accused Deukmejian of being racist. "It happens to be a fact that these judges are the only black, the only Hispanic and the only foreign born—Otto Kaus was born in Austria—members of our court."[27]

Bird was always Deukmejian's primary target. She symbolized everything he had long despised about the "liberal" judiciary, whose members claimed to be above politics and yet issued decisions shot through with what he saw as political ideology. In October 1980 he called her "an elitist, not a democrat," adding, "The people . . . want to know that their courts have been sensitive to the rights of victims, as well as the rights of defendants." The next year, he accused Bird of "engaging in partisan politics."[28]

Deukmejian also put Bird front and center in his gubernatorial campaign, accusing his Democratic opponent, Los Angeles mayor Tom Bradley, of being "a strong and outspoken supporter" of the chief justice. And when the high court ruled the Briggs jury instruction unconstitutional, Deukmejian blamed Bird. During an appearance at a $1,000-per-plate dinner, he accused her of using "every possible means of thwarting" California's death penalty law.[29] His election emboldened him further; for the remainder of his political career and beyond, Deukmejian continued to make Bird his go-to reference whenever he wanted to make a point about wrongheaded liberalism or bad judges.

It is unclear why Deukmejian chose to focus so intently on Bird, since a majority of her fellow justices—even, occasionally, conservatives— voted with her on criminal cases. Clearly, he was catering to his political base, who five years after her investiture continued obsessively to track all of her judicial opinions, which they saw as overwhelmingly biased toward defendants. In one case, for example, she had voted to overturn a teenager's conviction because it had been based on the uncorroborated testimony of an accomplice. And she was skeptical about the use of hypnosis in trials.[30]

Additionally, some of his campaign contributors—namely growers and large agribusiness interests—still harbored grudges against Bird for her part in enacting the Agriculture Labor Relations Act. As governor, Deukmejian would consistently work to gut the funding for the agency tasked with mediating disputes and setting union elections for farmworkers.

Deukmejian's campaign consulting firm also may have encouraged him to emphasize Bird. Spencer-Roberts had managed Ronald Reagan's campaigns. Stu Spencer and Bill Roberts were extraordinarily successful at mining data for issues designed to elicit emotional responses from voters. Bird had high name recognition and had revealed some personality traits that consultants and politicians could easily summarize in short sound bites designed to draw negative reactions: "soft on crime," "arrogant," or "out of touch."

The latter might be viewed as a subtle reminder that she had never married, or borne children, allowing opponents to frame her as a "women's libber" who felt superior to and could not identify with women who chose not to pursue careers. Feminism had given women like Bird opportunities they never could have imagined in earlier periods. By the 1980s, however, antifeminists had gained traction by branding career women unnatural beings who challenged tradition and nature by abandoning their roles as wives and mothers in their constant striving to be just like men.[31]

Finally, Bird often played into the hands of her opponents with judicial opinions and speeches that seemed unnecessarily antagonistic. In a July 1982 speech to the California Labor Federation, for example, Bird accused the "right wing" of "attempting to impose a new rule of law on the judiciary, the rule of extortion and the law of the jungle." Did Californians really want "a system that simply reflects the views of whoever can harangue the loudest, bully the best, make his threats felt the most forcibly?" One could argue that some percentage of them did, but this was a decidedly impolitic remark from one who needed public support to keep her job.

She sometimes used biting humor to make her points. Describing women's professional gains in law, she recalled a time when male judges told aspiring female lawyers that the "paramount destiny and mission of women are to fulfill the noble and benign office of wife and mother. This is the law of the Creator." Without skipping a beat, she added: "I always say to that, who asked Her?" Such comments reinforced critics' contention that she was "out of touch" with mainstream values.[32]

When Mathew Tobriner died in April 1982, only three months after leaving the court, Bird was distraught; she had relied on his counsel and friendship. In many ways, he was the father she never had, someone she could look up to and emulate. In a testimonial she extolled Tobriner, who had possessed, she declared, "the heart of a lion and the soul of a dove." But the essay also offered a hint as to how Bird hoped history might judge her.

Tobriner had been, she wrote, "a man of uncommon grace. He was unselfish and forgiving. He believed deeply in the ultimate goodness of everyone. There was a harmony to his life that sprang from his sensitivity to both the abstraction of the law and the needs of people. He saw life as the delicate balancing of order and liberty, mercy and justice, passion and compassion."[33]

Her friends and supporters often expressed puzzlement over the continuing acrimony toward the chief justice. After all, her immediate predecessors had all been staunch civil libertarians. Former chief justice Donald Wright was stumped as well. Bird received the kind of negative attention "that neither I nor my predecessors ever felt," he said. Even though Wright had authored the decision ending the death penalty in California, "with few exceptions, I never read an editorial about my performance or the performance of my predecessors that was anywhere near the type that are written about her almost repeatedly. I was never ... an object of publicity for anybody running for public office. I think it's been an unfair attack. I venture to say that 90 percent of those who are attacking her have never read a complete opinion that she's written. ... They are, on the whole, very well done."[34]

Some of her strongest partisans went out of their way to describe the Rose Bird they knew as warm, earthy, and kind. She loved watching movies and reading novels and then recounting their plots to friends.

Don Vial had worked with Bird since her days at the Agriculture and Services Agency, and she often had dinner with his family. "It wasn't easy to get her out of that work syndrome," he said, "but when you did, she's a totally relaxed person. You could talk to her about anything. She's very charming and sensitive and appreciates the values of home and the warmth of a family. I don't think of her as chief justice, she's just Rose."[35]

Alexandra Leichter, a family law attorney in Los Angeles, later recalled Bird as a "stunning, brilliant woman" and a caring friend, who also possessed a zany sense of humor. Bird "remembered every birthday or holiday occasion with a piece of jewelry, a funny card . . . or something exotic." Leichter was Jewish. Once, when she and Bird rode in a cab together, the driver began spewing "a barrage of anti-Semitic remarks." Bird insisted on immediately leaving the cab. She "threw her arms around me, apologizing for the hurtful comments of this total stranger."[36]

When journalists asked Bird why she declined to reveal this side of herself in interviews, she responded in the way she always had to media questions, with dissembling and quasi-lectures. "Okay, I could sit back and tell you all the nice things that I did for this person and that person. But what kind of a monster does it make of me that I exploit all that? And exploit my mother and exploit my dogs." The revelation that she had dogs, which needed walking and picking up after, might have made her seem much more like other people, but "my role isn't to be politically smart and figure out what is the politically smart thing to do. My role is to do what's right under the Constitution. And if that's politically unpopular, so be it."[37]

Bird had long been under fire, but the emergence of George Deukmejian altered the trajectory of her career in ways no one could have foreseen. "The only way they'll get me out of here is feet first," she had declared after her near loss in 1978. She, like many others, undoubtedly underestimated Deukmejian, who possessed a killer instinct when it came to capitalizing on the political weaknesses of others.[38]

He understood that being elected governor might enable him to push the state in a more conservative direction, at least with regard to issues such as crime and the death penalty. Others might argue that the court should be above politics, but not Deukmejian. He strongly believed that the state supreme court justices had for too long waved the flag of "judicial independence" while thumbing their noses at the electorate. When he took office in January 1983, five of the seven justices were Brown appointees; he hoped ultimately to replace them with his own. His main focus was Bird, and he hoped that keeping her under an unrelenting spotlight might help to facilitate her downfall.[39]

Without some context, the obsessive focus on violent crime in the late 1970s and early 1980s seems difficult to understand. Members of the public seemed convinced that hundreds and possibly thousands of predators roamed the streets at will and that only long prison sentences and ramped-up executions would stop their numbers from growing. This mentality can largely be attributed to the ability of conservatives to frame the debate following high court decisions that eliminated the death penalty in 1972.[40]

Abolitionists had been making inroads in California and nationally for more than a decade before the rulings, but most people pegged their chances of actually ending the death penalty as minimal at best. Then came Chief Justice Wright's February 1972 opinion declaring its application to be arbitrary and capricious and thus "cruel or unusual."[41]

Wright's opinion sparked public outrage, particularly because it invalidated the death sentences of all 107 death row inmates in California, including cult killer Charles Manson; Sirhan Sirhan, convicted killer of Robert F. Kennedy; and Gregory Powell, the "Onion Field" slayer of a policeman, made famous by writer Joseph Wambaugh in a book of the same name. "People began to wake up to the fact that the court was out of control," Christopher Heard, head of the Criminal Legal Justice Foundation, told a reporter.[42]

As California struggled with new death penalty laws, a number of chilling murders captured public attention and spawned sensational media coverage. Reporters quickly gave the perpetrators nicknames—"The Freeway Killer," "The Hillside Strangler," "The Night Stalker"—that seemed designed to ramp up the fear factor. Capital punishment proponents claimed that only the prospect of execution could deter brutal killers. "There are a lot coming, more and more and more. And you and all of us hiding behind a barrier, a little guardhouse up the hill, isn't going to stop it," one prosecutor warned during a trial.[43]

Media outlets were quick to capitalize on public fears, and reporters sought out experts to explain the perceived increase in crime. The *Los Angeles Times*, for example, conducted a "random survey" on the topic in the early 1980s. "The coroner has so many bodies, he doesn't know where to put them," said Armand Arabian, a superior court judge later named by Deukmejian to the state supreme court. Criminals "don't have a fear of apprehension, they don't have a fear of conviction and they don't have a fear of penalty," he added. Police captain John Salvino knew exactly where to place the blame: "The courts are the main problem with the justice system today, and Rose Bird is the main problem with the courts."[44]

At the same time, the emergence of media-savvy victims' rights groups forged bonds of sympathy between ordinary citizens and crime victims' relatives. Doris Tate may have created the first such organization, Citizens for Truth. Tate's daughter Sharon had been murdered in August 1969 along with four others under orders from Charles Manson. The crime riveted America: it occurred in a wealthy Los Angeles enclave, and Tate had been married to film director Roman Polanski and was eight months pregnant at the time of her killing. Manson's followers murdered two other Los Angeles residents the following night.[45]

The commutation of Manson's death sentence enraged Doris Tate. "Since when do we not have to pay penance for the things we do?" she asked in an interview. "Sharon was stabbed 16 times and hung by the neck." To maintain her sanity, Tate turned her energies toward lobbying lawmakers and raising money. She also befriended news reporters and the Los Angeles district attorney; until her death in the 1990s, she attended every prison hearing for incarcerated members of the "Manson Family." (Her surviving daughter, Debra Tate, has continued her mother's work.) Doris Tate blamed the state supreme court for taking too long to execute condemned inmates. "What happened to the Manson family was that while the court was sitting on their appeals, the death penalty was overturned."[46]

Patti Linebaugh also created an organization, Society's League Against Molesters (SLAM), to pressure lawmakers to keep pedophiles in prison. Linebaugh's two-year-old granddaughter Amy Sue Seitz had been kidnapped from her babysitter's front yard in 1978, sexually assaulted, and murdered by Theodore Frank, a recidivist sexual predator. Frank "had seven prior convictions," Linebaugh told a reporter. "There was nothing I could do as far as Amy was concerned, but I felt a responsibility to the public and to the families of victims." By the early 1980s, SLAM had chapters in more than forty states, and Linebaugh spoke with reporters and law enforcement officials throughout the country.[47]

The Orange County judge who sentenced Frank to death predicted that he would "die of old age" in about fifteen years, not in the gas chamber. "I'd bet on it."[48] Yet Linebaugh was stunned when the court actually overturned Frank's death sentence, and she vowed "to continue every effort that I can possibly extend to see Theodore Frank die." Stanley Mosk wrote the majority opinion in the case. Police had illegally seized private diaries without obtaining a search warrant, he wrote. In her concurrence, Bird noted that "the freedom from governmental intrusion into an individual's papers has long been recognized in law."[49] Republican state senator Ed Davis called the ruling "a classic case of the continuing, incredible misinterpretation of the search and seizure amendment."[50]

Groups such as Tate's and Linebaugh's provided a venue for death penalty proponents to vent and also served as a reminder that terrible crimes could happen to anyone, even people married to famous movie directors. If executions could deter even one perpetrator from committing a crime, capital punishment was worth it. Many, if not most, of the victims' groups were led by mothers, a factor that made them even more effective politically and served as an additional reminder of how significantly Bird deviated from the "traditional" woman. According to this long-held stereotype, by natural instinct women were supposed to react emotionally and viscerally when it came to crimes against children.

But Bird's job required her to approach horrific crimes with a detached and clinical mindset. Gender clearly played some role in these calculations, since the same standards did not apply to her male colleagues, all of whom had children and yet approached criminal cases with the same detachment. Away from public view, Bird said more than once that "my heart goes out to Amy Sue's grandmother. . . . There's nothing I can say in terms of assuaging the pain that she's gone through." She understood, she said, how someone experiencing such a tragedy "might never understand the need to uphold legal procedures, even in cases involving defendants such as Frank."[51]

Death penalty advocates did not want to hear judges or legal experts blame "constitutional requirements" and "complexities" for the lack of executions. They demanded justice, providing a vocal and supportive audience for conservative politicians, whose numbers continued to grow through the early 1980s. The U.S. Supreme Court seemed to reflect this changing climate by retreating from two decades of rulings favoring defendants' rights. In July 1983, for example, the court overruled the California Supreme Court with regard to the Briggs Initiative's provision for informing jurors that life sentences could be changed to something less. Ronald Reagan's first appointee—and the court's first woman justice—Sandra Day O'Connor wrote the 5–4 decision finding the jury instruction constitutional.

Notifying the jury of governors' ability to commute life sentences "invites the jury to assess whether the defendant is someone whose probable future behavior makes it undesirable that he return to society," she declared. At the same time, however, O'Connor suggested that California courts might revisit the initiative's constitutionality using state rather than federal constitutional grounds. The California court did just that, ruling that the jury instruction violated due process guarantees of the state's constitution. The state court also reinforced the requirement that intent to kill be present to confer a death sentence on a defendant.[52]

What could justices do to assuage critics under these circumstances? Laws governing capital punishment were too difficult to explain in a thirty-second sound bite, or even a thirty-minute speech. How to explain, for example, that enacting two separate death penalty laws a year apart significantly complicated the decision-making process? As law professor Gerald Uelmen saw it, the Briggs Initiative was shot through with "contradictions, ambiguities, ignorance of precedent, inconsistencies and erroneous citations all around."[53]

Californians might complain that the court "dragged its feet" on capital cases, but many death row inmates went months or years without attorneys willing to represent them, since the state authorized payment of only thirty-five to forty dollars per hour, and few private attorneys earning up to ten times that amount were willing to take on the work. That meant public defenders, already loaded down with cases, had to add more. Additionally, the numerous grounds that existed for appeal at both the state and federal level allowed condemned individuals to string out their appeals for years.[54]

Earl Lloyd Jackson's case offers a window into the process. It took more than a year for him to go on trial after his 1977 arrest. In January 1979 jurors sentenced him to death, and state supreme court justices heard his case in early 1980. His appellate attorneys covered familiar ground in their argument: trial counsel had been incompetent, prosecutors engaged in misconduct, and the judge improperly admitted evidence. None of this swayed the majority of justices, who upheld his death sentence. Jackson's attorneys then appealed to the U.S. Supreme Court, maintaining that race had played a role in Jackson's sentence—he was black and his victims were white. It took another year for the court to deny this petition, whereupon his attorneys filed another appeal with the state supreme court, declaring that evidence had been improperly suppressed.

The case and Jackson's death sentence were still in limbo when Deukmejian took office in January 1983, vowing to push capital cases through the pipeline. Death penalty advocates could not have known that, despite a second sentence affirmed by the state high court, Jackson would continue appealing in federal and state courts until in 2008 a federal court overturned his death sentence but not his conviction. Another jury then decided that he should, in fact, be executed. As of 2016, Earl Lloyd Jackson remained on death row at fifty-eight years old.[55]

In many cases federal courts issued most of the rulings that kept condemned inmates alive. For example, jurors in San Diego condemned Robert Alton Harris in March 1979, and less than two years later the state supreme court upheld his death sentence. Over the next decade, his attorneys made dozens of appeals (mostly to federal courts) before the U.S. Supreme Court finally put a stop to them. Among the issues: severe abuse Harris suffered as a child that led to brain damage and the state's refusal to pay for necessary psychiatric tests. When Harris died in the gas chamber in April 1992—fourteen years after his conviction—he became the first executed inmate in California since 1967.[56]

As the clamor for executions increased, Bird tried to remain above the fray. She appeared in public only on rare occasions, mostly to make speeches and accept awards. In 1984 she accepted a "Distinguished Woman of the Decade" honor from the organization Women in Business. In her remarks, she lauded the increasing numbers of women judges. "When I took office, there were few women on the bench in any state. Now in California we have 125 women on the trial and appellate benches, and of course, a woman on the Supreme Court."[57]

But she obviously felt the pressure. While not directly addressing the death penalty, in a June 1983 essay for the *Los Angeles Times* she offered an instructive lesson on how, from her perspective, the judiciary operated in the general sense. Judges were like umpires, Bird wrote. "They observe the facts … and apply the rules of the game fairly and evenhandedly. … When an umpire has called 'strike three,' the batter is out, no matter how loudly he, his team or his team's fans may protest. … Were the umpire to do otherwise, there would be no order left in the game."

Many readers found the essay irritating and condescending and its tone flippant and self-righteous. In retrospect, it also revealed a certain naiveté, since Bird seems not to have anticipated any hostile reaction. In fact, readers flooded the *Times* with letters. "The increasing attacks on the courts have come because there is a feeling that they have turned a blind eye to the legitimate concerns of the public," wrote one respondent. "Right-wing politicians did not create public concerns about the role of the judiciary, they merely exploit them," wrote another. A third accused Bird of "consistently giving the known criminal a fourth strike."[58]

By the mid-1980s, anger toward the court in general, and Rose Bird in particular, had intensified. Between 1979 and the end of 1984, 125 men had been condemned. Yet the supreme court had issued rulings in only 45 cases. As Bird supporters often pointed out, however, California was not alone with its backlog of cases: death rows nationally held more than 2,700 condemned individuals. The thirty-eight states with capital punishment had executed a total of 50 people between 1977 and 1985.[59]

Opponents were not swayed by statistics showing that the court had upheld the vast majority of convictions, nor by the fact that all of the condemned remained on death row pending the outcome of their penalty phase retrials. Bird had declared that she "took an oath to uphold the Constitution. I have faithfully tried to keep that oath," but she alone among the seven justices had never voted to uphold a single death sentence, an action that seemed to belie her words.

The pressure compelled justices eventually to address the growing clamor. Bird declared capital appeals "the equivalent of sometimes five to ten separate opinions because there are so many issues that have to be researched."[60] Just before he left the court in 1983, Frank Newman suggested cutting down the backlog by eliminating the requirement that all capital cases go directly from the trial court to the state's highest court. Instead, cases that raised no new constitutional issues could go to the court of appeal.[61]

Mosk reminded critics that capital appeals represented only a small part of the justices' overall responsibilities. They also dealt with non-capital criminal cases and civil matters. If politicians wanted the capital appeals decided faster, Mosk suggested, they should add four justices to the court and divide the workload between civil and criminal cases. Nothing came of his suggestion, or Newman's, but in 1982 the state legislature authorized the creation of a permanent staff of attorneys to help with the increased workload. These lawyers largely replaced annual law clerks and student interns, and they worked for the court as a whole rather than for individual justices. Eventually the central staff grew to thirty, with half working on criminal matters and the other half on civil cases.[62]

Opponents were less concerned about the court's ability to handle capital appeals than they were with the results. By early 1985 justices had upheld only three death sentences, and two of those—Earl Lloyd Jackson's and Robert Alton Harris's—had come before 1982.[63] Critics pondered publicly: What did it take to get a death sentence upheld? The court, for example, had deemed *People v. Ramos* an "almost perfect" trial, and yet justices overturned Marcelino Ramos's death sentence not once but twice.

Ramos had worked as a janitor at a Taco Bell in Santa Ana. One night he decided to rob the restaurant. He forced two employees into a store cooler and then, after telling the victims to "say your prayers," shot both in the back of the head. One survived and testified against Ramos, who was condemned and sentenced to die. The state high court first heard Ramos's case in late 1981. Tobriner acknowledged that the trial had been exceptionally well-handled by all parties, at least until the judge issued the disputed Briggs Initiative instruction informing jurors that a life sentence did not necessarily mean Ramos would die in prison.

Citing the jury instruction, the court overturned Ramos's death sentence while upholding his conviction. Ramos remained on death row while his case went back to the original court for a new penalty hearing. A second jury sentenced him to death. In November 1984 the case went back to the supreme court, which again invalidated his death sentence. The court had deemed intent to kill necessary for a death sentence, and it was unclear whether Ramos had intended to actually murder his victims.[64]

Los Angeles district attorney Robert Philibosian blasted both *Ramos* decisions. He placed the blame squarely on Bird, despite the fact she had not authored either ruling (but she had concurred without comment in both). And the decisions had been unanimous. Nonetheless, he accused her of "waging a war on prosecutors." In November 1986 Bird and four other justices would appear on the statewide ballot for confirmation. Philibosian and other opponents vowed that this time, she would not win a new term, and in speeches throughout the state, he began urging California voters to take care of "the problem."[65]

Within weeks of the second *Ramos* ruling, Republican campaign consultant Bill Roberts announced that he planned to lead the charge against Bird under the auspices of a newly formed group, Crime Victims for Court Reform. Roberts's leadership meant this effort would differ from earlier campaigns to oust Bird. Roberts was a well-connected consultant with a stable of high-profile clients, including Ronald Reagan and George Deukmejian. He also had a vast network of contributors and access to the most powerful media outlets. Others might snarkily refer to "Rosie and the Supremes," chant slogans such as "Bye-Bye Birdie," or brandish photos of stuffed turkeys named "Rosie." Roberts would labor—not altogether successfully—to maintain decorum and seriousness and tightly control his message.

Bird was Roberts's primary target, but conservatives understood by early 1985 that they had to defeat more than one justice to garner a conservative majority. Malcolm Lucas, Deukmejian's former law partner, joined the court in early 1984, replacing Richardson. Yet the ideological makeup remained the same—six liberals and one conservative. Opponents began to eye Cruz Reynoso and Joseph Grodin. Getting rid of three justices at once would enable George Deukmejian to put an end to the four-decade reign of liberals on the storied California institution. Conservatives had longed dreamed of this possibility; by 1985 the goal seemed eminently achievable.[66]

Big Business v. Rose Bird 8

It was just after midnight in November 1974 when Charles Bigbee left his job as a custodian at Los Angeles City Hall and drove to a pay phone outside a convenience store to call his girlfriend. As the pair spoke, Bigbee looked up to see a car barreling toward him, out of control. Frantically, he tugged at the accordion glass doors, but they had jammed. He covered himself with his coat, braced for impact, and began reciting the Lord's Prayer. The speeding car slammed into the phone booth, covering Bigbee with shards of glass and partially severing his right leg. Doctors ultimately had to amputate.

Bigbee sued the car's driver and the Hollywood Turf Club, which had sold drinks to the inebriated motorist. After receiving a small settlement, he decided to file suit against Pacific Telephone and Telegraph Company, which maintained the phone booth, as well as other companies involved in its manufacture and operation. The pay phone had been installed too close to a busy highway to be safe and the company had failed to properly maintain it, his lawyer declared.

The defendants claimed that *Bigbee v. Pacific Telephone and Telegraph Company* had no merit; how could they predict that a drunken driver might lose control and plow into the booth? A superior court judge agreed with the defendants and issued a summary judgment, terminating the lawsuit. Bigbee decided to take his case to the California Supreme

Court. It seemed a long shot, but justices accepted the case. In June 1983, nearly nine years after the accident, the court overturned the summary judgment. Bigbee had every right to sue for negligence, Chief Justice Rose Bird wrote in her 6–1 decision.

"It is not uncommon for speeding and/or intoxicated drivers to lose control of their cars and crash into poles, buildings or whatever else is standing alongside the road they travel, no matter how straight or smooth that road may be." Defendants had placed the phone booth, "which was difficult to exit, in a parking lot 15 feet from the side of a major thoroughfare and near a driveway. Under these circumstances, this court cannot conclude as a matter of law that it was unforeseeable that the booth might be struck by a car and cause serious injury."

The lone dissenter was an Alameda County superior court judge sitting on the high court just for the case. "To hold that defendants could be found liable for locating the booth where they did is tantamount to holding that one may be found negligent whenever he conducts everyday activities on or adjacent to the public sidewalk," wrote Robert H. Kroninger.[1] The case never went to trial, however. After the high court decision, the companies involved settled with Bigbee for an undisclosed, though "not insubstantial," amount of money.[2]

Few people in California paid much immediate attention to the *Bigbee* decision, since it did not involve a death row inmate, a victims' group, or a violent crime. To corporate executives, however, it seemed to be another example of "justice" run amok, one more in a long string of adversarial judicial decisions that—wrongly, in their eyes—punished businesses.

In reality Bird broke no new ground with *Bigbee*; previous California Supreme Courts had issued forty years of proplaintiff rulings. In fact, an earlier court had pioneered the concept of strict liability. Justice Roger Traynor, as he had done in so many other areas of jurisprudence, led the way. The initial case, from 1944, involved an exploding Coca Cola bottle that seriously injured a Merced waitress as she removed it from a restaurant refrigerator. A jury awarded the waitress damages, but Coca Cola appealed, arguing that the accident had not been due to negligence on its part. The supreme court upheld the jury award. In a concurrence that went further than the majority opinion, Traynor declared that "negligence should no longer be singled out as the basis of a plaintiff's right to recover" damages. A manufacturer incurred "absolute liability when an article he has placed on the market proves to have a defect that causes injury."[3]

Nineteen years later, another opinion by Traynor expanded the concept of strict liability with a declaration that as a general principle the rights of consumers should be privileged "over the interests of manufacturers of consumer goods."[4] This time the plaintiff was a dentist who had been struck in the head by a piece of wood while he worked with a power tool. The company argued that the plaintiff had failed to heed the warranty's requirements for filing a lawsuit. Writing for a unanimous court, Traynor said it was "not necessary for a plaintiff to establish an express warranty. . . . A manufacturer is strictly liable when an article he places on the market, knowing that it is to be used without inspection for defects, proves to have a defect that causes injury to a human being."[5]

These and other decisions served as the foundation for broadening the definition of liability to include many kinds of personal injuries, such as those from traffic accidents. In 1969 the California high court deemed State Farm Insurance Company liable for an accident, even though the company had canceled the driver's policy for lying about a prior license revocation. State Farm had rescinded the policy only after learning of the accident.[6]

Two years later, the court held a tavern owner liable for injuries caused by a drunken patron who left the premises, drove down a narrow mountain road, and crossed over into the other lane, where he hit an oncoming car head-on, injuring the driver.[7] And in a case involving a motorist seriously injured after his new Ford suddenly and inexplicably swerved on a busy road, Traynor wrote that manufacturers and retailers "could not escape liability by tracing the defect to a component part supplied by another."[8]

Emotional distress also came to reside under the doctrine of strict liability. In 1968 the court authorized payment for damages to a woman who watched a driver hit and kill her young daughter as the girl crossed the street near her home. The trial court had dismissed the case because the woman had not personally been in danger. But the supreme court disagreed. The woman's mental suffering made her eligible for damages.[9]

Such rulings compelled businesses to purchase liability policies from insurance companies. By the 1960s standardized policies covered "legal obligations arising from death, injury or property damage caused by an 'accident' involving 'goods or products manufactured, sold, handled or distributed by the named insured.'" As the number of lawsuits proliferated in the 1960s, premiums rose significantly.[10]

Initially, the designation "tort reform" referred to judicial efforts to provide monetary relief to injured consumers, but over time, business groups including chambers of commerce and the Business Roundtable co-opted the term. According to this new designation, courts were "anti–free enterprise" and needed to be reined in via legislative and other reforms of the tort system.[11]

Corporate leaders and others railed at Traynor and his fellow liberal justices for their consistently proconsumer rulings, but their outrage seldom went further than a few sputtering speeches, editorials, or essays. It was not simply Traynor's elite status or stellar reputation that protected him. He was savvy enough to avoid using his legal opinions to challenge or confront individuals or groups who advocated tough-on-crime measures and who strongly supported "measures as popular and viscerally important as the death penalty."[12] Timing worked for him as well: he left the court before capital punishment became the lightning-rod issue in California politics.

Bird's willingness to challenge both the business and prosecutorial establishments significantly enhanced her vulnerability because it gave corporate leaders incentive to join forces with groups already targeting her rulings in criminal cases. Thus was born an alliance among Republican politicians, business leaders, law-and-order activists, and campaign consultants. All of them held one goal: gaining control of the California Supreme Court. Firebrands such as H. L. Richardson and, to a lesser extent, consultants such as Bill Roberts provided the emotional rhetoric; corporate interests provided the cash.

In some ways, the charge that Bird was antibusiness and proplaintiff seems a more valid characterization than the accusation that she favored criminals. She did vote to overturn every death sentence that came before her court, but provisions of the Briggs Initiative could be construed as legally questionable at best and unconstitutional at worst. Bird was not alone in espousing this viewpoint. Besides, no death row inmate—or any inmate, for that matter—ever got out of prison because of Rose Bird. And in both capital and noncapital cases, she voted to uphold criminal convictions.

Civil plaintiffs, on the other hand, tended to fare exceedingly well on her watch. And there was a strong subtext to her opinions: rich and powerful individuals exploited and mistreated poor and middle-class people who had no political connections and thus needed someone to stand up for them. Bird—raised by an impoverished, exploited single mother—now had political connections, and she intended to use them on behalf of others. As her colleague Cruz Reynoso put it, Bird "knew life as those without power live it. The perspective of those who do not have power guided her."[13]

Corporate executives had an additional incentive for targeting the court's rulings. By the late 1970s and 1980s, the proliferation of class-action lawsuits had upped the stakes financially. Such cases involved hundreds of plaintiffs injured or killed by a particular product. "Until the late 1970s, tort claims had been pursued on an individual, case-by-case basis," wrote Linda S. Mullenix in the *Northwestern University Law Review*. "But with massive exposure to toxic chemicals such as Agent Orange, the pervasive incidence of asbestos-related illness, and the large numbers of women [and men] suffering adverse effects of pharmaceuticals or medical devices, plaintiffs' attorneys turned to procedural means for aggregating the claims."[14]

The Bird court had, in fact, opened the door to a class-action suit itself in 1980 with an opinion by Stanley Mosk. The case involved diethylstilbestrol (DES), a drug taken by as many as six million women beginning in the 1940s to prevent miscarriages. Decades later, many of their now adult daughters had begun developing vaginal and cervical cancers, and in 1971 the Food and Drug Administration ordered the manufacturers to stop marketing and promoting DES.

In the late 1970s, two cancer-stricken daughters of women who had taken DES filed suit in California alleging that the manufacturers had known of potential problems. A majority of high court justices—including Bird—agreed. The companies had "failed to test DES for efficacy and safety," Mosk wrote. With this decision, one reporter noted, the court established "a sweeping new doctrine of product liability."[15]

Even though lawsuits might not be settled for years or even decades, the prospect of multimillion-dollar verdicts upheld on appeal terrified corporate executives. And the suits themselves might affect stock prices, or even send a company into bankruptcy. Decisions such as *Bigbee* thus carried far more freight than those reached by earlier courts. On the defensive about potentially shoddy or dangerous products, corporate spokesmen blamed "greedy" plaintiffs' lawyers who sought out victims, overly generous juries, and courts for what they feared might become an onslaught of similar cases, filed under even the flimsiest of pretenses.

In other times, business owners might have sought relief from California legislators, lobbying to get laws enacted limiting damages. But this scenario seemed unlikely by the early 1980s. Voters may have elected a conservative Republican governor, but Democrats controlled both houses of the state legislature. Consumer lawyers earned their livings from big-money verdicts for the plaintiffs, and they contributed heavily to Democrats, who seemed likely to remain in power for the foreseeable future.

Every decade California lawmakers redrew maps that set the boundaries for state legislative and congressional districts. Whichever party controlled the legislature nearly always configured districts to ensure a continued majority. The influx of new residents to California in the 1970s meant the creation of new districts, making the process of redistricting even more fraught than usual. When Democrats revealed their new plan in 1981, it gave them additional seats in both houses of the state legislature and in Congress. Republicans cried foul, and in early 1982 they successfully gathered signatures for three ballot referendums to nullify all of the changes. Meanwhile, they wanted old districts used in upcoming elections. Democrats sued, and the case wound up before the state's highest tribunal.

In January 1982 Bird wrote the decision for a divided court. The referendums could go forward, she said, but the newly configured districts had to be used in both the June primary and the November 1982 general election. "Maintaining the old election districts for the upcoming election would raise troubling questions about the future of reapportionment in our state," she wrote. "It would create a serious risk that every reapportionment plan would be delayed at least two years before it could be implemented."[16]

Republicans reacted with dismay. "In a blatantly partisan action, the Rose Bird court in effect has placed a stamp of approval on clearly unconstitutional reapportionment plans," one letter writer complained in the *Los Angeles Times*.[17] The referendums passed handily but became moot when legislators tweaked the new districts, reconfiguring them to protect incumbents of both parties. The Bird court was forced to weigh in a second time, after one disgruntled Republican lawmaker sought to qualify another measure to make the process "fairer," he said. In September 1983 justices ruled against his plan. Once-a-decade redistricting had already occurred and, by law, could not be visited again.

No justice affixed her or his name to the latter decision, but the wording did not seem designed to allay suspicions that the court worked hand-in-glove with Democrats. "In this case we are called upon to determine the constitutionality of an attempt—novel in the history of this state—to readjust state legislative and Congressional district boundaries through the statutory initiative process after the Legislature has already done so," justices declared.[18]

With both the legislature and the state's top court seemingly stacked against them, corporate leaders had few options, at least in the short term. Looking to the future, however, they saw opportunities. If George Deukmejian were to win a second term, and if Bird—and possibly other justices—were to be defeated in 1986, the Republican governor could replace liberals with conservatives. With Republicans in charge of two branches of government, the composition of the state legislature consequently would matter less.

But they had to carefully craft their messages and strategies. Business leaders understood that many ordinary Californians often felt aggrieved and abused by industrial behemoths. They cheered when "little guys" fought back and won. They felt gratitude toward juries, judges, and justices who finally seemed to be taking their side; they had to be carefully nudged toward the notion that judicial opinions favoring plaintiffs might adversely affect the lives of average citizens.

Tough-on-crime proponents could use scare tactics, such as the prospect of vicious criminals roaming suburban neighborhoods. Corporate executives and their lobbyists had to craft subtler messages and carefully choose their battles. In one 1980 case, for example, the court had ruled in favor of a plaintiff who had been fired by Atlantic Richfield Co. for refusing to participate in a gasoline price-fixing scheme.[19] Declaring decisions such as this one to be the product of "greedy trial lawyers" or "liberal justices" was not a winning public relations strategy.

Since the Bird court's civil rulings seemed focused on the notion of "fairness," the message from business had to raise the question: fairness to whom? With each new ruling, the Bird court seemed bent on raising the bar higher; at some point, this approach might be framed as likely to have an adverse impact on consumers as well as business.

The court's decisions favoring tenants gave business representatives an opening to test this message. In 1974 the court under Chief Justice Donald Wright had charged landlords with a contractual obligation to maintain their buildings in "habitable" condition—a somewhat vague concept but one the court under Bird came to use as a baseline for significantly enhancing renters' rights.

In February 1981, for example, the court determined that tenants could withhold rent and stave off eviction if landlords failed to adequately maintain their property. The case involved a group of residents of a Venice, California, apartment building. In 1977 the building's new owners notified residents of plans to substantially raise rents. Tenants protested, citing wall cracks, peeling paint, water leaks, broken windows, and rodents, among other problems.

In response, the landlords sent eviction notices to tenants, ordering them to either pay up within three days or move out. Ultimately, they evicted three tenants. The tenants sued, and a lower court ruled in favor of the apartment owners. The fact that tenants had not relocated despite substandard conditions suggested they had willingly accepted the status quo; thus the owners had every right to expect tenants to pay higher rent without protest or repairs.

Writing for a 5–1 majority, Bird disagreed. Their status automatically placed renters at a disadvantage. Additionally, a housing shortage in the Los Angeles area meant people often had to remain in less than ideal—even unsafe—conditions, she wrote. The tenants' failure to relocate did not absolve the owners of a contractual obligation to provide decent conditions. The majority also disagreed with the new owners' argument that their predecessor had been responsible for making repairs.[20] The Legal Aid Society of Los Angeles lauded the decision, which it deemed "very pro-tenant and sweeping in extending the right to tenants to ensure landlords meet their fundamental obligation to provide livable conditions."[21]

Nine months later, Bird wrote for a unanimous court in the case of an Orange County woman evicted from her apartment after telephoning police to report that her landlord had molested her nine-year-old daughter. The following week, the landlord raised the woman's rent from $200 to $600 a month. She refused to pay. The landlord was retaliating against her, she charged. The landlord evicted her; a superior court judge upheld the eviction, but the supreme court disagreed.

"California has a long history of protecting those citizens who report violations of criminal laws," Bird said in overturning the judge's decision. "Criminal laws . . . would be meaningless if citizens who reported crime were not protected from vindictive retaliation." The plaintiff's attorney called the high court ruling a "landmark. Until this decision, nobody was sure of the extent of tenants' protection" from retaliatory actions, she said.

The landlord eventually pleaded guilty to a misdemeanor in connection with the molestation accusation but continued to assert his innocence.[22]

Bird did not author the landmark decision in February 1982 that barred apartment owners from refusing to rent to families with children, though she signed on to the majority opinion. "A society that sanctions wholesale discrimination against its children in obtaining housing engages in suspect activity," Mathew Tobriner wrote in one of his final opinions before retiring from the court.

The case had been brought by the parents of a six-year-old; the family had been evicted in 1977 from an adults-only apartment in the beach community of Marina del Rey. A lower court judge sided with the landlord. Children, according to the judge, were "rowdier, noisier, more mischievous and more boisterous than adults." Tobriner cited the Unruh Act—named after former Democratic assembly speaker Jesse Unruh—which barred "all arbitrary discrimination" by businesses, including apartments, "based on class distinction—such as race or religion." Children were part of a protected class, Tobriner wrote, even if they were "noisier, rowdier, more mischievous and more boisterous than adults."

Richardson and Mosk dissented from the majority opinion. "Do our middle-aged or older citizens, having worked long and hard, having raised their own children, having paid both their taxes and their dues to society retain a right to spend their remaining years in a relatively peaceful and tranquil environment of their own choice?" Richardson asked. "The answer . . . is, why not?"[23] The owner of the apartment complex appealed Tobriner's ruling to the U.S. Supreme Court, but the federal court let the decision stand. In 1983 the California Supreme Court extended its ruling to cover children living in condominiums.

David Lane, an attorney representing real estate interests, wrote an essay for the *Los Angeles Times* targeting the ruling on children in apartments. Who might the court decide to protect next? he pondered. For example, would they deem homosexuals part of a protected class? The state supreme court earlier had "established the right of homosexuals to frequent bars and restaurants," Lane wrote. "In the wake of this decision, landlord rights to discriminate on the basis of other characteristics will be questioned." Lane cited a recent case where "a Los Angeles court held that an apartment owner could not discriminate against tenants on the basis of their homosexual orientation." He also cited the case of a man with quadriplegia who was evicted after his landlord learned his tenant had hired a lesbian as his attendant. The tenant had sued, Lane said, though he offered no particulars of the case or its outcome.

Such opinion pieces seemed clearly designed to elicit anxious and fearful reactions from readers who might not be renters themselves but were encouraged to see the handwriting on the wall. At a time when the "homosexual lifestyle" was being debated throughout society as a result of the burgeoning AIDS epidemic, the subtext was not difficult to see. If landlords could not evict gay people from apartments or condominiums, ultimately employers would not be able to fire them, and realtors and homeowners' associations would be forced to accept them as residents in middle-class neighborhoods. Thus Bird and her fellow liberal justices could be accused of privileging "deviance" over traditional values.[24]

Business representatives also strongly protested a 1985 decision that found landlords liable for tenant injuries occurring on their property, even if the landlord was unaware of potentially dangerous conditions. The case involved a Bay Area tenant who was injured when he slipped in his apartment's shower and fell against the shower door, which shattered. "Within our marketplace economy the cost of purchasing rental housing is obviously based on the anticipated risks and rewards of the purchase," Associate Justice Allen Broussard wrote for a 5–2 majority. Housing costs "reflect the anticipated costs of protecting tenants, including repairs, replacement of defects and insurance."

Deukmejian appointee Malcolm Lucas dissented. "Any landlord, even one renting the family home for a year, will now be the insurer for defects in any wire, screw, latch, cabinet door, pipe or other article . . . despite the fact that he neither installed the item or had any knowledge or reason to know of the defect." Ronald Brower, the landlord's lawyer, claimed that the decision "increases the number of people that an injured tenant can sue. There is a greater likelihood that he will be able to recover something from someone."

Brower predicted rising insurance rates as well, due to a likely onslaught of lawsuits. "A larger number of plaintiffs will have the opportunity to sue, so there will be a greater legal expense involved," he said. Also, "landlords will be inspired to sue the original installer of the products and landlord-tenant litigation will be made more complex and costly." In other words, virtually no one was safe from liability.[25]

James M. Udall, a property manager, defended landlords. "If a landlord knows something needs fixing, he'll fix it. But how can you fix the unknown before somebody gets injured? You're getting to a point that a person is not responsible for his own conduct anymore. And to respond to unknown defects without having any reason to know if such defects [exist] is really asking too much."[26]

And renters did not benefit from this decision, according to business representatives. Charles A. Isham, executive vice president of the Apartment Association of Greater Los Angeles, declared that "Rose Bird raised rents. Landlords will have to go out and get additional insurance and the rate they will have to pay will be higher. The major impact will be to increase rents," he said.[27]

The court's rulings requiring gender equity in private establishments opened the door to a new kind of charge: justices were involved in "social engineering." In 1985 Bird authored a decision barring businesses from offering women special discounts. The case actually involved an Orange County car wash but was dubbed the "Ladies' Night" ruling, since it also prohibited nightclubs from setting aside certain times when men paid cover charges to gain entry while women got in for free. Businesses had to charge women and men the same price, the chief justice said. That same year, the court compelled a Santa Cruz boys' club to admit girls.

The court, in both cases, based its decisions on the Unruh Act. In the "Ladies' Night" case, plaintiffs charged that the price differential violated the act's prohibition against gender discrimination. Business owners argued that the act only barred establishments from excluding prospective patrons. That argument "lacked merit," the court found.[28]

Such rulings played into the hands of both conservative law-and-order proponents and corporate executives. Ordinary people did not care about "obscure" laws or statutes—how might such a decision affect them? And what might come next? UC Berkeley professor David Kirp pondered the possibility that the Boy Scouts and Campfire Girls might become the "Child Scouts" and the "Campfire Persons." "Next time it may be my privacy, my right to decide how to live my life, that the judges will take away," Kirp said.[29]

The medical profession also came under the Bird court's review, guaranteeing a new group of unhappy court watchers: doctors. The 1970s saw an explosion in medical malpractice suits, partly as a result of diminishing deference toward doctors who, like judges and politicians, were now viewed as fallible and thus candidates for litigation when procedures went wrong or when they made the wrong diagnosis. In one case, justices said a male plaintiff could seek damages after a doctor mistakenly diagnosed his former wife with syphilis. Both members of the couple understandably had experienced severe emotional distress. The wife believed her husband had gotten the disease from another sexual partner and had to undergo painful medical treatment. The stress eventually broke up the marriage.[30]

In another case, the court ruled in favor of a woman whose boyfriend had told his therapist he planned to kill her. The therapist failed to warn the woman, and the boyfriend subsequently ran her car off the road and shot her through the leg, though she survived. Therapists had an obligation to inform potential victims about threats even if patients had not been deemed dangerous to public safety, Associate Justice Joseph Grodin wrote for the majority. Failure to do so "is as much a basis for liability as is a negligent failure to warn a known victim once such diagnosis is made."[31]

The court also consistently ruled for employees in lawsuits against employers. For example, it required companies who offered vacations as part of their employment packages to provide prorated vacation pay to workers who left before qualifying for all of their benefits. A worker earning a two-week vacation for each year of employment thus would qualify for one week if he or she left after six months. Justices also forbade companies from disqualifying workers from employment because of physical disabilities. The case in question involved a man denied employment because of chronic hypertension.[32]

Several cases involved employee rights to join unions, to collectively bargain, or to strike. Interns and residents at University of California hospitals often worked one hundred hours per week but did not have the right to bargain for better conditions since the schools labeled them students, rather than employees. A decision by Bird declared them to be employees who, like other medical personnel working at university hospitals, had the right to be represented by unions. The ruling affected more than half of all interns and residents in California, since most doctors trained at public universities. Hospitals complained, but a spokesman for residents at UC Irvine said: "This gives us an avenue to speak with the administration on a more equal basis."[33]

A decision granting public employees the right to strike drew more attention—both negative and positive—than perhaps any other case involving employee-employer relations. Public sector jobs in sanitation, safety, road construction and maintenance, teaching, and utilities, among others, impacted virtually everyone in California. Public employees had gained collective bargaining rights in the 1940s and 1950s, but the state legislature had long "maintained a stony silence" when it came to allowing strikes, which potentially posed "substantial and imminent threat[s] to the health and safety" of communities. In a 1985 decision by Associate Justice Allen Broussard, the court broke the silence when it deemed public employee strikes "a basic civil liberty" and declared them legal, "unless or until it is clearly demonstrated" that they "created a substantial and imminent threat to the health and safety of the public."[34]

The case involved workers at sewage treatment plants and dumps in Los Angeles County. The sanitation district that employed them had cut back overtime pay. In 1976 the employees—members of the Service Employees International Union (SEIU)—struck in defiance of the ban on work stoppages. After three weeks the workers called off the strike. The sanitation district subsequently sued the union and won $246,904 in damages.

The SEIU appealed to the state's highest court. Six justices determined that the workers had a right to strike. In a concurrence, Bird declared the right to strike "an essential protection against abuses of employer power." Without that right, "working people would be at the total mercy of their employers.... Such a condition would make a mockery of the fundamental right to pursue life, liberty and happiness."[35]

Workers' rights advocates cheered the decision. Leo Geffner, lawyer for the SEIU, called it "extremely important." Ten other states allowed public employee strikes but only for workers in jobs considered "non-essential," such as golf course maintenance. "It has been an unresolved question ever since public employees started bargaining almost a generation ago," Geffner said.

Critics saw the situation differently. Writing in the *Los Angeles Times*, Robert Sherwood of Hemet castigated Bird's claim that the decision represented the culmination of a long struggle to gain workers' rights. Douglas Collins of Canoga Park dubbed public employee strikes "abhorrent. They cut off services to citizens." Unlike in the private sector, this "leave[s] no alternative source of such services to the affected public."[36]

Governor Deukmejian expressed outrage. "This is the type of decision that Californians have come to expect from this court," he said. Malcolm Lucas, his sole appointee to date, had been the lone dissenter. Lucas accused his colleagues of being "so enamored with the concept of the public strike that [they elevate] this heretofore illegal device to a basic civil liberty."[37]

As the 1986 election slid toward the horizon, critics of the Bird court's business rulings knew they needed a more unified approach. Individuals and small groups had tried to raise concern about "undesirables" as neighbors, increased rents, government intrusion into the practices of private organizations, and the prospect that employee strikes might cut off crucial services. Corporate spokesmen also needed to disseminate a singular message designed to resonate with the largest possible number of voters.

The issue of insurance rates seemed most promising. Decades of plaintiff-friendly rulings in California had made liability insurance mandatory for anyone doing business in the state: day care centers, hair salons, banks, pharmaceutical companies, hospitals, and department stores. Premiums rose dramatically in the late 1970s and early 1980s, in some cases as much as 25 or 30 percent in a single year. Some businesses faced policy cancellations.

The reasons for the increases were complex. Some sources attributed them to risky underwriting practices in the 1970s, a period of extraordinarily high interest rates. But corporate spokespeople offered a simple explanation: excessive litigation resulted from the state supreme court's willingness—even eagerness—to do the bidding of any and all plaintiffs' attorneys. To counteract this alleged phenomenon, a coalition of business interests joined together in early 1986 to create the American Tort Reform Association (ATRA).

The group began by pressuring state legislators to enact laws that included capping jury awards in civil liability cases with the goal of eliminating trial lawyers' incentive for taking them. ATRA members also placed stories in sympathetic publications, such as the *Wall Street Journal*. In one editorial, the paper blasted proplaintiff rulings for causing "skyrocketing insurance costs" and charged liberal judges with using civil lawsuits to "redistribute wealth." But the *Journal* had a relatively small impact, since its circulation was limited mostly to a well-off audience focused on financial issues.[38]

To garner wider attention and influence, tort reformers needed a spokesperson not linked in the public's mind to the strict liability issue. They found one in Washington DC. President Ronald Reagan knew a thing or two about crafting winning messages. His folksy good humor, nostalgic references to an America of small towns and white picket fences, and his twinkling charm entranced many Americans. But campaign donations from wealthy corporate titans had put him first in the California governor's seat and then in the White House. Like Reagan, these men detested government bureaucracy, liberal state legislators, and judges who often branded them—unfairly, they believed—as uncaring and selfish individuals who lacked concern for anyone not wealthy or powerful.

Reagan had paid little attention to tort reform—which, after all, required government action—until his attorney general, Edwin Meese, pushed him in that direction. During Reagan's years in Washington, Meese grew to be one of Reagan's most influential advisors, particularly after William P. Clark left Washington to return to his California ranch.

Meese's disdain for Bird went back to her first judicial retention election in 1978, when he had penned articles charging the court with delaying decisions in controversial criminal cases. His strong influence could be seen in a speech Reagan gave to ATRA in early 1986. The Charles Bigbee telephone booth decision was by then nearly three years old, but it provided an opportunity for Reagan to tag Bird as the symbol of a court system that needed to be reined in.

"Twisted and abused, tort law has become a pretext for outrageous legal outcomes," Reagan charged, "that impede our economic life, not promote it." He understood why Bigbee might sue, he told his audience. "But you might be startled to hear whom he sued: the telephone company and associated firms. That's right, according to Chief Justice Rose Bird of the California Supreme Court, a jury could find that companies responsible for the design, location, installation, and maintenance of the telephone booth were liable.... I suppose all this might be amusing if such absurd results only took place occasionally. Yet today, they have become all but commonplace."[39]

Reagan's public indictment of Bird thrilled her opponents in California, since it guaranteed national attention and a large influx of cash from deep-pocketed campaign contributors. It also lent credibility to Deukmejian's longstanding opposition to Bird. By early 1985 he had begun to focus on business as well as crime in his stump speeches. He urged business leaders to use their influence to help unseat the chief justice. In appearances across the state, he warned voters that businesses "consider a lot of factors when they are making a decision about whether or not they are going to invest hundreds of millions of dollars in either expanding their operations here or coming into the state."

At one point, he released a list of thirty-one cases—compiled by business groups at his request—that he claimed "allowed added taxes on business, made it easier to win large judgments against business, damaged landlords, forced business to pay added compensation to injured employees and made it easier for labor to picket companies." Eventually, Deukmejian suggested, businesses might relocate to other states where the climate was more welcoming, costing Californians desperately needed jobs. This implied threat soon became a conservative mantra.[40]

Deukmejian's participation encouraged other court critics to pile on as well. Stephen Barnett taught tort law at Boalt Hall. He was a vociferous Bird critic and a dependable source for journalists seeking out quotes criticizing high court rulings. Deukmejian should have added two more cases, Barnett told journalists after the governor unveiled his list. The decision barring adults-only apartments, for example, represented "an expansive interpretation of anti-discrimination law, one that would have been better dealt with by the Legislature." Bird's majority opinion on vacation pay, meanwhile, "invoked principles of equity and justice. Yet, while the decision might seem economically fair, the court's reading of the statute was both problematic and surprising."[41]

Bird's supporters were fighting on two fronts and had to quickly and strongly respond to the governor and to his business allies. "I could spend a half hour and find a number of decisions that are pro-business," said attorney Robert Seligson. Several of the cases cited by opponents involved injured workers, he added. "To say that the court being protective of the rights of people who have lost their bodies means that [it] is anti-business—I don't see how you can make that jump."[42]

Others argued that earlier courts had been even friendlier to plaintiffs. Additionally, fourteen of the "anti-business opinions" cited by Deukmejian had been written by justices no longer on the court. Mathew Tobriner had authored seven of them; Frank Richardson, a Reagan appointee, had written two. And many rulings came without the participation of the targeted justices. Reynoso had not participated in nineteen of the thirty-one cases; Grodin had not participated in twenty-two. And Bird, who wrote just two of the decisions, had not been involved in at least three of the cases Deukmejian cited.

Supporters also argued that justices had proved themselves willing to revisit cases and to tweak or even overturn decisions when they believed circumstances warranted changes. For example, they had done this in

1979 with the "use a gun" law that had spawned the 1978 Election Day debacle and the Commission on Judicial Performance hearings.

In 1982 they had overturned a law passed by the legislature that allowed doctors and hospitals to make periodic, rather than lump-sum, payments to successful plaintiffs in malpractice suits when damages amounted to more than $50,000. Plaintiffs might die before receiving their entire settlements, Stanley Mosk wrote for the majority. Just two years later, however, the court reversed itself. Hospitals could make periodic payments after all, a new majority decided. Both Mosk and Bird had dissented, however, and both accused the majority of "diminishing the rights of victims." Bird noted that upon a plaintiff's death, the payments stopped. A plaintiff owed $100,000 and paid $25,000 a year would lose $25,000 if he or she died three years after winning a settlement.

The court tweaked the medical malpractice payment issue a third time in 1985. Associate Justice Otto Kaus declared that "there are limits on what lawyers may collect in probate matters . . . and for lawyers pressing claims for veterans and Social Security benefits." But Bird again dissented. The law, and the court's ruling, called "into question the fairness of the judicial process itself," she wrote. "Attorneys may avoid these problems by refusing to represent medical malpractice victims. Only those lawyers not sufficiently competent or well-established" would be willing to represent injured people of limited means.[43]

By the end of 1985 the entire political establishment of California, it seemed, had come to focus on a single individual: Rose Elizabeth Bird. Everyone had an opinion on the embattled chief justice, who by this point seemed more a symbol than a real person. To conservatives she embodied the ideological and elitist arrogance of liberalism. To many—though not all—liberals she represented courage and the willingness to stand against the greed and punitive approach of conservatives. She sometimes waxed wistful about her desire to be depicted in more "human" terms, but she seemed incapable of following a course designed to accomplish that goal.[44]

In summer 1985 she reluctantly hired political consultant Bill Zimmerman, who specialized in representing progressive candidates. Despite the fact that she despised politics, Bird said she understood the necessity for a "full-blown" campaign to hold on to her job. She "was prepared to fight fire with fire in terms of rousing public support with dramatic and emotional commercials." Zimmerman found her "very appealing," he said.

"To a degree rarely seen in a public official, Bird put the people's good before her private concerns, maintained absolute standards of honesty, of integrity and contrary to public image, was disarmingly open and personable." Zimmerman hired a fundraiser, a pollster, and a direct-mail expert to help with the campaign. Within weeks, however, Bird had a change of heart and fired Zimmerman. She did not want to use emotional pitches to sell herself, participate in negative advertising, or engage her opponents in debate. Despite the powerful forces lined up against her, she had decided to run her own campaign.[45]

Virtually everyone acquainted with Bird knew of her nearly pathological suspicion of the media and her obsession with not revealing any personal information. Thus her decision to sit down with a reporter for *Vegetarian Times* magazine in summer 1985 took acquaintances and some friends by surprise. It also irritated and angered reporters for large, mainstream media outlets who had tried unsuccessfully for years to garner interviews.

Several factors seem to have played a role in her decision. First, she needed to establish some public presence—hopefully positive—preparatory to the 1986 election; a small, specialty niche publication, one not focused on politics, undoubtedly seemed a safer choice than some others. Additionally, the magazine centered on an issue she cared passionately about—the relationship between healthy eating and physical and emotional well-being. The article proved surprisingly revealing; cancer was the focus. As it turned out, Bird had experienced not one but two recurrences after her initial 1976 mastectomy.

For the first time, she revealed publicly how terrified she had been at the initial diagnosis. "It is almost impossible to put into words the shock and terror you feel when you have this dreaded disease." She was doubly stunned, she said, because no one in her family "as far as I was able to learn" had ever had cancer, and her own medical experience to that point had been limited to a childhood tonsillectomy, performed in the doctor's office. She had always eaten healthy foods. "My mother was always a stickler for having a balanced diet, which, in American terms, usually means eating a large amount of animal protein in addition to vegetables, salads and the rest," she told the *Vegetarian Times* reporter. Initially, doctors "told me my cancer was a one-time occurrence; they had caught it early and there wouldn't be a problem. But then I had a recurrence."

Bird emphasized stress as a significant factor in her cancer: stress from her single-minded focus on work, impossibly high expectations of herself and others, and obsession with maintaining control at all times. She had returned to work just two weeks after her initial mastectomy. This decision was, she acknowledged, a serious mistake. "After my [first] operation, I submerged myself in my work and became the picture of the traditional workaholic, falling prey to a sort of 'macho man' complex." And both her recurrences had come during particularly stressful times: the first in 1978, as she prepared to face voters in the November election, and the second less than a year later, in the midst of Commission on Judicial Performance hearings.[46]

Both times she had minor surgery to remove cancerous nodules. Doctors had pronounced her cancer-free, but the threat of future recurrences remained. Each time, she refused chemotherapy, as she had done after her first surgery, but did not explain her reasons for making this somewhat unusual choice. Instead she had radically altered her diet, completely removing meat and dairy products and taking large doses of vitamin C.[47]

She acknowledged the difficulty of this approach, given the number of venues in which she took meals. She gave speeches all over the state and beyond, often having to eat lunch or dinner while seated on a dais in front of hundreds of people. Courthouses where justices heard oral arguments offered additional challenges. The court's Los Angeles branch, for example, "has a very nice cafeteria for the judges, but most of the food is meat and potatoes. I'm not surprised that judges have heart attacks on a regular basis," she said.

She also meditated to reduce stress, she told the magazine's reporter. "I have tapes which basically help you to be thoughtful and look inward for awhile." Meditation also helped her get in touch with her "inner sea of calm," Bird said. The practice helped her deal with the ever-present spotlight, which she called "cruel and unusual punishment." And it made her even more determined to live her life on her own terms, following her own principles, and helped her appreciate the irony in comments depicting her as "the cancer at the top of the court," she said.[48]

Readers of the magazine were among the first to view the beginnings of a months-long and extraordinary transformation in Rose Bird's appearance. No longer favoring the "nun" or "schoolmarm" look, she was morphing into a glamorous woman. The woman featured on the cover of *Vegetarian Times* was slender, with curly, shoulder-length dark-blonde hair. She wore makeup. By early 1986 Bird sported layered, slightly teased and blow-dried, streaked blonde hair worn off her face; carefully shaped eyebrows; and eyeliner, mascara, and lipstick. Her crooked teeth had been straightened and capped.

Virtually everyone paying attention to Bird and the court would come to ponder her motivation for embarking on such a dramatic change. Scholars, meanwhile, used the transformation to examine how voters perceived looks in female political candidates. Their study, instead, revealed that Bird's decision to so dramatically alter her appearance led to confusion. Respondents studying three separate photos of Bird at different periods failed to recognize their subject as the same person.[49]

Critics also took note of Bird's changing appearance, though they were careful not to make negative comments. Her looks, however, proved less important than her quoted remarks, such as her references to "an inner sea of calm." She also said that "being a vegetarian makes one much more pacific as a person." Such statements enabled opponents to label her a vain and out-of-touch elitist who—judicial decisions notwithstanding—had no idea how average people lived and thought.

"I was shocked and dismayed to find Rose Bird on the cover of my September issue, with an accompanying five-page spread depicting her as some sort of beatific humanitarian," wrote Santa Cruz resident and

Vegetarian Times subscriber Burt Bailey. He added: "Recent polls among California voters suggest an overwhelming anti-Bird sentiment, with a majority prepared to toss her out of office next year." The magazine should have waited until after the November 1986 election to feature Bird, Bailey suggested, when she would be an ex–chief justice.[50]

9 *The People v. Rose Bird*

Rose Bird was speaking to a group in Los Angeles in late 1985 when she noticed a man wearing a trench coat enter the room from a side door. He carried a small bag "and some kind of bulky object" beneath the coat. Since the temperature in the packed room hovered near 90 degrees, she became somewhat alarmed, particularly as she watched the man move along the wall toward her. "For one split moment, well it goes through your mind that this could be possibly the last time that you would speak." There turned out to be no threat, but Bird could be forgiven for seeing trouble at every turn. As the years passed, she had received more and more death threats, and they had rattled her to the extent that she had moved her elderly mother out of the Palo Alto home they had long shared.[1]

At one point, Bird began receiving batches of what would become several thousand postcards bearing scrawled messages calling her a "Black-Robed pervert," "lousy criminal lover," "mistress of [African American state assembly speaker] Willie Brown." Some warned the chief justice to "watch out" or said the writer hoped that she would be raped or die. She also received envelopes containing bullets. The effort obviously was designed to intimidate and had been organized by an anti-Bird group, though none took credit. Some part of her must have wondered whether her job was worth fighting for, given the immense personal costs and the probability—growing greater every day, it seemed—that she faced ignominious defeat at the polls in November 1986. If she had these thoughts, however, she kept them to herself.[2]

A year before the election, the campaign against Bird had expanded far beyond its ultraconservative origins, though individuals such as H. L. Richardson continued to make waves and headlines. Several organizations led the effort to oust her. Two were run by high-priced political consultants based in Southern California.

Bill Roberts headed Crime Victims for Court Reform. Originally a partner in the firm Spencer-Roberts and former campaign manager for Presidents Ronald Reagan and Gerald Ford, as well as Governor George Deukmejian, by 1985 he had his own firm, the Dolphin Group.

Roberts's strategy was to put crime victims and their families front and center. Murdered toddler Amy Sue Seitz undoubtedly proved to be Roberts's strongest weapon. Advertising spots featured photos of the little girl posing in front of flowering trees, wearing pigtails tied in ribbons and a ruffled pink dress. Viewers could not help but juxtapose the sunny photos to her brutal end at the hands of a recidivist sex offender.[3]

Californians to Defeat Rose Bird purported to be a grassroots organization, led by Howard Jarvis and Paul Gann, the two men most identified with Proposition 13; Orange County Republican lawmaker Ross Johnson; and former Los Angeles police chief Ed Davis. But Butcher-Forde, an Orange County consulting firm, organized and ran the campaign. Their primary emphasis was building a fundraising juggernaut using direct mail solicitations that started with individuals who had donated money to previous anti-Bird efforts and expanded from there.

Stu Mollrich of Butcher-Forde said the company sought to "build credibility" by demonstrating that "there are a lot of people . . . willing to express their feelings. . . . If you've heard directly from someone, you're more likely to take what they have to say seriously." The company sent letters signed by Jarvis and Gann to potential donors. "Thank you for helping to build the largest citizens' organization in the history of California," read one. Ignoring solicitations did not mean a recipient was scratched off the list, however; the consultants simply changed their tactics. "Have you had a sudden change of heart?" they wrote to one former donor. Further silence might garner an additional letter warning that "a dangerous killer may be let out of prison, free to roam the streets ... unless you act immediately."[4]

By late 1985 smaller groups had joined the anti-Bird effort as well. One, made up of conservative activists, called itself the Bird Watchers Society. Lawyers at O'Melveny and Myers, a leading California firm specializing in corporate clients, also opposed her, based largely on her rulings in civil cases. The firm had helped to create the so-called white paper often cited by Governor Deukmejian and others as evidence that Bird was "antibusiness."[5]

Nearly nine years after her confirmation, her opponents had thoroughly succeeded in shaping her public image as an "extremist," "judicial activist," and an all-around unsympathetic individual. Furthermore, they had made her an issue in virtually all Democratic campaigns for 1986. Explicit or even tacit support for Bird could get one immediately targeted by Republican candidates and media consultants, whose accusations were then picked up by reporters and inserted into news stories carried widely in newspapers and television broadcasts throughout the state. Republican senatorial candidate Ed Zschau linked his opponent, Democratic senator Alan Cranston, to Bird at every campaign stop. "It's hard to tell the difference between the two," Zschau said. "They both ignore the will of the people and they both oppose the death penalty."[6]

Some Democrats quietly hoped that Bird would resign from office. Not surprisingly, many candidates—including Los Angeles mayor Tom Bradley, running for a second time against George Deukmejian for governor—remained mute in the face of nearly constant queries. Other Democratic leaders, such as San Francisco mayor Dianne Feinstein, who planned to run for governor in a few years, declined invitations to fundraisers for Bird. Barry Keene, a Democratic state senator, said he "was probably the only Democrat in a contestable district up for election" who openly supported Bird and her two colleagues. "There were billboards up and down Highway 80 and up and down [Highway] 101 saying, 'Barry Keene Supports Rose Bird.'" The support did not hurt him politically, however.[7]

Yet, in the face of unrelenting attacks, Bird chose to forge ahead without the services of paid consultants. From a distance of thirty years, it is impossible to know whether she really was as naïve as she seemed, whether her lifelong distrust of situations she could not control made it impossible for her to put her destiny in someone else's hands, or if her rock-solid principles made compromise impossible no matter what the consequences. Bill Zimmerman, the consultant she had hired and then fired, insisted that she wanted to win, and badly. "Few candidates I've met wanted to win more. It was precisely her desire to win that led her to insist on personal control over every aspect of the campaign."[8]

Zimmerman, along with many others, saw Bird's decision as thoughtless as well as foolhardy, since it also adversely impacted two other justices—Joseph Grodin and Cruz Reynoso—but it was decidedly in character. Despite her status and power, she remained at heart a loner. As one journalist put it, "The most enduring image of Rose Elizabeth Bird is that of a woman alone—the plucky schoolgirl pedaling long miles to school in the rain; the teen-age idealist working for Adlai Stevenson . . . the legal ingénue defending accused rapists and murderers . . . the recluse of the Brown Administration who worked late, skipped the Sacramento parties and went home to her mother."[9]

Bird always insisted that she wanted to remain "above politics," but the fact that she had to run for periodic retention made her office innately political. Additionally, in the two decades following her graduation from law school, the definition of politics had expanded to encompass virtually every facet of life having to do with power relationships, even those deemed personal and private.[10] Every judicial ruling produced a winner and a loser, thus every ruling was political by definition. And at the dawn of the era of 24-7 news, "politics" had come to assume an outsize significance in public discourse.

Bird did have strong partisans who cared for her personally and worked on her behalf. On the personal level, she had close friends and longtime aide Stephen Buehl. As death threats increased against his boss, he took karate lessons and accompanied her virtually everywhere. A decade younger than Bird, he also kept her apprised of popular music trends, lending her albums by Bruce Springsteen, Joni Mitchell, and Elvis Costello; she sometimes made reference to pop lyrics in her speeches.[11]

A campaign organization, Committee to Conserve the Courts, headed by state bar president Anthony Murray, raised money and sought out prominent surrogates to publicly confront critics. Bird also had a spokesperson, Steven Glazer, a former advisor to Jerry Brown. Glazer arranged appearances and interviews and issued press statements that had been vetted by Bird. Surrogates included actors Warren Beatty and James Garner; television producer Norman Lear; women's groups, including California Women Lawyers; and prominent trial lawyers, including San Francisco attorney Melvin Belli. Bird's surrogates charged opponents with being "overtly partisan" and using scare tactics to subvert justice.[12]

They also expressed fear at what such an unprecedented and destructive campaign might mean for judges across the country. Would the judiciary itself become a permanent ideological battleground? At one fund-raising dinner, Beatty told his audience: "If we let the far right prevail here in California . . . they are going to push to apply a political and ideological litmus test to judges all over the country. Their dream is freedom's nightmare."[13]

Former governor Jerry Brown also weighed in. He had spent much of his postpolitical life traveling, volunteering, and working in the slums of India with Mother Teresa. He warned against using emotion in voting for or against judges. "The issues raised by electoral confirmation or rejection of Supreme Court justices involves more than politics and the fate of a few judges. At stake is a choice about fundamental principles and the kind of government we want. How independent should our judiciary be? And how much should the power of the state be constrained in the pursuit of justice? . . . Our heritage sees in judicial independence an ingenious method of limiting the natural tendency of governmental power."[14]

To Bird supporters, the future of an independent judiciary was the most crucial issue of the election season. Every statewide official in

California would appear on the November 1986 ballot, but Bird would receive virtually all of the attention. "Move over Governor Deukmejian. Step aside Senator Cranston. Your reelection campaigns are important, sure," wrote Richard Bergholz in the magazine *California Journal*. "But for long-term historical significance, nothing can match the battle for control of the state Supreme Court.

"It's an election battle like you've never seen before," Bergholz added, "far beyond the usual judicial confirmation contest tucked far down on the ballot."[15] As Pat Nolan, Republican leader of the state assembly put it, "Every eight to ten years an issue comes along that so focuses the public's attention that all other issues become secondary." In 1986 the vote to confirm or defeat Rose Bird would be that issue.[16]

Obviously, Bird had to become actively engaged in her own campaign if she had any hope of winning retention. Specifically, she needed to make herself available to reporters for general interest publications, her best chance to reach voters. Yet, "I've never seen a public official or candidate so reluctant to be interviewed or so suspicious of the motivation of reporters," said her former consultant Zimmerman.[17] But one sympathetic reporter said she could understand Bird's extreme wariness. Ever since her appointment, "she has been treated as some sort of freak show."[18]

In late November 1985 Bird decided to approach journalists on her own terms and turf. A press conference might have been the best approach, with reporters from all over the state and perhaps beyond showing up at a specific time and place to ask questions. Bird chose instead to handpick eight news outlets and give back-to-back one-hour interviews with individual reporters in her court chambers. Trouble started even before the interviews began. Representatives for publications not selected expressed outrage; her choices seemed arbitrary. For example, she had invited the *San Francisco Examiner* but not the *San Jose Mercury-News*, arguably a larger and more influential paper.

The interviews failed to soften her image; in fact, they might have had the opposite effect. Dan Morain of the *Los Angeles Times* recalled his hour with Bird as "grueling." She began by describing the court as "an incredible institution, taking the beating we have over and over again. . . . It is incredible what this court has been able to withstand." She criticized the media for focusing on "frivolous" issues, such as her "hairdo, the way I walk, the way I dress," and for turning death penalty rulings into "a grisly body count."

She blamed her troubles on the right wing, led by "bully-boys" such as President Reagan's attorney general Edwin Meese. "Why do we have to have Eddie Meeses all over here? He doesn't have a corner on the truth." She also refuted the notion that she might resign to save the jobs of Grodin and Reynoso. "You know what they will do if you turn tail and run?" she asked. "They will beat up everyone else until they get every single seat they want."[19]

Bob Egelko of the Associated Press said his "biggest frustration . . . was that . . . there wasn't one minute of dialogue. She talked at me and sometimes shouted at me for the better part of an hour. I came out of there shaken." Afterward, Bird expressed regret at the way she had handled the interviews. "I should have phrased [the answers] more precisely and less personally," she admitted.[20]

She subsequently gave a few interviews to news outlets she viewed as supportive, such as *San Francisco Focus*, a publication affiliated with that city's public television station KQED. She predicted large numbers of executions in California should she, Grodin, and Reynoso be defeated. Again, she blamed "the far right" for her predicament. This time she focused on Moral Majority leader Jerry Falwell and conservative activist Richard Viguerie, "[who] have made me their prime target, nationally. And they must see somehow in my defeat a way in which to turn around this society to be the kind of society where their views will be the only ones accepted."[21]

She accused her opponents of exploiting the families of crime victims and criticized the media for shallow and superficial coverage. "It's very hard to talk in terms of substance in an age where everybody's focus is on personality. I mean, if I want to get a front-page story, I could go out and cut my hair. But if I want to talk about the middle class being priced out of the system I can't get the newspapers to cover it at all." Some reporters and readers must have pondered why she had so dramatically altered her appearance and then expected the transformation to go unmentioned. And at least a few opponents must have wondered whether they needed to bother raising money and campaigning to defeat Bird, since she seemed perfectly capable of irritating and alienating voters herself.[22]

Polls taken at the end of 1985 showed 48 percent of respondents opposing her retention and 35 percent favoring it, with 17 percent undecided. Her numbers had slipped significantly from February 1985, when 35 percent viewed her negatively, 30 percent positively, and 35 percent were undecided. Voters had a somewhat better opinion at this point of associate justices Grodin and Reynoso. Grodin had support from 35 percent of potential voters, while 15 percent said they opposed his retention. But 50 percent said they could go either way. Reynoso faced opposition from 32 percent of respondents, while 23 percent said they favored his retention and 45 percent were undecided. Stanley Mosk had waited until the last minute to announce that he planned to seek reconfirmation. Polling showed him running far ahead of his liberal colleagues, and court critics said they planned to drop any effort to defeat him.[23]

Her dismal numbers rattled Bird, who expressed regret in early 1986 over her sometimes "inartful" comments and her inability to connect with journalists and with ordinary Californians. She attributed her media troubles to inexperience. At the beginning of her tenure as chief justice she "had no experience with the press at all. I had no press people. My own view was that if you did anything worthwhile, people would eventually see it and write about it."[24]

Meanwhile, anti-Bird forces were successfully raising large sums of money, nearly $4 million by February 1986. Contributors included actor Clint Eastwood and Los Angeles newscaster Jerry Dunphy, the father-in-law of Republican lieutenant governor Mike Curb and himself a robbery victim. Major business interests also contributed, including banks, real estate firms, insurance companies, manufacturers, and oil companies. Bird had raised slightly more than $1 million, mostly from trial lawyers, but had spent very little.[25]

As if Bird needed something else to worry about, in March 1986 *People* magazine featured her in an article titled "The New Look in Old Maids," which pegged her chances of ever finding a mate at less than 1 percent. This statistic came from a study by Harvard and Yale researchers that detailed how women's marriage opportunities dropped precipitously with each passing year. By age thirty there was a decline to 20 percent and by thirty-five to 5 percent. Bird was in good company. Other "old maids" included newscaster Diane Sawyer, actor Diane Keaton, and rock star Linda Ronstadt. Bird told the reporter that she didn't "take any of these studies seriously. I take each day as it comes." At forty-nine, she was too old to bear children, but "I would definitely like to adopt a child," she said.[26]

The *People* article might have humanized Bird somewhat, but it also reflected the antifeminist contention that elite female achievers lived in a different universe than "regular" women. And it reinforced Bird's image as out of the mainstream, since she did not discount the possibility of becoming a single mother. It might have been much more helpful to her cause if a mass-circulation magazine had run a story on how she had contacted a stranger—the friend of a friend—suffering from cancer. "If you ever need someone to talk to," Bird had told the woman, "just call."[27]

In April 1986 Bird left California and the United States for two weeks to travel to New Zealand and Australia. The trip did not count as a vacation, aides insisted, since in Australia she would be the guest of local officials observing Law Week in Sydney. It is possible, however, to see her departure as an effort to take a break and distance herself from the relentless news coverage.

Seven months before the election, interest in her campaign had spread beyond California. The same month as her trip abroad, the *Washington Post* had interviewed Bird. Reporter Cynthia Gorney asked her to imagine how a grieving mother might feel about justices who overturned the death sentence of her child's killer. "You've pinpointed the very difficult process that the court has to deal with," Bird acknowledged. "If the trial has an error in it, our history has told us that what you do is, you don't release the person. You reverse the [sentence] and it goes back for a proper trial, so that when you put that person behind bars, or when you take that person's life, you do it with a clear conscience."

She continued in a reflective vein: "You know, you have to read these things. And you can't turn your face away from them. You have to look at them. And I think it hurts all of us up here to have people truly feel that we don't feel for them."[28]

Even 7,500 miles from home, however, she drew media attention. Australian reporters were decidedly more conciliatory and flattering than their California counterparts. "By any objective assessment, she has conducted herself with wisdom, principle and efficiency," wrote a Sydney reporter. "Let's face it," one Australian lawyer explained, "there's a lot more interest in her not just because she is a woman judge … but because she is a different sort of woman. She makes an effort to look like a woman and not the sort of doddering fossil we tend to think of when we think of lady lawyers."[29]

Bird was relaxed and engaging during her trip. "Does your scalp itch?" she asked one bewigged Australian judge. She visited the zoo, museums, and nightclubs. Asked about her campaign, she said: "The most we try to do is keep [opponents] honest on the facts, and they will say what they want anyway." Asked if she thought she would prevail, Bird said, "Yes, I think so."[30]

Her trip abroad angered some California journalists, however. She had arranged to let a *Los Angeles Times* reporter accompany her and her aides to Australia but had denied requests from other news outlets. A San Diego newspaper sent a reporter anyway; Bird and her retinue limited her access to only the most public events. Chief aide Stephen Buehl explained that the *Times* had made arrangements far ahead of time, while the San Diego paper had not. His explanation failed to mollify critics.[31]

Upon her return to California she largely disappeared from public view, though she gave speeches as an invitee of groups in settings that were open only to attendees. And she appeared at private fundraisers. On these occasions, she exhibited wit and a dry sense of humor. After offering serious observations about the court and its battles, she asked the group Women in Business, "How do you like my new hairdo? It is the same style I wore when I was four, but I'm wearing it again to convince the press that I'm really conservative."[32] At one fundraiser, she took the stage following Warren Beatty. She looked the actor up and down and then remarked: "I see how kind Mother Nature was to put such a fine mind on such a fine body." She quickly apologized to him "for my sexist comment."[33]

In the few interviews she gave, however, she often slipped back into the negativity that had characterized most of her conversations with journalists. In one she complained: "If somebody wants to be critical of the way I dress, the way I speak, my personality, all the way up to my decisions, they get front-page coverage." Not so for substantive issues, she lamented. Ironically, these comments came in a story in which even some critics praised her for improving administration of the courts. One conservative appellate judge lauded her for lifting "the courts of appeal out of cronyism" by implementing "civil-service-type hiring" and increasing the number of staff and librarians.

The story also credited Bird with promoting the California Appellate Project, which paid private attorneys to represent indigent defendants. And it noted how the Judicial Council under Bird's direction had initiated a procedural change that allowed supreme court justices to weed out all but the most crucial issues in cases appealed from lower courts, as a way to speed up the appellate process.[34]

In May 1986 CBS *Evening News* featured Bird's retention campaign, which, anchor Dan Rather predicted, "could make or break careers far beyond the California judiciary and make judges nationwide think twice about politics, pressures, and principles." The three-minute piece interspersed stock footage of the court at work with comments from supporters and detractors and short clips of Bird talking about her job and her prospects for retaining her seat. "It will be very difficult," she conceded. Like many others, correspondent Terry Drinkwater could not resist mentioning Bird's transformation from "traditional somber robes to plunging necklines." And he attributed part of her opposition to the fact she was "an outspoken woman in a job usually held by old men."[35]

In early summer Bird began writing thirty-second television spots to appear in six of California's largest media markets. She wanted to craft them herself to make certain, she said, that they were not shallow or mean-spirited. The spots would be filmed in her chambers, which, according to syndicated columnist Ellen Goodman, "held enough plants to fill a health food restaurant."

In a June 1986 column, Goodman described Bird as "the daughter of a widowed factory owner . . . colorful, complicated, strong-willed and articulate . . . and determined to campaign her own way, as herself. She has modified neither her opinions nor her free-flowing talk about 'the journey of life,' language rarely found in judicial chambers." Supporters had urged Bird to uphold "just one execution," Goodman noted, but she had refused. Quoting Bird, she wrote that "when judges become one-issue candidates, when they make decisions with one eye on a pressure group and a pollster, this will be a different society."[36]

Slightly more than a month later, Bird authored the 4–3 decision that overturned the fifty-sixth death sentence to come before the court during her tenure. The case involved Ronald Smallwood, condemned in 1979. He had been charged with two separate murders, but the trial judge had refused to sever the cases. The jury could not reach a verdict in one case but convicted and condemned Smallwood in the other. The judge's refusal to separate the cases represented grounds for reversal, Bird wrote. Both Grodin and Reynoso signed on to the decision, but Mosk joined Malcolm Lucas's dissent.[37]

Grodin and Reynoso had never faced the same level of scrutiny and hostility that Bird had experienced, but opponents ramped up their criticism as the months wore on and the potential for taking down three justices seemed tantalizingly possible. By late summer they had begun to refer to the trio as "the gang of three," who voted as a bloc on every significant case. Both men tried to separate themselves from Bird without overtly criticizing her. This proved difficult. "I knew of no way to distance myself from her without doing things that I thought would be wrong and unprincipled," Grodin said later.

The growing threats led both men—reluctantly—to hire campaign consultants and to raise money, approximately $1 million apiece. They traveled the state, giving interviews and speeches, and appeared in television ads. Reynoso stressed his humble beginnings, which had taken him from summer work as a farm laborer to community college, Pomona, and then Berkeley's Boalt Hall for law school. He had served in the military and had worked as an attorney, as a law professor, and as director of California Rural Legal Assistance. Grodin didn't have Reynoso's up-by-the-bootstraps narrative, but he had an impressive resume, including both a law degree from Boalt and a PhD from the London School of Economics. Both men found it difficult to explain how the court worked in thirty-second spots—"I mean really impossible," Grodin said. The fact they could not make campaign promises or discuss specific cases made their outreach efforts more difficult.[38]

Though they did not overtly criticize Bird, both men insisted that they did not march in lockstep with the chief justice. A *California Journal* study verified this assertion. It examined all of the rulings the state high court had issued in 1984 and 1985—a total of 277 cases. In none of the cases did Bird, Grodin, and Reynoso vote as a bloc without support from at least one other justice. In all but three of the cases, the trio had been joined by at least two other justices.

Reynoso was Bird's most consistent ally; he had joined her opinions 74 percent of the time in 1984 and 63 percent in 1985. Reynoso agreed most frequently, however, with two "moderate" justices—Otto Kaus and Allen Broussard. Grodin had signed the same opinions as Bird less than half the time, the study found. He more often agreed with the court's most conservative member, Malcolm Lucas. In fact, Lucas agreed with his fellow justices 70 percent of the time in 1984 and 60 percent in 1985. Most surprisingly, one-quarter of the court's rulings came on unanimous votes. "It can be stated without equivocation that there is no common front composed of Bird, Reynoso and Grodin," the study concluded.[39]

By the end of August, Bird's television spots were ready to air. She had made five separate ads under the auspices of the Committee to Conserve the Courts. In each, she sat, relaxed at her desk, wearing a blue dress. The camera filmed her from a three-quarters angle. A lamp behind her right shoulder cast a warm glow over the room. Each ad carried its own caption, identifying the topic. They included "Backbone," "Politicians," and "Hip Pocket." For "Backbone," Bird cited America's tradition of constitutional guarantees and judges "with back bones" who upheld them. "I've been watching some television lately," she began in "Politicians," and "you'd think I ran every branch of government.... Why are [politicians] so afraid of a chief justice who follows the law?"

She also celebrated the state's diversity, insisted that no condemned individual had ever been released from death row, and assured viewers that justice was not for sale in California. She signed off each spot with the words, "That's a California tradition worth keeping." Campaign spokesperson Glazer noted, "We are raising the level of debate with these commercials," but polls continued to show Bird losing ground at the end of August with 57 percent planning to vote "no," 33 percent planning to vote "yes," and 10 percent still undecided. Grodin and Reynoso had lost ground as well.[40]

The sinking poll numbers led Stanford law professor Barbara Babcock to muse on the campaign against Bird. Opponents may have portrayed her as "standing between Californians and the death penalty. But for a conviction to be reversed, other justices must join the chief justice." And not just Reynoso and Grodin; it took four votes to overturn a death sentence. More importantly, according to Babcock, "the chief justice's opinions in death penalty cases, like her other opinions, are legally creditable. Her main concern has been that no one should be executed if the conviction or death penalty was the result of a serious malfunction in the judicial process."[41]

Comments like Babcock's reflected the success of anti-Bird forces in framing the election as a referendum on the death penalty; in reality, much of the money flowing to campaign coffers came from business interests angry with the court majority for its proplaintiff decisions. *New York Times* writer Anthony Lewis recognized the court campaign as a potential game changer, setting a precedent for future campaigns to get even nastier via emotional pitches to voters, direct mail, and scare ads.

The attack on Bird, Grodin, and Reynoso, said Lewis, "challenges the whole American tradition of reliance on an independent judiciary to protect the system from abuse of power." Bird was from the "old school," and she could not (or would not) adapt to political exigencies that required candidates to be steeped in the use of images and symbols no matter who they were or what office they sought. He quoted Bird's statement that "courts are an aristocratic institution in a democracy. That's the dilemma for an institution that has the function of reviewing the will of the people. We're bound to be 'anti-majoritarian.'"[42]

Tom Wicker of the *New York Times* issued an even blunter warning: "Don't believe for a moment that the campaign to oust Chief Justice Rose Bird from the California Supreme Court is a spontaneous public uprising. . . . Don't believe either that the effort . . . is nonpartisan. . . . Don't believe, finally, that the anti-Bird campaign is about the death penalty. . . . [T]he death penalty is only the trumped up excuse for the anti-Bird campaign—the actual purpose of which is clearly to put a conservative majority on the California Supreme Court." Federal judges had lifetime appointments, but their Senate confirmations could become more strident and partisan in the future, Lewis predicted.[43]

With so much on the line, Bird's allies agonized over her continuing inability to gain traction. By fall, polls consistently showed her with support from only a third of prospective voters. Worse, by this point it seemed likely that she would bring Grodin and Reynoso down with her. Discussing her predicament with Anthony Lewis, she expressed sorrow at that prospect, particularly with regard to Reynoso, whose support had dropped as low as hers, to 33 percent. The "good" news was that 45 percent of those polled said they remained undecided about Reynoso. "It would be a great tragedy if [Reynoso] were defeated," she said. "He is the only person from the Hispanic community in statewide office. He is a role model. Defeating him would be a clear statement, an ugly statement."[44]

Florence Bernstein, a Los Angeles superior court judge, was a long-time friend and associate of Bird. In fact, the chief justice had officiated at Bernstein's marriage and had appointed her to the Judicial Council and a number of other positions. But Bernstein expressed dismay at Bird's inability to effectively counter any of her opponents' arguments. Bird's "destructive, pathological suspicion" and obsession with exerting "complete control" over every situation had led her "to run an isolated, ineffectual campaign that could have been won had she been willing to accept the help of politically experienced supporters," Bernstein wrote in a *Los Angeles Times* essay. Bird responded through Stephen Buehl. "It saddens me that some do not understand that the process by which you attempt to win public office is as important as winning itself. I do not feel comfortable in following a course that stresses the negative [and] that ruthlessly attacks your opponents."[45]

In a subsequent letter to the editor, Bernstein insisted that she had not meant to criticize Bird's work on the court but simply wanted to voice her frustration with the campaign. "She has attempted a statewide campaign without a campaign manager because she is not a 'manageable' person; that may be the very quality that makes her a great chief justice." Other letter writers also praised Bird for remaining above the fray. "It's not worth destroying your own soul and dishonoring yourself," wrote one. "It is clear that our chief justice is a judicial officer first, last and foremost, and not a politician. That is to her credit," wrote another.[46]

But Bernstein's point was a valid one. When Bird spoke to groups, she chose only those who already seemed primed to vote for her, such as African American churches and unions. To Los Angeles seniors, she said the election was "about an institution and who's going to run it. It's about whether you are going to have judges who are independent or . . . whether you're going to have sycophants sitting there who have pre-recorded messages inside [telling] them exactly how to vote without ever looking at the issues."[47]

By early October Bird seemed resigned to defeat. She traveled the state visiting editorial boards of major newspapers, but the sessions were pro forma affairs, with editors sitting on one side of large conference tables and Bird, Stephen Buehl, and (frequently) campaign spokesperson Glazer sitting on the other side. No one drank the proffered water or coffee. Editors asked predictable questions, and Bird gave predictable answers. During one session, she became animated only when recounting how often reporters published erroneous information about her family. One reporter, for example, had mentioned her father's abandonment of his family. More than forty years later, she remained sensitive about this event. "My father did not abandon us," she said. "My parents separated."[48]

Meanwhile, her opponents continued pouring on, with new thirty-second spots featuring relatives of murdered children. In one, Marianne Frazier of Huntington Beach sat next to a photo of her smiling, blonde daughter Robin Samsoe as a small music box played softly in the background. Robin had been twelve when Rodney Alcala kidnapped her in 1979. "Robin never got to her ballet class," Frazier said to the camera, "but the man who kidnapped and killed her is still alive. Rose Bird, Cruz Reynoso, and Joseph Grodin overturned his death sentence as they have for so many brutal killers." She urged voters to turn all of them out of office.[49]

George Cullins, the father of another murder victim, traveled the state giving speeches blasting Bird. The killer had not yet gone to trial, but Cullins predicted that "the defendant will never be properly punished."[50] H. L. Richardson acknowledged the cynical strategy of Bird's opponents when he noted that "the public is . . . simplistic about how it looks at the criminal justice system. They see a guy who murdered somebody and nothing happens to him. They don't look at the little nuances."[51]

By mid-October Bird had become the focus of virtually all political news coverage in California—and much of it beyond. "If I look a little tired," she told one group of supporters, "it's because it's awfully hard to run for governor, lieutenant governor, controller and the U.S. Senate."[52] Even the *Times of London* weighed in, noting that "barring a miracle," the chief justice was "about to be booted out of office by the voters. . . . The reason is simple . . . she has failed to execute anyone." Reporter Deirdre MacDonald noted that the "campaign against her has been a multi-million dollar marathon, masterminded by two key groups rooted in professional political consultancy."

On the other hand, MacDonald said, the "chief justice's self defence has been all too dignified." She, like virtually all other reporters, could not resist commenting on Bird's looks, describing her as "a tall, extremely handsome woman. She dresses with panache, a flair that falls on the tasteful side of [*Dynasty* television character] Krystle Carrington. . . . She likes films, exercise, good food, books, people, her country (though she is concerned about it), her work and her job."[53]

Deukmejian had made Bird's defeat the centerpiece of his gubernatorial reelection. Political operatives had linked Bird, Grodin, and Reynoso, but the governor had refrained from publicly announcing his intention to oppose the two men until late in the election season. "A thorough review of the opinions and votes cast by Justices Bird, Grodin and Reynoso on death penalty cases indicates a lack of impartiality and objectivity," he said in announcing his opposition. He intended to back the three other justices on the ballot, including Mosk. All possessed "sensitivity to the will of the people and the intent of the Constitution," the governor said. Former governor Pat Brown called Deukmejian's action "an obvious effort to control the Supreme Court and I think it's a disgrace."[54]

Mosk no doubt was pleased to have the governor's backing, but he defended the court. He had worked with Bird for nearly a decade and still had a somewhat complicated relationship with the chief justice. Nonetheless, in a speech to the Los Angeles Press Club he said he feared what the bitter battle might portend for the future of the judiciary. Despite critics' charges about leniency, crime had actually decreased in California, Mosk declared. He blamed the "poorly worded" 1978 Briggs Initiative for many death sentence reversals. "Anyone can qualify an initiative for the ballot, and then have it passed, no matter what it pertains to," Mosk said, "then we have to straighten it out."

Mosk also distanced himself from the rough business of campaigning. Together, both sides had raised and spent nearly $10 million. Mosk had been responsible for none of it, he said. His only expense had been for filing papers to run for retention. "I have a non-campaign, with a non-chairman and non-committees," he said. Since he had solicited no contributions, "my friends will take my calls."[55]

Deukmejian's opposition obviously had an impact. By October a statewide telephone survey of 1,200 voters showed Reynoso's support slipping to 20 percent, with 26 percent opposing him. Only 21 percent of voters supported Grodin, while 24 percent opposed him. Grodin spokesperson Abby Haight said she was "absolutely surprised" by the poll results. "He can't be lumped together with Bird on the death penalty; he has voted to affirm seven cases. This just goes to show the opposition isn't just interested in capital punishment, but political and economic issues as well."[56]

Deukmejian's announced opposition to both Grodin and Reynoso raises some questions. He had targeted Bird since his days as attorney general, and during his many campaign stops around the state he seldom mentioned anyone but Bird. "We need the death penalty, we don't need Rose Bird," he intoned in his usual stump speech. Two of the justices on the ballot—Malcolm Lucas and Edward Panelli, who replaced Otto Kaus—had been appointed by Deukmejian, so the governor only needed to convince voters to defeat one justice in addition to Bird to gain a court majority.

Possibly he feared charges of racism if he opposed only Reynoso. *Los Angeles Times* editorial writer Frank del Olmos, in an essay for the paper, had declared opposition to Reynoso to be "subtle racism. . . . It indirectly suggests that because Reynoso came from a large family of farm workers, he's not quite as capable as judges from different backgrounds."[57] Deukmejian had voted against Reynoso's appointment to the supreme court, but as a member of the Commission on Judicial Appointments he had supported Grodin's appointment to three separate judicial offices, including the supreme court. Thus his opposition represented a distinct change of heart.

The governor was, in fact, sensitive to charges of racism, and may have been seeking to deflect them. Tom Bradley, his Democratic opponent in both 1982 and 1986, was African American. In the waning days of the 1982 campaign, polls showed Bradley leading Deukmejian. Campaign consultant Bill Roberts believed the polls to be inaccurate and raised the specter of a phenomenon that came to be called "the Bradley effect." Voters might tell pollsters they were "undecided" or planned to vote for minority candidates so as not to appear racist, Roberts said, but in the privacy of the voting booth, many of them ended up voting for the white candidate. Deukmejian fired Roberts for the comment, but in the end he defeated Bradley by a very narrow margin.[58]

Racial sensitivities may have been a factor in Deukmejian's decision to oppose Grodin, but gender had long been the elephant in the room.

In the months leading up to the election, numerous commentators had made allusions to gender, including Terry Drinkwater of CBS News when he noted that "old men" usually held Bird's job. Bird only infrequently mentioned it in speeches or talks and then mostly when others directly asked her about it. In one talk to a senior citizens' group she was asked about gender as a factor in the campaign against her. "We've come a long way, but some people in this society still have a difficult time seeing a woman in power. Do you hear people remark about [former U.S. Supreme Court] Chief Justice Warren Burger's hair? Do people wonder what it would be like to be married to him?" she asked.[59]

As the long campaign wound down, she became somewhat more forthcoming. As she told one interviewer, "Women in positions of authority are still perceived as vulnerable. And I think that is partly why the focus comes so heavily here." Perhaps trying to bridge the chasm between herself and "ordinary" women, she sometimes spoke wistfully about how different her life might have been had she made more traditional choices. For example, she regretted not having had a family of her own. "I've missed out on that part of life," she said. "I'm sorry about it, though I think now I would be a much better wife and mother than I would have 20 years ago. I think I am a much more tolerant person." She also reiterated her interest in adoption.[60]

In an interview with *Ms.* magazine just before the election, she let down her guard, revealing—with bitter resignation—how significant a role she actually believed gender had played in all of her troubles, stretching back to the beginning of her tenure as chief justice. "Women have always had to submit at some level to a man. The real problem occurs when you're a woman who can't be defined by a man. They use the fact that I'm not married against me because I don't have to even submit to a husband, what a 'terrible, terrible sin.'"

Bird had achieved a number of firsts in her life, she said, but she "never really understood what the problems of women are in this society until I came into *this* office." She might have fueled some of the problems herself, however. For example, she had insisted that, as head of the Judicial Council, she should be called "chairperson," rather than "chairman." And she had refused to back down despite a heated and prolonged debate.

And her refusal to allow reporters access to her personal life also had had a calculated gender component. "If I truly wanted to have an image that would be useful politically," she told reporter Deidre English, "I'd take you home and have my nieces and nephews there, I'd be baking cookies, I'd have my dogs jumping up and down, I'd have my 82-year-old mother there telling wonderful anecdotes about my childhood. That's what works in this society right now."[61]

Other women also expressed outrage at her treatment. "Rose Elizabeth Bird has become the focus of the California hate campaign," said a writer for the feminist publication *Off Our Backs*.

> As chief justice of the State Supreme Court, she is the first and only woman to sit on that court. She is personally and politically a feminist. She has spoken out publicly for women's rights, workers' rights, an end to racism and a tolerant, diverse society. She has survived sexist challenges to her competence and judicial performance. . . . Now right wing "Bird-Watchers" have targeted Rose Bird. . . . The smears, lies, and sexist belittling have increased. Slogans of "Bye Birdie" mask a concerted attempt to destroy the political independence of justices who have consistently voted for women's rights.[62]

The National Organization for Women (NOW) also added its voice, calling the "campaign against Chief Justice Rose Elizabeth Bird an instance of sexism gone rampant." NOW president Eleanor Smeal called the focus on the death penalty a "smoke screen" covering up the opposition's real issue—"Bird's opinions on behalf of women's, civil and consumer rights."[63]

Rose Bird had long refused to directly engage Deukmejian and continuously insisted that she sought "the high road," but in the final days of the campaign, she took off the gloves. It was too late to save her job, but she hoped she might save her two male colleagues. She had offered money to both from her own campaign treasury, but both had refused to take it. She traveled the state charging Deukmejian with trying to turn "a house of justice into a house of death." The governor was "ignorant of the way courts are supposed to function in society," she said. At one stop, she lectured him. "You do not understand at a very fundamental level what our society is all about, what the rule of law is all about and what constitutional government is about."[64]

As evidence, she cited a letter that then attorney general Deukmejian had sent Reynoso in 1982 after Jerry Brown nominated Reynoso to the court. The letter asked Reynoso's views "on a number of cases." Reynoso had replied that it would be unethical to talk about pending cases, and Deukmejian subsequently voted against him when he appeared before the Commission on Judicial Appointments.

Deukmejian responded angrily to Bird's criticism. "I am a private citizen just like everyone else. I have a right to vote in this election. I think it's important that somebody who is in my position tell the people how he intends to vote."[65] Both Grodin and Reynoso distanced themselves from Bird's remarks. They were "not helpful," a Grodin spokesperson said. "We don't talk about the governor," said Reynoso's campaign manager.[66]

In the end, the unrelenting campaign against Rose Bird brought down all three justices. The results were not close for any of them. Bird won only 34 percent of the vote, Reynoso 40 percent, and Grodin 43 percent. Their defeat meant that Deukmejian, who swept to a second term with 62 percent of the vote, had three new court appointments to make, bringing his total to five. Meanwhile, the three justices supported by the governor all won lopsided victories: Malcolm Lucas with 79 percent of the vote, Mosk with 74 percent, and Ed Panelli with 79 percent.

Less than two hours after the polls closed on November 4, as ballots were still being counted, Bird walked into the room where the court heard oral arguments in Los Angeles. For the last time, she took her seat in the center of seven plush, dark-blue chairs to resounding applause from the standing-room-only crowd of supporters. She looked regal as she faced her audience, her blonde hair swept off her face, makeup perfectly in place, wearing a tailored gray dress and dazzling earrings. Her concession speech was both wry and serious; her voice was strong, though it occasionally wavered. She began by addressing "an issue which was raised with me earlier and that I suspect was on the minds of the press as well: How am I taking this? My answer is, 'just like a man.'"

She thanked the "millions of California voters who voted today to retain the justices of the California Supreme Court and specifically voted for me.... I know you believe deeply in the ideal of justice and believe it is possible to have it as an ideal in this day and age.... I say to those who voted for us today that although my voice will go silent, yours will not." Acknowledging that voters were impatient about the pace of death penalty appeals, she said, "I don't think anybody in this state will sit easy if in fact this becomes a court that ensures nothing but executions to appease the overweening and insatiable appetite of ambitious politicians."[67]

Neither Grodin nor Reynoso made public statements, though many others did. Bill Roberts of Crime Victims for Court Reform said, "The public is very unhappy with the judicial system generally. Too much attention has been paid to the needs of the criminals and not enough consideration has been given to victims and the general public." However, both Grodin and Reynoso had been "in the wrong place at the wrong time," Roberts acknowledged. He said he hoped Deukmejian would appoint a woman to replace Bird and a Latino to replace Reynoso.[68]

Californians to Defeat Rose Bird denied that big business had bankrolled the campaign. The organization's direct mail solicitations had garnered donations from 150,000 people, mostly middle-aged and giving less than one hundred dollars, said spokesperson Stuart Mollrich. Donors were "the kind of people you'd see running an ABC plumbing or an ACE real estate brokerage."[69]

Not everyone bought Mollrich's assertion, particularly since campaign spending reports showed significant contributions from corporate sources, including growers, oil companies, and real estate and insurance interests. "It would be inaccurate, if not naïve, to assert that Bird brought all her troubles on herself," wrote *San Francisco Examiner* reporter John Jacobs. "Her liberal rulings angered some of the state's most powerful business interests, particularly the insurance industry."[70]

In a letter to the *Los Angeles Times*, Catherine Doyle of Los Angeles wrote: "I trust that the people of California who voted against Rose Bird, Cruz Reynoso and Joseph Grodin are satisfied. But how do you explain to all those voters that they were not part of a 'grass roots' movement to remove the justices and that it was not the people who instigated the campaign? They were but the pawns of several wealthy industries [that] have much to attain—at the expense of the people."[71]

In a press conference, Deukmejian said he was "gratified" by the voters' decision to oust the three justices. "There is a great need in my view to restore credibility and confidence in the Supreme Court." He said he would announce Bird's replacement within a month, though it was no secret that he planned to appoint his old law partner Malcolm Lucas. In early December he did just that, and on February 5, 1987, in San Francisco he swore in Lucas as California's twenty-sixth chief justice. "The election was a difficult time," Lucas told his audience, in somewhat of an understatement. "What this court needs is a quiet time to heal itself and reconstitute itself free from political turmoil."[72]

Deukmejian had spent nearly a decade stalking Rose Bird, and he would be forever linked with her in the public's mind. He "really didn't have a whole lot going for him and would not have had much of a record in eight years" without her, said one fellow Republican. "The legacy of George Deukmejian ... was going to be strictly [based] on the judicial branch of government. That's what he wanted. And the circumstances in terms of changing the court ... it was phenomenal."[73]

Soon after Lucas's swearing-in, the governor named three new justices to fill the court's remaining vacancies. All were appellate judges appointed to earlier posts either by Deukmejian or by Ronald Reagan. John Arguelles, like Reynoso, was Latino; Marcus Kaufman, like Grodin, was Jewish. But Deukmejian did not immediately name a woman to the court. Instead, he tapped David Eagleson, who had presided over some of the most high-profile criminal trials in Los Angeles County. Grodin and Reynoso soon became law professors—at Hastings Law School in San Francisco and at the University of California, Davis, respectively. It was unclear in early 1987 where Bird would land; rumor had it that she planned to join the law firm of feminist attorney Gloria Allred, but she denied it.

In her last public appearance as chief justice, Bird spoke to a gathering of law school deans in Los Angeles. "We sometimes must stand in the way of the most powerful groups in our society—governments, presidents, governors, legislatures, special interests—in order to do what our oath of office demands of us," she said. "We are not an institution which can achieve that acceptance by the use of slick public relations gimmicks and entertaining news hooks. We have no way of pandering to the public or pampering the press." Asked "what the most difficult part about being chief justice" had been, Bird offered a light-hearted response: "I think it's eating lettuce in front of 1,000 people on a dais. I finally learned how to do it and I lost my job."[74]

As the California Supreme Court entered its new, post–Rose Bird era, it remained unclear to what extent the new majority would depart from decades of "liberal," pro–civil libertarian decisions and whether politicians, campaign consultants, and voters in general would continue to care about its rulings, even on the death penalty, in the absence of its lightning-rod chief justice. More important was the issue of the election's wider impact. It ultimately had cost nearly $10 million. But was it an anomaly whose success had required a female target possessing thin skin, a hypersensitive, prickly personality, and an unyielding sense of how she believed the law should work? Or, as some pundits had suggested, did it represent the vanguard of a larger movement aimed at challenging the judiciary itself?[75]

High Courts and Political Footballs 10

On July 1, 1987, President Ronald Reagan nominated Robert Bork to a seat on the U.S. Supreme Court. If confirmed by the Senate, Bork would replace Associate Justice Lewis Powell, a moderate "consensus builder" appointed in 1971 by Richard Nixon. Announcing Bork's nomination, Reagan called the sixty-year-old federal appellate justice "a premier constitutional authority. His outstanding intellect and unrivaled scholarly credentials are reflected in his thoughtful examination of the broad, fundamental legal issues of our times."

Whatever one thought of Bork, he was not generally described as a "consensus builder" but as the author of outspoken and sometimes inflammatory opinions. Edwin Meese, Rose Bird's nemesis and Reagan's attorney general, had recommended Bork to Reagan, and journalists predicted he would face "a difficult and prolonged confirmation fight." However, "his eventual approval does not appear in doubt."[1]

Pundits and prognosticators correctly assessed the first part of the equation but got the second part wrong. Bork would face a tempestuous confirmation hearing. He would not, however, serve on the U.S. Supreme Court. Reagan might have depicted him as "thoughtful" and as "a premier constitutional authority," but liberals viewed him as an "extremist" whose reading of the Constitution was years, even decades, outdated. Opponents cited Bork's views on race and gender but specifically homed in on the notion of the right to privacy, which sat at the heart of several seminal 1960s and 1970s high court decisions. Bork viewed "privacy" as a legal nonstarter, since the term appeared nowhere in the Constitution.[2]

Debate began soon after Bork's nomination, and it reflected the deep cultural divide among Americans, with the judiciary as a touchstone for both sides. Conservatives flooded the Senate Judiciary Committee with letters. "Don't wait—act now!" Dr. Robert Grant, chairman of a group called Christian Voice, urged lawmakers. "We must return the law of our land to godly foundations while we have a chance." New York Republican congressman Jack Kemp appealed to his supporters to promote Bork's nomination by noting that "abortion, school prayer, business regulation, product liability and civil rights plus public health issues brought on by the AIDS epidemic will be settled before the Supreme Court."[3]

The New York Times editorial page, on the other hand, offered a long list of objections before noting that "most judges subscribe to . . . judicial restraint. Judge Bork carries the idea to mechanistic extreme." Harvard University law professor Laurence Tribe claimed that Bork's "judicial philosophy . . . seriously threatens constitutional values that have proven fundamental to American history."[4]

The Senate hearings began in September and carried over into October 1987. Opinion polls tried to gauge public sentiment toward Bork as television networks covered the proceedings. Moderate Republican Robert Packwood met with Bork and then announced his opposition. "I am convinced that Judge Bork . . . will do everything possible to cut and trim, and eliminate if possible, the liberties that the right of privacy protects." Utah Republican senator Orrin Hatch, meanwhile, called Bork "one of the most qualified and impressive individuals, it seems to me, ever nominated to the Supreme Court." In the end, the Senate rejected Bork by a vote of 58–42; seventeen Republicans joined with Democrats to defeat the nomination.[5]

To those closely following the news, the Robert Bork saga, coming less than a year after Rose Bird's historic election loss, must have seemed like déjà vu: allegations of ideological judges issuing "radical" rulings;

judges with prickly, acerbic personalities and thin skins; intensive media coverage of and public interest in what usually was the dull, pro forma process for selecting jurists.

Both battles even featured some of the same players. Ronald Reagan and Edwin Meese had advocated against Bird based on her judicial opinions but castigated opponents of Bork for doing the same thing. Liberals, meanwhile, happily attributed conservatives' change of heart to hypocrisy, while they shifted gears as well. Voters should not have focused on Bird's opinions, supporters had declared during her retention campaign. But Bork's opinions should be held against him. Journalists took note of the similarities. "The parallels made activists of the left and right squirm, but they are unmistakable," wrote David Broder of the *Washington Post*. "Bird lost because of the multi-million-dollar direct-mail campaign mounted by her opponents, and if Bork goes down it will be for the same reason."[6]

The undeniable similarities made it easy to overlook crucial differences between Bird's and Bork's circumstances. Bird's electoral defeat removed her from the bench. Bork might not sit on the country's highest court, but he could keep his seat on the Washington DC Court of Appeals, where he enjoyed lifetime tenure. And the defeat of Bird, Joseph Grodin, and Cruz Reynoso at the hands of California voters had been unprecedented.

Historically, most U.S. Supreme Court appointees easily won confirmation. But fifteen Supreme Court hopefuls before Bork had been rejected by the Senate. Richard Nixon saw two of his high court appointees turned down. And Reagan might have had a second nominee rejected if the candidate had not withdrawn first.[7] Anthony Kennedy, Reagan's third choice, sailed through the confirmation process in early 1988. A federal appeals court judge and Sacramento law professor, he was known for his calm, low-key demeanor and moderating influence.[8]

Bork's case was different in one way from those of all other rejected federal nominees, however. None of them had experienced the relentless glare of media exposure. Bird's confirmation had opened the door, it seemed. In a media-saturated age, personalities and perceived temperament had come to play an outsized role in judicial confirmations, which could be "sold" to the public as political theater.[9]

Bork certainly saw it that way. Four months after his defeat, he resigned his appeals court seat because, he said, he wanted to "speak out without restraint on the process by which Supreme Court nominees are reviewed by the Senate." He planned to write a book about his experience, he said. He also joined a prominent conservative think tank, American Enterprise Institute, and began traveling the country speaking bitterly about his experience. In one speech to the American Bar Association, Bork called his ordeal "the first national election campaign ... for control of our legal culture." Sounding a lot like Bird, Bork warned that efforts to politicize the court "could taint the judiciary," which needed to preserve its independence.[10]

To Joseph Grodin, however, Bork's experiences paled before his own and those of Bird and Reynoso. "The politicization of the Bork campaign and its portent for the future integrity of the judicial branch were small-time compared to the nature and political impact of a full-blown judicial election such as my colleagues and I went through in 1986," he wrote in his autobiography.[11]

Early in 1989 Bird and Bork agreed to appear together in a distinguished lecturer series at the University of California, Irvine; the University of California, Davis; and El Camino College. Each received $30,000 for the three appearances. At the sold-out Irvine gathering, Bird presented Bork with flowers, and Bork smiled and bowed in gratitude. If the nearly five thousand attendees expected fireworks, however, they were disappointed. Instead, they were treated to a somewhat cautious exchange. At one point, Bork surprised the audience with the revelation that he favored gun control—or at least it seemed that way.

"I'm not an expert on the Second Amendment," he said, "but its intent was to guarantee the right of states to form militias, not for individuals to bear arms." Bird told the audience that "courts are faced with an ever-more complex society that the framers of the Constitution could never have envisioned. . . . Once we get into very rigid viewpoints on any of these issues, we begin to lose the dynamics of what our system is all about."

Both became animated, however, when discussing their own experiences. "We are now witnessing a war for control of our legal culture, and most particularly for control of our Constitution," Bork said. Bird blamed her court's 1983 reapportionment ruling in part for putting a bull's-eye on judges. "Once there were major decisions in the area of redistricting, politicians realized that they needed sympathetic judges on the bench."[12]

By the early 1990s Bird and Bork had become part of the political lexicon, their names used by politicians from both sides of the spectrum. All Republican candidates in California had to do was mention Rose Bird in campaign ads or mailers and Democrats fled as if to escape a swarm of angry bees. Bork, meanwhile, had become a verb. To be "borked" meant that one had reached for and been rejected for high political office.[13]

Bork may have been bitter, but professionally he had fared much better than Bird. Just after leaving the court, she said that it "felt like being 20 again" with new options and choices ahead. But thirty years had passed since her days as a stellar college student. She had reached the pinnacle of her profession and was on the downhill slope. She soon went into a tailspin both personally and professionally. She found rewarding and remunerative work hard to find. Her notoriety made many legal firms skittish about employing her. "The kind of substantial offers one might expect would be forthcoming to a former chief justice do not seem to be there for her," said one friend. She thought about writing a book, but literary agents and prospective publishers wanted a gossipy, tell-all rendition of her difficult years at the court; she refused to take this approach.[14]

A brief foray into television had not worked out either. A month after leaving the court, in February 1987, she made a single appearance on *Superior Court*, a syndicated series that featured actors as lawyers and litigants and real judges as presiding court officials. Bird appeared during "a weeklong celebration of the Bicentennial of the U.S. Constitution." Other prominent jurists included former California appeals court judge Bernard Jefferson and Associate Justice Harry Blackmun of the U.S. Supreme Court.[15]

In early 1988 she agreed to appear as a twice-weekly political commentator on two California affiliates of the national ABC television network. She would provide a "liberal" perspective and act as a counterpoint to conservative pundit and sometime political candidate Bruce Hershensohn. Promotional spots touted her as "the most controversial woman in California," but her commentaries did not live up to the hype. Her first appearance featured a rhyming commemoration of Japanese internment during World War II:

> A day of remembrance, that's why we're here
> Remember when justice was once ruled by fear?
> Remember when freedom was clear[ly] your right?
> Provided you proved that your skin was pure white.

A television executive from a competing station called Bird's debut "bizarre. I think people were pretty stunned." A news director at another station said, "I've never seen a rhyming commentator before. It's a novel approach." Bird explained that she had hoped to get her point across without sounding "too harsh to the ear" but said she did not plan future poems.

Her second commentary focused on surviving breast cancer. Other topics included Jesse Jackson's bid for the presidency and the winner-take-all mentality of the Olympics. Asked about her somewhat offbeat approach to commenting, Bird said she was not an ideologue, despite what her opponents claimed. "My views can't be particularly categorized, especially today when so many things are in flux. . . . My goal is to get viewers to listen and think about something for a moment."[16]

Los Angeles Times television critic Howard Rosenberg lauded her performance. "For one thing, it's exhilarating to see a female commentator in a field dominated by men," he wrote. Rosenberg acknowledged that Bird was still somewhat stiff in front of the camera. "Far better a relative TV novice with something to say, than a noodle-minded smoothie who merely sounds and looks good." But her employer courted controversy and conflict, and after a few months Bird was let go. Considering her strong feelings about the media in general and her obsession with privacy, her foray into television seems an odd choice for a second career.[17]

She had an additional circumstance that made finding work difficult: caring for her elderly mother. Anne Bird was in her eighties and in failing health. As her mother's primary caregiver, Rose Bird could not travel far from the San Francisco Bay Area; she taped her television commentaries for both news outlets at the San Francisco affiliate of ABC. She might have accepted an academic appointment, but the university had to be in the Bay Area. For parts of two years she taught constitutional law at Golden Gate University, where she won plaudits from students, but it was only a part-time position. So she mostly remained at home in Palo Alto, gardening, caring for her dogs, making audio tapes of books for blind law students, and taking her mother to medical appointments and to church.

In her last year as chief justice, Bird had earned more than $93,000, but afterward she got by on savings and a pension of about $1,000 a month, plus occasional speaker's fees. She distanced herself from many former acquaintances and friends with no explanation. "I think the story of Rose Bird is an American tragedy," said Judge LaDoris Cordell. "I don't imagine she ever conceived she'd go from the top of the world to . . . become a virtual pariah. . . . I think it's very, very sad."[18]

Though she had left the public sphere, Republican candidates in California continued to find Bird extremely useful for fundraising and direct mail purposes. As one commentator phrased it, "Ms. Bird's name remains a kind of reflexive shorthand in California for 'soft-on-crime liberal.'" Former San Diego mayor Pete Wilson was particularly apt to cite Bird at every opportunity. He had won a U.S. Senate seat in 1982. Eight years later, he ran as the Republican candidate for California governor to succeed George Deukmejian. In campaign stops across the state, he brought up Bird's name at every opportunity, accusing his Democratic opponent Dianne Feinstein of supporting Bird and opposing the death penalty. Feinstein insisted she supported the death penalty but acknowledged that she considered Bird "a friend." Wilson narrowly won the election.[19]

Dan Lungren, Republican candidate for attorney general in 1990, branded his Democratic opponent Arlo Smith "a Rose Bird liberal," causing Santa Clara law professor Gerald Uelmen to lament: "Rose Bird is becoming the perennial bogyperson that the political right drags out of the closet whenever it wants to get a little hysteria going."

As one friend told a reporter, "the campaign against her was meant to destroy her. She may be the first person so devastatingly destroyed in a political sense that just mentioning her name conveys negative thoughts."[20]

On rare occasions, Bird contributed opinion pieces to newspapers and magazines. In 1987, to commemorate the bicentennial of the U.S. Constitution, the *Washington Post* asked five noted individuals, including Bird, to write essays on various aspects of the founding document. Bird wrote about gender. Her own experiences "only mirrored a harsh national reality," she wrote. "In this year of our Constitution's bicentennial, 'We the People' are not yet at a point where the fundamental promise of equality for women is a legal fact." She went on to describe the travails women experienced in law—underrepresentation as lawyers and judges, difficulty finding acceptance from male peers—which "reflects in microcosm the larger struggle of all women in this country to secure equal rights."

Women entering the courtroom as defendants, jurors, or litigants were at a distinct disadvantage, Bird wrote, because they had little understanding of how the legal system worked. She had tried to address this problem by focusing on gender bias in "selection of court-appointed counsel at the trial and appellate levels; the language and pattern of jury instructions"; and "methods to overcome gender bias in the courtroom behavior of judges, counsel, court personnel and witnesses." But much work remained to be done.[21]

Meanwhile, the California Supreme Court—as expected—shifted rightward, particularly in criminal cases. In June 1987 prosecutors asked justices to abandon a Bird court program to study racial disparities in death sentences; in October they obliged. That same month, justices overturned a 1983 Bird court ruling mandating that juries had to find that a defendant had intended to kill before conferring a death sentence. Six justices signed the majority opinion, written by Stanley Mosk, who declared that the earlier opinion had been reached in error.

The case involved a man who had strangled two women. Justices overturned his death sentence, however, because the trial judge had given jurors the disavowed Briggs Initiative instruction that a sentence of life without parole could eventually lead to parole. Associate Justice Allen Broussard dissented from the majority opinion, noting, "When the political winds gust in a new direction, it becomes necessary to remind all concerned of the virtues of a steady course."[22]

In August 1987 the Lucas court unanimously upheld its first death sentence. By December 1990 justices had affirmed 84 of 109 death penalty cases, a nearly 75 percent affirmation rate. In comparison, the average for all thirty-six states with the death penalty was a 41 percent affirmation rate. And death penalty appeals took up more of the court's time—39 percent, compared to 11 percent for the Bird court. If the public wanted death sentences pushed through the pipeline, the Lucas court seemed willing to oblige.[23]

But the increased number of capital cases meant that justices heard fewer appeals in other kinds of cases. In 1989, for example, the court granted petitions for hearings in only eighty non-capital cases, less than a third of the number of such cases heard annually by the Bird court. And the new court proved somewhat more favorable to business interests than the Bird court had been. For example, it overturned the court's 1985 opinion making landlords liable for injuries suffered by tenants and ruled that mobile home parks had the right to exclude children.[24]

In cases involving civil liberties and some other issues, however, the Lucas court "blunted, but did not reverse the direction of the high court under Bird." For example, it ruled that prayers at public school graduations violated the U.S. and California constitutions, mandated buffer zones in front of abortion clinics to protect patients, barred private clubs from discriminating against women and minorities, and allowed the battered-women defense in some criminal cases. Some of these decisions elicited surprise, a few protests, and charges that the new court still was engaged in "social engineering."[25]

By 1990—only three years after their appointments—two of Deukmejian's replacement justices had left the court. John Arguelles retired in 1989. Deukmejian named appeals court judge Joyce Kennard as his replacement; she became the court's second female justice. Born in

Indonesia at the beginning of World War II, Kennard had a youth even more deprived than Bird's. Her father died in a Japanese prison camp during the war, and in the 1950s, she and her mother moved to the Netherlands. A tumor in her right leg led to a partial amputation when she was only a teenager. She immigrated to the United States in 1961 and worked her way through the University of Southern California both as an undergraduate and as a law student. Shortly after Kennard's appointment, Bird sent her a congratulatory note, and the two women became friendly. Though not as predictably liberal as Bird, Kennard soon revealed a strong independent streak.[26]

Marcus Kaufman left the court in early 1990. In a parting shot, he accused the Bird court of having held up death sentences because of opposition to capital punishment. He suggested that its inaction on capital cases had created a massive backlog that created problems for the Lucas court, which often had to work seven days a week to catch up. The work had exhausted him. "To use dastardly means so that the death penalty cannot be implemented is really a disgrace," Kaufman said. His remarks represented only his opinion, he added.[27]

Bird consistently refused to criticize her successors. "I felt I was under a microscope—it's an enormously painful and difficult process, so I won't comment on the new justices and their decisions." Others did not share her reluctance. Joseph Grodin blamed the backlog on the Briggs Initiative of 1978. The court had spent years trying to untangle its provisions. "When Justice Kaufman got there, there wasn't all that much to do," Grodin said.

Cruz Reynoso suggested that the U.S. Supreme Court's involvement in determining the constitutionality of California's death penalty statutes also had played a role in the backlog. And Allen Broussard, who still served as an associate justice, said that when "Justice Kaufman was on the court, I frequently had to bite my tongue; maybe it's just best to continue to bite my tongue."[28]

The renewed emphasis on capital punishment had not resulted in any executions by the time Kaufman left the court, and polls found that more than three-quarters of Californians were anxious to see killers executed. Robert Alton Harris was first in line. Following his sentence for murdering two teenage boys in San Diego, he spent more than a decade on death row, as his attorneys filed dozens of state and federal appeals. His execution finally had been scheduled for April 1990, but the federal Ninth Circuit Court of Appeal issued a stay with only hours to go, postponing it yet again. Deukmejian had hoped to preside over the state's first execution in a quarter century, but Republican Pete Wilson sat in the governor's office when Harris finally went to his death in San Quentin's gas chamber in April 1992.

Harris's execution brought renewed attention to Bird and her record on death penalty cases. She had been out of office for more than five years but still had not found steady work. Her mother had died in 1991, so she was free to commute, or even to relocate, but no offers had emerged except for a semester-long stint teaching at the University of Sydney in Australia. She let her membership in the California bar association lapse. She gained weight, often dressed in jogging suits, and seldom wore makeup. Some friends described her as a recluse, but others noted that she still enjoyed dinners out and movies with a few chosen people. One was Associate Justice Joyce Kennard, with whom she occasionally had lunch. Kennard described Bird as "gracious, warm and witty."[29]

Reporters still sought interviews. They phoned, wrote letters, and showed up at her Palo Alto home without warning. They took note of the "quiet cul-de-sac," the "robust ferns hanging from a gracious old tree above a picnic table in the front yard." They braved the closed gate and the "No Admittance" and "Beware of Dog" signs to knock on her front door. Dogs barked inside, but no one answered. Once, a reporter spied a woman who looked suspiciously like Bird walking her dogs. The woman brusquely said she did "not know the addresses" on the street and strode away quickly.[30]

One day in 1992, Bird stopped into the East Palo Alto Community Law Project—which offered legal services to low-income litigants—and volunteered her services. The staff of young attorneys failed to recognize the state's first female chief justice, who asked them to call her Rose. They happily handed her documents to photocopy. A law school dean eventually alerted them to the identity of their diligent volunteer. Horrified, they apologized and asked her to take on a bigger role, but she demurred. She was no longer licensed to practice law and did not like to attend meetings.

Over time, however, Bird became close to several of the young women attorneys and gave them advice about how to navigate a still male-dominated profession. She told one to wear lipstick and professional clothing. "I learned you have to play those games," Bird said. She told another to be more assertive, to not let men interrupt her, and to "feel comfortable looking out for yourself."[31]

In the decade following voter rejection of Bird, Grodin, and Reynoso, California justices continued to appear on the ballot for confirmation. None faced organized opposition, and all easily won retention, albeit by somewhat smaller margins than in the days when justices routinely won 75 to 80 percent of the vote.[32] In fact, few people paid attention to judicial elections, and only reporters covering the court on a regular basis wrote about the justices or their decisions.

Virtually no one outside legal circles took note of Malcolm Lucas's retirement in 1996. Governor Pete Wilson appointed Ronald George—a former Los Angeles prosecutor, superior court and appeals court judge, and associate supreme court justice—to replace Lucas. It began to look as if, despite projections of continuing conflict, Bird's rejection had been an anomaly, just a blip on California's radar screen. Even so, some writers still predicted there would be "repercussions of a system driven by ideological true believers and attack ads."[33]

The ideological battles had continued at both the federal level and in other states. In summer 1991 Republican president George H. W. Bush nominated Clarence Thomas, former head of the Equal Employment Opportunity Commission (EEOC), to fill the U.S. Supreme Court seat vacated by Thurgood Marshall. Whomever Bush nominated undoubtedly would have faced tough questioning; Marshall was a civil rights icon who had argued *Brown v. Board of Education* before the court in the early 1950s. Thomas, like Marshall, was African American. He also was an unabashed conservative.

His grueling confirmation hearing in fall 1991 illustrated how far the yardstick measuring "appropriate" topics for discussion and consideration had moved since the rejection of Bird and Bork just a few years earlier. The intervening time had seen the downfall of Democratic presidential candidate Gary Hart due to disclosures of marital infidelity, and now issues pertaining to sex had moved to the forefront of politics.[34] Bird and Bork had complained about the circus-like atmosphere surrounding the judicial retention and selection process. Thomas called his appearance before the Senate Judiciary Committee—and an audience of millions—"a high-tech lynching."

Early debate centered on Thomas's legal philosophy. Liberal groups initially targeted Thomas for his opposition to affirmative action and abortion, and some women's groups threatened to "bork" him. But the hearings soon pivoted to another topic: sexual harassment. Oklahoma University law professor Anita Hill had worked for Thomas at the EEOC, and in testimony to the committee she offered graphic details of uncomfortable conversations between herself and Thomas relating to pornographic films and other sexual matters. In the end, the Senate confirmed Thomas by a razor-thin margin, 52–48.[35]

By the early 1990s some state judicial elections had become fraught affairs as well. Texas had long been Democratic-leaning, angering business interests and others who believed the state supreme court was too plaintiff friendly. Led by conservative campaign strategist Karl Rove, beginning in the late 1980s they fought back. Texas jurists are chosen via partisan elections. Under Rove's direction, "trial lawyers" became a term of derision and political efficacy.[36]

Conservatives in other states soon targeted justices for being "soft on crime." In 1992 Mississippi associate justice James Robertson lost his seat in part because of a ruling that rapists could not be sentenced to death unless they killed their victims. Robertson's opponent took the victory by incessantly touting his "law and order" credentials.

Four years later supreme court justices in Nebraska and Tennessee lost their seats following bitter election campaigns. David Lanphier lost his retention bid in Nebraska after a group called Citizens for Responsible

Judges targeted him for two unpopular rulings. One overturned the state's term-limit law and another deemed "malice" a requirement for finding defendants guilty of second-degree murder.[37]

Penny White was defeated in Tennessee following a campaign charging her with being "soft on crime" based largely on her ruling overturning the death sentence of a man charged with murder during a rape. She had voted to uphold the conviction. Victims' rights groups led the campaign. One family traveled the state brandishing a photo of their murdered daughter even though White had not been involved in that particular case. She believed, she said, that the Republican governor had targeted her because he wanted to appoint a judge more sympathetic to his own point of view.

Citing the judicial code of ethics, White refused to fight back. At one point, when the attacks against her became too vicious, she sold her television set to avoid having to flip through channels or turn it off each time a negative ad appeared. Some of the attacks were based on gender. For example, she was criticized for not having taken her husband's last name. Churches told members not to vote for White because she lacked "family values." One editorial cartoon depicted White in her judicial robes reading a law book while, over her shoulder, two overweight male lobbyists muttered to each other. "Look at her, deliberately ignoring us," one said. The other responded: "Uppity woman—we'll show her." White later called the experience of trying to retain her seat "hideous."[38]

Whatever thoughts Rose Bird had about Clarence Thomas, or any of the defeated state justices, she kept to herself. By 1996 she still had no steady work but had regained her voice. She cowrote a book on constitutional law with Santa Clara professor Russell Galloway and penned opinion pieces in California newspapers generally focused on high-profile events and criticizing the media for its superficial, sensationalist coverage of the courts and of politics in general. It is possible to read Bird's bitterness at her own treatment in her essays describing the experiences of others.

The arrest and trial of former NFL star O.J. Simpson for killing his former wife Nicole Brown Simpson and her friend Ronald Goldman seems to have served as a catalyst for Bird's willingness to again take up her public persona. From the moment of Simpson's arrest, Americans became obsessed with the case. It had everything: sex, race, celebrity, high-profile attorneys (including famed lawyer F. Lee Bailey and DNA expert Barry Scheck of the Innocence Project), colorful witnesses, and a glove that appeared not to fit. When the jury pronounced Simpson not guilty, many whites howled in protest; the African American defendant had "gotten away with murder."

Bird also became hooked on the case. Not surprisingly for a former defense attorney, she believed the jury had gotten it right; the prosecution had not proved its case. "It was the media that played up the fact that one victim was a beautiful white woman," she wrote in an essay for the *Los Angeles Times*. Reporters "knew that this touched historical chords in the white community." Seeming to channel Clarence Thomas, she added, "It wasn't very long ago that black men were castrated and lynched for looking at white women. Is this part of our collective psyche?" Did they "care that the white community might convict this man for a double murder based solely on white revulsion at the domestic discord, the abusive words, the graphic pictures? If the white community doesn't understand the verdict rendered, then the press and television have failed in their responsibility."[39]

Six months later Bird wrote about the suicide of navy admiral Jeremy Boorda, who came under scrutiny for wearing two medals that critics claimed he had not earned. It was perhaps her most personal piece. She understood exactly what Boorda had gone through, she said.

If you have never experienced life under a microscope, it is almost impossible to understand any of this. Those who live a public life are no longer seen as human beings. Rather, they are objects to be examined, worked over, manipulated, ridiculed and sometimes even hated. Someone else defines who they are as men and women and what they stand for as public figures. And that image often has little to do with the real person.

The personal lives of our public figures are scrutinized in the hope of finding some flaw, some misstep, some instance that can be blown up out of proportion, to make or break those individuals. Then their ideas and programs can be killed without any real public discussion.[40]

Several months later Bird learned that her cancer had returned for a fourth time. In November 1996, twenty years after having her right breast removed, doctors removed her left breast. The day after her release from the hospital, she drove more than one hundred miles round-trip from Palo Alto to Oakland to speak at the memorial service for her former court colleague Allen Broussard, who had died of cancer. "He was a scholar of the law," she said. He was also "fun to be around and that's a blessing on a court that often took itself too seriously."[41]

Broussard had died the same day that California voters passed Proposition 209, limiting the use of affirmative action in education and hiring. The measure had been heavily promoted by Republican governor Pete Wilson. Bird took to the pages of the *San Francisco Examiner*, bemoaning what she called "California-style apartheid," which would result in fewer African Americans and Latinos on college campuses. "What a shame.... California is world famous for its system of higher education. However, no one can expect legislators to fund a system that represents only part of the citizenry. And no one can expect minority legislators and other officeholders who believe in diversity and equality to fund a non-representative system."[42]

She took a wry tone in an April 1998 piece for the *San Francisco Examiner*, which came in the midst of sensational media coverage on President Bill Clinton's sexual relationship with White House intern Monica Lewinsky. Bird's missive purported to be a memo to anyone planning a campaign for president. "Establish a legal defense fund of at least $10 million to ensure you can pay the bills for all the lawsuits and criminal investigations against you or your spouse.... Remember that in politics you don't make friends, only alliances. And those are momentary at best." If elected, the successful candidate should "abolish the intern program at the White House.... Never let a woman under

85 near you. And never hug anyone, not even your mother. . . . Make certain your spouse has no opinions on anything and can stand for hours gazing lovingly at you."[43]

That same month, Bird traveled to Los Angeles to accept an American Civil Liberties Union Conscience Award. She virtually never attended such gatherings, and those present gave her a standing ovation. Some reporters also attended, hoping to finally interview the elusive former chief justice. She evaded their questions, except for one from a journalist who queried why she was not working. "You have to be asked," Bird replied.

ACLU of Southern California executive director Ramona Ripston said that Bird had "paid dearly for her conscience." Among those participating was Mike Farrell, human rights activist and star of the television series *M.A.S.H.* In his introduction, Farrell called Bird "certainly one of the great figures in California on issues of equality in society." He assured the former chief justice that she had not been forgotten.[44]

This came as no news to Bird. A dozen years after her defeat, Republican candidates still used her as a cudgel to beat on their opponents. In 1998 Republican attorney general Dan Lungren was running for governor against Gray Davis, formerly chief of staff to Jerry Brown. "I won't go back to the Jerry Brown-Gray Davis years when [they] were putting people like Rose Bird on the court," Lungren told one audience. "If you listen to my opponent right now, he can barely remember Rose Bird. . . . Give me a break."[45]

The reference was relevant for another reason, however. In 1998, for the first time since 1986, conservative groups had targeted two California high court justices—Associate Justice Ming Chin and Chief Justice Ronald George—on the November ballot. Both were appointees of Pete Wilson. The death penalty was not at issue this time, since the court had upheld 85 percent of the more than three hundred death sentences it had heard, and the state had carried out five executions. But George and Chin had angered antiabortion forces when they voted to strike down a 1987 law—never enforced—that required girls under eighteen to obtain parental consent before having abortions.

In his majority 4–3 opinion, George acknowledged vast differences of opinion on the topic. But "the morality of abortion is not a legal or constitutional issue," he wrote. "It is a matter of philosophy, of ethics, and of theology." In the final analysis, the law was unconstitutional because it violated the right of privacy guaranteed by the California Constitution, he wrote.[46]

The California Pro Life Council quickly announced an effort to defeat George and Chin. The group garnered widespread attention and some funds, mostly by harkening back to the Bird court. But its campaign gained little traction. George announced his intent to fight back and traveled the state talking to a wide variety of groups and individuals. Both justices raised money—approximately $1 million apiece.

Newspapers editorialized about the differences between the 1986 and 1998 antijudiciary campaigns. The prolife forces were attempting to defeat justices based on a single decision, wrote Berkeley law professor Stephen Barnett. Bird, meanwhile, had voted to overturn more than sixty death sentences that came before the court during her tenure. In the end, both George and Chin easily won confirmation.[47]

By the 1998 election, every justice but Stanley Mosk—by then eighty-six years old—had been appointed by George Deukmejian or Pete Wilson. The court still handed down decisions that pleased conservatives, but it was not always predictable. For example, it ruled against employers who sought the right to randomly drug test employees and watered down the state's draconian "three strikes" law, which mandated life sentences for anyone committing a third felony, no matter how minor.

When Gray Davis defeated Dan Lungren in the November 1998 governor's race, he became California's first Democratic chief executive in sixteen years. He understood that he had to tread carefully when it came to judicial appointments, lest he unleash a reprise of the acrimonious battle over "soft-on-crime" judges. "The shadow looming over Davis' appointments is that of Rose Elizabeth Bird," wrote one journalist. Davis moved quickly to quash potential trouble, sending out a member of his transition team to promise that the governor would appoint only judges who understood that the death penalty was settled law in California.[48]

In an ordinary time, Rose Bird might have cheered Davis's election, despite his efforts to distance himself from her. The two had, in fact, been friends, and Bird had presided over the wedding of Davis and his wife Sharon. She also might have been pleased by the decision of the group Death Penalty Focus to honor her work, via the annual Rose Elizabeth Bird Commitment to Justice Award. In early 1999 the organization announced that Norman Jewison, a film director specializing in socially conscious films, was that year's recipient.[49]

By early 1999, however, she faced extremely serious health problems. The second mastectomy had not eradicated her breast cancer. She decided against further treatment, and by summer she had largely come to terms with the fact that her life might be measured in months, rather than years. In late summer Claire Cooper, a reporter for the *Sacramento Bee* who had covered the court for two decades, penned a letter to Bird. She was writing a story for a magazine and had some questions. Would the former chief justice be willing to talk to her? "I was surprised . . . by her call when she got my letter in September," Cooper wrote. She arranged to meet Bird for lunch at a Palo Alto restaurant.

The woman who greeted her was "gaunt and unsteady." She occasionally mixed up her words, as when she said "General Motors" when she meant "General Mills." She was "in good spirits," but thirteen years after her ouster, her experiences on the court still haunted her. She wanted to set the record straight. She admitted to some mistakes, particularly to being politically "naïve," such as when, as agriculture secretary, she told lawmakers she would take no amendments to the Agriculture Labor Relations Act.

When it came to her tenure as chief justice, however, Bird mostly blamed the entrenched political system. The "old boys' network" viewed everything as a "power grab," she said, particularly her efforts to diminish the influence of the "dangerous shadow court"—administrators who actually ran the judiciary from behind the scenes. At judges' meetings, "wives would say hello to me, but men didn't know what to call me. Three-quarters of the battle is looking the part. Nobody knew what a woman justice was supposed to look like." As Cooper phrased it, Bird was "a symbol of change that threatened domination of the courts when the women's rights movement was young."

Bird knew early on that she would not be reconfirmed in 1986, she told Cooper. "The forces were so powerful against me and I had no political or economic base." The notion that she might have tried to save her job by voting "differently if I knew it would keep me in" was a nonstarter. "It was never an option. I made choices and I was willing to live with them." It had been difficult to live on so little money afterward, she acknowledged, but "I learned to scale down and live like a student again, to get down to values." It was to be her last interview; Bird died at Stanford University Hospital on December 4, 1999. Hers had been a particularly complex type of breast cancer, according to her doctors.[50]

Virtually every major newspaper in the United States took note of her passing, as did some publications outside of the country. All described her trail-blazing career, her votes against the death penalty, her humiliating rejection by voters, her reclusive postcourt life, and her role in changing the way politicians and the electorate viewed judges.

The *New York Times* recalled that Bird "came of professional age at a time when major law firms still resisted hiring women" and quoted federal appeals court justice Stephen Reinhardt, who reflected on her "total passion and commitment," which was "not always the best way to function and get along in this world in a political environment."[51] The *San Francisco Examiner* remembered Bird as a "brilliant pioneer for women in law, California's first woman chief justice and perhaps the most controversial figure in the state's political history."[52]

The *Washington Post* called her a "young, brilliant and combative jurist." The *Guardian* combined a personal reminiscence on Bird with a discussion of the impact of her confirmation loss on the judiciary as a whole. Writer Christopher Reed said he had spoken with Bird during her 1986 campaign, and she had shared with him the immense personal costs of trying to keep her job: "the daily deluge of letters threatening to kill or rape her, how they got hold of her [home] telephone number," and how she had to move her "terrified" elderly mother out of her home. Writer Harold Jackson described the "chilling effect" of "the sacking of a chief justice. Every subsequent judicial appointee seemed to peer nervously toward the electorate."[53]

A few writers proved willing to challenge the maxim that one should not speak ill of the dead. Debra Saunders of the *San Francisco Chronicle* reminded members of "the Bird fan club that voters gave Bird the boot not because she was principled, but because she put her principles above the law."[54] Two pointed remembrances discussed the price that Bird had paid for her devotion to principles. Writing in the *Orange County Register* and other papers, syndicated columnist Peter H. King noted that writers of her obituaries

> have presented anecdotal evidence that the former chief justice actually might have been a human being.
>
> Though best known for a job that was taken from her, Bird, in fact, was stripped of something far greater . . . her humanity. For more than a dozen years and long after voters removed her in 1986, she was battered by politicians looking for a cheap way to define themselves. . . .
>
> She became a bumper sticker, political invective, campaign shorthand. . . . She became an 'ism. Why? Because it worked.[55]

Patt Morrison of the *Los Angeles Times* wrote in a similar vein:

> At some unknown transformative moment, Rose Bird ceased to be a person.
>
> Instead, she became, in the pidgin of politics, a cause célèbre, a litmus test, a hot button. . . . [H]er name is still carried down from the attic and dusted off whenever candidates get hooked up to the political polygraph: Do you support the death penalty? Did you oppose Rose Bird?
>
> Her defeat woke a slumbering giant. Until Bird, judges had barely registered on voters' radar. . . . The legacy of Rose Bird . . . is not outlawing the short-handled hoe or bolstering tenants' rights, but embodying the warning that henceforth, beneath the robe of a jurist, there better beat the heart of a politician.[56]

A few weeks after her death Bird's friends and former colleagues held memorial services in Los Angeles and Palo Alto. Hundreds of friends and former colleagues remembered Bird not as a tragic figure but as a warm and generous woman, always there to help celebrate a triumph or mourn a tragedy. One friend remembered her annual phone call when she sang off-key birthday greetings, accompanied by her dog Nellie.[57]

In March 2000 the state supreme court gathered in San Francisco to memorialize Bird. Former justice Cruz Reynoso said that Bird "knew life as those without power live it. The perspective of those who do not have power guided her sense of justice." Associate Justice Joyce Kennard remembered the former chief justice as "a woman of intellectual brilliance, extraordinary courage, compassion and grace" and noted that Bird had "forever left her imprint on California's history." She also had a strong impact on Kennard. Bird's friendship, Kennard said, "enriched my life."[58]

Paying for Justice 11

Marsha Ternus was working as a civil litigator in 1993 when Republican governor. Terry Branstad appointed her the first woman to serve on the Iowa Supreme Court. Seven years later her male colleagues unanimously selected her as the court's first female chief justice. For more than fifteen years Ternus's work won high praise, and she faced scant opposition. Then in 2009 she authored a unanimous decision overturning a law that barred gay marriage in Iowa; it violated the equal protection provision of the state's constitution, she wrote.

Within weeks, a coalition of conservative groups announced that they planned to target Ternus and two male justices in the 2010 election. Money poured in. Opponents carried signs declaring: "It's we the people, not we the courts." Ads depicted "pictures of a church, a boy scout, hunters and children pledging allegiance to the American flag." In the end, all three justices went down to defeat. Ternus later called her opponents' tactics "intimidation and retaliation utterly inconsistent with the concept of a judiciary charged with the responsibility to uphold the Constitutional rights of all citizens."[1]

Oliver Diaz, a Republican, was appointed to the Mississippi Supreme Court in 2000; two years later, after a bitterly fought race, he won a six-year term. But he quickly ran afoul of business interests who saw him as too plaintiff friendly. Over the next several years, opponents managed to have Diaz charged with bribery and tax evasion, leading to two trials that ended in acquittals. His legal troubles kept him off the bench for three years, and in 2008 he lost his retention bid. Speaking to Amy Goodman on NPR's *Democracy Now* several years later, Diaz said: "What we've seen lately are these corporations coming in, putting money into judicial races, and they're promoting candidates who tend to support corporate interest."[2]

In Illinois, probusiness opponents targeted Chief Justice Thomas Kilbride after he voted to overturn limits on medical malpractice awards. Perhaps recognizing that malpractice would not bring out enough voters to defeat Kilbride, critics also accused him of being "soft on crime." Kilbride fought back, traveling the state and raising more than $2.7 million. He retained his seat.[3]

In 2012 three Florida justices managed to fend off a high-wattage effort to oust them because of a ruling on "Obamacare." The justices had voted to remove a measure from the statewide ballot that allowed Floridians to opt out of mandatory health care coverage. It contained "misleading and ambiguous language," they ruled. R. Fred Lewis, one of those targeted, told the *New York Times* that he was "very, very stressed at the whole circumstance. This is a full frontal attack . . . on a fair and impartial judicial system, which is the cornerstone and bedrock of our democracy."[4]

The 2014 election season featured campaigns in several states against high court justices. In Tennessee, the Republican lieutenant governor led a campaign to defeat three supreme court justices appointed by a Democratic governor. They were "antibusiness" and "soft on crime," he charged. The three judges counterattacked, joining forces to raise money and run ads under the auspices of a group called Keep the Tennessee Supreme Court Fair; all three won by narrow margins.[5]

Two Kansas justices also won retention despite an effort by conservative groups to remove them for voting to overturn two death sentences. Eric Rosen and Lee Johnson had been appointed by former Democratic governor Kathleen Sebelius, and their defeats would have enabled Republican governor Sam Brownback to appoint their successors. After the election, Rosen thanked the electorate, noting that "of far greater importance than our personal retention is the retention of the court's independence and autonomy."[6]

Back in the 1980s the campaign to remove Rose Bird, Joseph Grodin, and Cruz Reynoso had seemed an anomaly, based on a unique set of circumstances. Bird and a few others warned then that the California contest was the opening salvo in what would become a large and costly battle to control the nation's courts. Few paid attention. Yet today, virtually every election cycle brings another effort to remove state supreme court justices. Thirty-nine states elect justices, either in contested or uncontested races. Spending on judicial campaigns "has exploded in the last two decades," Jeffrey Toobin wrote in 2012. "In 1990 candidates for state supreme courts only raised around $3 million, but by the mid-nineties campaigns were raking in five times that amount. The 2000 races saw high-court candidates raise more than $45 million." Since 2000, $275 million has gone to judicial campaigns.[7]

Some have dubbed the movement to defeat justices "robe rage." Anyone with a grievance, it seems, might mount an effort against a judge. Appointment to the bench no longer automatically confers status and prestige; instead, it almost guarantees emotional distress. Rose Bird was targeted for a body of work over nearly a decade. Today, it takes only one controversial ruling to threaten a justice's career.[8]

Nearly thirty years after Bird's defeat, nothing, it seems, is off-limits politically. Gloves-off fights over supreme court justices—and some lower court judges as well—have become as commonplace as Friday night football games, with each side rooting for its "team" and both sides using vitriolic slogans. In Michigan, conservative opponents of one judicial candidate accused her of helping to "free a terrorist." Another campaign claimed that a pro–gay rights candidate "sides with child predators." Liberals, on the other hand, accused a conservative judicial candidate of "denying benefits to cancer patients."[9]

As more and more judges have faced opposition and the campaigns have become increasingly expensive, ugly, and personal, the contests have become a serious topic of discussion in a wide variety of media. Law journals, blogs, newspapers, magazines including *Mother Jones* and the *New Yorker*, and television programs such as *60 Minutes* all have waded into the debate. Many ponder how all of this came to be. Explanations have been many and varied, with some commentators blaming the opposition to Rose Bird for pointing the way.

"Hundreds of thousands of voters have apparently been experiencing robe rage since 1978, the year opposition groups first began their ultimately successful efforts to recall California's then-Chief Justice Rose Elizabeth Bird," one writer opined. "We figured out a long time ago that it's easier to elect seven judges than it is to elect 132 legislators," said a consultant.[10] Other factors have played roles as well, including *Bush v. Gore.* The 2000 presidential election ultimately decided by the U.S. Supreme Court enhanced public awareness of the powerful role courts play in the larger political arena. Then there were U.S. high court decisions such as *Citizens United* and *McCutcheon v. Federal Elections Commission* that lifted caps on campaign spending.

Uninformed voters, who often know next to nothing about their state's supreme court justices or the issues they decide, can easily be manipulated by inflammatory campaign rhetoric, misleading slogans, and direct mailers. One survey featured interviews with voters who were asked about the qualifications of justices on the ballot. "I don't know the difference between one judge and the next," one respondent told an interviewer. "I don't think I should have voted, but I did."[11] As former California appeals court justice Mildred Lillie put it, "The public has great difficulty in evaluating a judge's qualifications or performance. The education of voters comes from special interest groups."[12]

More important to many jurists, scholars, and writers, however, has been the potentially game-changing impact on the judiciary of the ever larger infusion of cash needed to counter these attacks. Polls suggest that judges and members of the public alike have strong concerns about this issue. A survey by two groups, the National Center for State Courts and Justice at Stake, found that three-quarters of the public and half of state court justices worry that money influences judges' decisions.[13]

As retired West Virginia chief justice Richard Neeley put it in 2006,

"It's pretty hard in big money races not to take care of your friends. It's very hard not to dance with the one who brung you."[14]

Barbara Pariente survived the 2012 effort to oust her and two other associate justices from the Florida Supreme Court. "If judges think they have to put a finger to the wind, rather than decide cases based on the facts and the law, their ability to dispense justice will be compromised and democracy will be undermined," she said.[15] Theodore B. Olson argued the *Bush v. Gore* case before the U.S. Supreme Court in 2000 and became solicitor general under President George W. Bush. "The improper appearance created by money in judicial elections is one of the most important issues facing our judicial system today," he said.[16]

Sue Bell Cobb served as chief justice of the Alabama Supreme Court for four and a half years before resigning in 2011, largely because of her inability to persuade state lawmakers to change a judicial selection process that left her "feeling disgusted." Initially, Cobb reveled in her first-woman status, which "represented the pinnacle of success." But it had taken $2.6 million to get there. In Alabama, judges can ask anyone for campaign contributions, even lawyers who appear before the court. "Dignity and fairness are too often the first casualties in these kinds of endeavors," she wrote in 2015. Donors "want to know that investments they make . . . will yield favorable results."[17]

Former U.S. Supreme Court justice Sandra Day O'Connor has spoken out frequently about money and judicial campaigns. At one point she said: "In too many states, judicial elections are becoming political prize fights where partisans and special interests seek to install judges who will answer to them instead of the law and Constitution."[18] At a 2006 law conference, O'Connor declared that "the public needs to understand that the notion of independence is not only for the benefit of judges, judicial independence is for the benefit of all society."[19]

What can be done, if anything, to stop the juggernaut of money and destructive influences in judicial elections? Legal experts, politicians, and interest groups have wrangled with this issue for decades. One suggestion is the creation of nonpartisan campaign conduct committees. Judicial candidates and consulting firms would agree to avoid negative campaigning, and those stepping over the line would face sanctions. Another suggestion would eliminate the election and retention process, except in limited cases. Whenever a judge's term expired, a panel composed of state bar association representatives would assess her or his qualifications. Those meeting specified standards automatically would be retained. Those who fell short would face the electorate in retention elections, with a 60 percent affirmative vote required to keep their jobs.

Groups including Justice at Stake have begun to track the sources of money going into judicial campaigns. In Michigan, suggestions have included limiting justices to one term, listing the names of all contributors online, and requiring the secretary of state to maintain contribution records until justices leave the bench.[20] The U.S. Supreme Court has signaled its willingness to get involved in the issue as well. In April 2015 justices ruled that judges cannot solicit contributions when running for office. "Judges are not politicians," Chief Justice John Roberts wrote in his majority opinion.[21]

California began grappling with the ramifications of judicial elections in the immediate aftermath of the 1986 election. Following the defeat of Bird, Grodin, and Reynoso, many in the legal community and beyond "feared that the California judicial retention process was forever tainted." A "thoughtful and productive exchange" ensued. Suggestions included regulating campaign funding and expenditures.

California and a few other states require donors and fundraisers in judicial elections to register and report contributions, just like in other types of campaigns. Other suggestions have included public financing of judicial elections and the creation of standards and guidelines for appropriate campaign materials and tactics. These would be monitored by committees with authority to publicize violations. In 1998 the state removed from the ballot information on the number of years judicial candidates would serve, should they be elected. Studies found that judges seeking longer terms received fewer votes than those seeking shorter terms.[22]

As it turned out, 1986 was the last year that California Supreme Court justices faced any significant, widespread opposition. In the state that started it all, few people any longer pay much attention to the court, most people would be hard-pressed to name a single justice, and retention elections draw yawns and low numbers of votes, just as they did for decades before Rose Bird. In the 2014 election, for example, only about half of those casting ballots voted either for or against the three justices on the ballot. All three won handily.

Unimaginable even a decade ago, many people today find it difficult to recall Bird or her tumultuous tenure atop the court. References to Bird, even for people who lived through those years, are apt to elicit puzzled looks and, after a short pause, possibly an "aha" moment. What accounts for this dramatic change? Part of it can be attributed to short attention spans, courtesy of twenty-four-hour news, and to waning interest in capital punishment, the issue most connected to Bird in the public's mind. It would have been much harder, if not impossible, for consultants to fuel a groundswell against Bird without the death penalty.

California has executed thirteen men in the years since Bird left office. The first execution occurred in 1992 and the last in 2006, the same year a federal judge ruled California's cocktail of lethal drugs could cause inmates to "suffer inhumanely."[23] San Quentin prison now has three death rows, holding more than seven hundred men. Twenty women reside on their own death row in the Central California Women's Facility in Chowchilla. The last execution of a woman in the state took place in 1962.

The increasing number of DNA exonerations of condemned individuals has made more Californians—like their counterparts in other states—queasy at the thought of wrongful executions. In 2012 abolitionists succeeded in qualifying Proposition 34, a ballot measure to end capital punishment in California. It very nearly passed. Former San Quentin warden Jeanne Woodford led the effort. And in a situation that can only be deemed ironic, Donald Heller, who cowrote the 1978 Briggs Initiative, and Ron Briggs, son of the measure's namesake coauthor, traveled the state arguing for Proposition 34. The death penalty had become too expensive and essentially pointless, since it takes so long to execute anyone.[24]

That same year, current chief justice Tani Cantil-Sakauye, appointed by a Republican governor, said the death penalty in California was "not working. We know that." It "requires structural change and we don't have the kind of money to create the kind of change that is needed.... When the state decides to put somebody to death, gratefully, it takes time." No one has called for her removal or even criticized her.[25]

Declining support for capital punishment—and the pervasive belief among many Californians that voters and politicians went "too far" in their efforts to harshly punish all criminals, no matter how minor their crimes—has significantly diminished conservatives' power in the state and consequently their ability to shape debate and control the narrative on political issues in general. Meanwhile, the court itself has become much more diverse, more accurately reflecting the state's demographics.

Six of George Deukmejian's eight court appointments went to white males. Once he left office in 1991, more women and people of color garnered appointments. Meanwhile, the court that Deukmejian sought to mold into a bastion of conservatism began moving to the center politically. Some rulings even suggested that it had reverted to the liberal brand of jurisprudence practiced by Roger Traynor, Mathew Tobriner, and Rose Bird.

In May 2008 the court ruled that same-sex couples had the right to marry in California. In his 4–3 opinion, Chief Justice Ronald George— appointed by Wilson—referenced Traynor's 1948 ruling in *Perez v. Sharp*. "The right to marry is not properly viewed simply as a benefit or privilege that a government may establish or abolish as it sees fit," George wrote, "but rather [it] constitutes a basic civil or human right for all people."[26]

Conservatives took to the airwaves—and to social media—to castigate the court. They qualified a measure, Proposition 8, for the November 2008 ballot; the only valid marriage was between a man and a woman, it stated. Voters narrowly approved the measure, but victory was short lived. In 2010 a federal judge ruled Proposition 8 unconstitutional, and three years later the U.S. Supreme Court upheld his ruling.[27]

In an interview after his retirement from the court, George explained his evolving views on same-sex marriage. "Basically the argument was largely historical—'Well, it's always been this way.' But of course if we go back and we look at women's rights when they were basically the property of their husbands, we look back at school desegregation, these were all historically justified, but not constitutionally or morally justified. I ended up concluding that it was not enough to give it a different name, and that it was basically the equivalent of being allowed to sit in the bus, but sit in the back of the bus."[28]

Nothing demonstrates the state's political about-face more than the resurgence of Jerry Brown. When Bird died, Brown was mayor of the city of Oakland. Three years later, in November 2002, he won election as attorney general, marking his return to statewide office. In November 2010 California voters elected Brown governor for the third time, making him both the state's youngest and its oldest chief executive. In November 2014, forty years after his first campaign, he won an unprecedented fourth term.[29]

As of July 2015 Brown had made three state supreme court appointments: Goodwin Liu, associate dean of the Boalt Hall law school; Mariano Florentino Cuellar, a Mexican-born Stanford University law professor; and Leondra Kruger, an African American attorney in the U.S. Justice Department. All are young. At thirty-eight, Kruger is the youngest justice in the state's history. And all are liberal. For the first time, the court has no white male justices. It is composed of four women, two Asian American men, and one Latino. None of Brown's most recent appointees had previous experience as judges, and yet all won unanimous approval from the state's Commission on Judicial Appointments.[30]

A confluence of forces conspired to doom Rose Bird, and they no longer exist in California, at least not at present. Her tenure began at a transitional time when the federal and state courts had come under fire for decades of liberal rulings on issues such as affirmative action, school busing, plaintiffs' and defendants' rights, abortion, and the death penalty. Conservatives—and some moderates—sought a retrenchment, and yet Bird (and to a lesser extent Grodin and Reynoso) persisted in pushing the court even further in many areas. Previous courts, led by well-connected, longtime members of the judicial elite, had been considered bulletproof. The Bird court came to be dominated by neophytes and outsiders, and it was led by a woman with no previous judicial experience.

Bird's tenure also coincided with the media's obsessive focus on politics at all levels, and she headed the most significant state court in the United States. She always blamed the media for facilitating her downfall. It trivialized serious issues, she declared, turning everyone into a commodity and everything into a sound bite. She had a point, and it was a valid one. No previous chief justice had been subjected to the kind of media scrutiny she experienced or, in fact, much scrutiny at all.

But the pioneering nature of Bird's appointment evoked a high degree of curiosity, and her stubborn refusal to grant reporters access—and her not-so-veiled suggestions that even asking for interviews was improper—fueled more curiosity, irritation, and, at the dawn of the twenty-four-hour news cycle, more determination to get the story. When they could not get to Bird, reporters did the next best thing: they approached people who knew Bird. Some of them disliked her and were happy to talk.[31]

Finally, the importance of gender in Bird's downfall cannot be overstated. Her appointment—and those of other women, including state justices such as Rosalie Wahl of Minnesota and Shirley Abrahamson of Wisconsin, and Sandra Day O'Connor on the U.S. Supreme Court—represented a triumph for second-wave feminism. It signaled that women had "arrived" and could compete with men at the highest levels.

But the succession of female firsts elicited a strong backlash among those who feared women's success represented the beginning of the end for a white male–dominated society. Opponents hoped to stop the movement in its tracks, or better yet, reverse its course. "It was no mere coincidence that judicial races became hotly contested just as women and minority men ascended to the bench," Sally J. Kenney has argued. She might have added that the lessening of public esteem for judges in general also coincided with increasing numbers of female and minority judicial appointees.[32]

A variety of factors made Bird a particularly promising target for these efforts, though they cannot explain the viciousness with which her enemies attacked or their single-minded effort to destroy her both professionally and personally. She was single and childless, enabling critics to construct her as out of the mainstream and to posit her as an example of what feminists "really wanted"—to undermine longstanding traditional gender roles. Abrahamson, Wahl, and O'Connor, on the other hand, had married and borne children—in Wahl's case, five of them.

Bird was the third woman to sit atop a state supreme court, but the other two female chief justices had been much older and established at the time of their appointments. And both had close ties to members of the judicial elite in their respective states. In fact, both had ridden their fathers' coattails into office. Lorna Lockwood of Arizona had been an attorney for twenty-six years when she was first appointed to the superior court bench in 1951. She was in her sixties when she became chief justice of the Arizona Supreme Court, a position her father had held before her. Susie Sharp of North Carolina practiced law with her father in the 1930s. She became a superior court judge in the 1940s and an associate justice of the state supreme court in the early 1960s. In 1974 she was named chief justice of the North Carolina Supreme Court.

Bird had never had a male figure to show her, either through example or advice, how to navigate the rocky shoals of gender politics, or any sort of politics. She had been on her own since childhood. Once on the court, she modeled herself after Associate Justice Mathew Tobriner, but the timing was all wrong. Tobriner was in the twilight of his career, and his liberal judicial philosophy had gone out of fashion.

Bird was part of a generation of achieving women that experienced "profound exclusion" and alienation while climbing the professional ladder, but other women seemed more adept at avoiding the pitfalls—by using humor, for example, or embracing collegiality. She possessed a personality that gave her opponents extra ammunition. She insisted on living and working on her own terms, hence her refusal to make friends with individuals, including journalists, who might have softened her image. And she declined the services of an experienced campaign consulting firm that might have defused or countered allegations that she wished to see hardened killers released from prison so that they could murder innocent children.

Tani Cantil-Sakauye is California's second female chief justice, and she has not made the same mistakes as Bird. In fact, from the beginning she seemed to position herself as the "anti-Bird": friendly, accessible, and welcoming. "I hate to say it, but she's a charmer," appeals court justice Vance Ray told a reporter just after Governor Arnold Schwarzenegger announced her nomination in summer 2010. "She's just a very engaging person."

Both Cantil-Sakauye and Bird experienced similar straitened circumstances as children. Born in 1959, Cantil-Sakauye is the youngest child of Filipino immigrants, who worked in fields of California and Hawaii in their youth. She grew up in Sacramento and was in high school when Bird lived there and worked as agriculture secretary. She attended community college before transferring to the University of California, Davis, where she majored in rhetoric. To pay college tuition, Cantil-Sakauye waited tables, and she continued doing so as a student in UC Davis's law school, where she "devoted an incredible amount of time" to a program that encouraged other low-income students to attend law school. During summers she worked as a blackjack dealer in Lake Tahoe and Reno.

Even though she is a generation younger than Bird, Cantil-Sakauye found private law firms reluctant to hire her after law school; she was young, female, and an ethnic minority. Her first legal position came when Governor Deukmejian appointed her deputy legal affairs secretary in his administration. Soon she was on the fast track, appointed to the municipal court, superior court, and state appeals court. Chief Justice Ronald George appointed her to the state's Judicial Council. When he announced plans to retire in summer 2010, he recommended Cantil-Sakauye as his replacement.[33]

At a ceremony announcing her appointment, she marveled at her life's trajectory. Married to a Sacramento police lieutenant whose Japanese American parents had been interned during World War II, she spoke of her two daughters: "They have a set of grandparents who worked in the fields. They have a set of grandparents who were interned for four years. And their mother; is history remarkable or what?"[34]

In interviews Cantil-Sakauye disarmed reporters with self-deprecating anecdotes. She went to bed at night "in a tizzy," she said, but woke up each morning telling herself, "I can do this!" Despite her title, she never presumes that she "is the smartest person in the room." She modeled herself after the woman she most admires, Justice Sandra Day O'Connor, and in law school she and her friends formed a basketball squad dubbed the "Justice O" team. Asked by one reporter if she could offer a tip or two about blackjack, she said, "I could, I suppose, but I'm not any good or else I wouldn't be working for a living." In addition to her professional accomplishments, she also has been a Brownie leader.[35]

Cantil-Sakauye easily won unanimous confirmation in August 2010 but did not take office until the following January, when Ronald George retired. She immediately faced significant problems. The court system's budget had been slashed during the recession, and the state legislature threatened to wrest funding control from the court's central bureaucracy and shift it to state lawmakers and trial courts. She directly confronted legislators and visited newspaper editorial offices, calling such a plan "disastrous."

Like Bird, she immediately faced problems with court staff. Bird's involved a power struggle with longtime administrator Ralph Kleps, who soon resigned. Cantil-Sakauye's also involved the court's chief adminis-trator, who came under fire for "mismanaging a costly computer system" and for running a "financially reckless, secretive and bloated department." She eventually accepted his resignation but not before calling him "an invaluable resource."[36]

The appointment of a second female chief justice fueled inevitable comparisons with the first. One appellate judge called Cantil-Sakauye "a lot smarter and a lot better looking than Rose Bird." When Bird asserted judicial prerogatives, she had been "over-reaching" or a "polarizing figure." Yet when Cantil-Sakauye did the same, as when she confronted the state legislature over cuts to the judicial budget, she was absolutely correct in her actions. Bird "was polarizing because of her views on a very liberal Supreme Court," one attorney said.[37]

On the bench, Cantil-Sakauye is less predictable than Bird, though sometimes she seems to take a page from her predecessor. In one ruling, she said the public has a right to know the identity of police officers involved in shootings of citizens. In another, she said a young attorney in California illegally since childhood had a right to practice law in the state. The U.S. Department of Justice had deemed his illegal status sufficient reason to deny him a law license.[38]

In comments, Cantil-Sakauye suggested how much the professional climate has changed for women judges since Bird led the state high court. The public is now accustomed to women working as doctors, judges, corporate chiefs, and high-level politicians. Said Cantil-Sakauye, "In many ways I feel it was the wrong time" for Bird. "It doesn't seem like she had the tools to deal with all that was going on with the bench at that time, the acrimony. . . . Ultimately, it was the wrong timing for her, and I feel badly about that."[39]

The brutal campaign that cost Bird her job did not stop women from aspiring to the high court bench, governors from appointing them, or voters from electing or retaining them. Today, every state has had at least one woman supreme court justice, and judicial retention campaigns are equal-opportunity affairs; more than half of those challenged—and sometimes defeated—at the polls have been white men. And yet Bird's experience remains extraordinarily significant.

In 1982, four years before the election that removed her from the bench, she penned an article for the *Catholic University Law Review* in which she bemoaned the "instant society" where judges were pressured to make decisions aimed at pleasing the populace. She foresaw a future both depressing and inevitable. "As part of this process of serving up images," she wrote, "form often is exalted over substance, and oversimplification is mistaken for clarity of thought. The appearance of whatever is being packaged—be it food, news or even our political leaders—becomes far more important than the package's contents.

"Faced with such formidable obstacles, judges may well come to view any potentially unpopular decisions . . . as threats to their careers. . . . It is my hope that judges will be able to withstand these enormous pressures in the years ahead. However, that will not be a simple task. It is easy to be popular; it is difficult to be just. . . . Unfortunately, courage has become a devalued currency in the instant society. The coin of that realm is image and speed, and those who would place principle above expediency often must pay dearly for that choice."[40]

NOTES

INTRODUCTION

1. Paul Redinger, "The Politics of Judging," *American Bar Association Journal*, April 1, 1987, 54.
2. Faludi, *Backlash*, 11.
3. Maura Dolan, "Rose Bird's Quest for Obscurity," *Los Angeles Times*, November 15, 1995, A1.
4. John Balzar and Dan Morain, "Politically Reluctant Bird Hops aboard Campaign Wagon," *Los Angeles Times*, July 4, 1985, A1. *CBS Evening News*, May 21, 1986, accessed via YouTube. Anchor Dan Rather featured Rose Bird in a three-minute segment.
5. Nathan Crabbe, "Former Iowa Chief Justices Discusses Influence of Special Interest Groups," *Gainesville (IA) Sun*, September 10, 2012, accessed at Gainesville.com.
6. Sandra Day O'Connor, "Fair and Independent Courts: A Conference on the State of the Judiciary," presented to the Conference on the State of the Judiciary, sponsored by Georgetown Law and the American Law Institute, September 28–29, 2006.
7. Bert Brandenburg, "Justice for Sale: How Elected Judges Became a Threat to American Democracy," *Politico*, September 1, 2014, accessed at www.politico.com/magazine/story/2014/09/elected-judges.
8. Wiseman, "So You Want to Stay a Judge," 643.
9. Patt Morrison, "Bird Was Quixotic, Courageous, and a Little Too Naïve," *Los Angeles Times*, December 6, 1999, A3.

I. THE FIRST WOMAN

1. Cooper, "Rose Bird: The Last Interview," 38.

2. Cynthia Gorney, "Rose Bird and the Court of Conflict: California's Chief Justice, Embattled over a Reconfirmation Vote," *Washington Post*, April 8, 1986, C1.

3. Gorney, "Rose Bird and the Court of Conflict," C1.

4. Twelfth Census of the United States (1900), New Jersey, Belleville Township, Roll 969, 8B. Harry was married to Charlotte and listed three children, Samuel, Lottie, and Harry. Samuel does not appear on any subsequent census form. Thirteenth Census of the United States (1910), Essex County, New Jersey, Roll T624_882, B9. The form lists two sons, Robert and Harry, and a daughter, Lottie. In 1920 Harry was listed as still married to Charlotte, with Robert, Lottie, and James as his children. No mention was made of a son named Harry. Fourteenth Census of the United States (1920), Essex County, New Jersey, Roll T625_1030, 9B.

5. World War I Draft Cards, 1917–1918, Roll 1712104, Draft Board number 5.

6. Fifteenth Census of the United States (1930), Manhattan, New York, Roll 1581, 19A.

7. Sixteenth Census of the United States, Roll T627_112, 19B, lists the Birds with three children: Jack, 9; Philip, 4; and Rose, 3. FamilySearch.org shows an infant daughter, unnamed, who died in infancy in 1931.

8. Harry Bird is buried in Tempe's Double Butte Cemetery, according to information on the cemetery's website. No birth year is noted, but his age is cited as eighty.

9. Philip Bird, Rose's older brother, began making online inquiries seeking information about his father in the late 1990s. He included the information that his father might have used different names, suggesting that Harry Bird was not always forthright when providing information about himself. Ancestry.com Message Boards, June 1, 1999.

10. Frank Clifford, "Bird Rises Above the Fray in a Visit Down Under," *Los Angeles Times*, April 26, 1986, C3.

11. Lamson, *In the Vanguard*, 193. Anne Bird offered extensive observations about her daughter, the last time she did so for publication. Lamson's book reinforces the family's sensitivity about Harry Bird. The author noted that Harry's ill health made his wife's employment necessary. The source of this information is unclear, since it is not attributed to anyone.

12. Many writers have focused on the post–World War II gender ideology. They include Coontz, *The Way We Never Were*; May, *Homeward Bound*; Cohen, *A Consumers' Republic*. Cuordileone discusses some consequences of deviating from this ideology in *Manhood and American Political Culture in the Cold War*.

13. Lamson, *In the Vanguard*, 193.

14. I have found no indication that either Jack or Philip Bird moved with their

mother and sister to New York, though media accounts of Rose Bird's upbringing imply that they did. Jack Bird would have been twenty years old in 1950 and Philip sixteen. Classmates of Bird's recall her living with her mother; there is no mention of siblings. Yearbooks from Sea Cliff do not show Philip attending the high school there. Neither man has ever given interviews or discussed their sister for publication. Jack Bird died in 2003.

15. Author email interviews with Wallace Kaufman and Edwin Gauld, July and August 2015. Kaufman moved to Sea Cliff in 1947 and grew up there. He did not know Rose Bird, but he described the town, its ambience, and its residents. Gauld, another former resident, discussed the racial and class composition of the town.

16. Author email correspondence with Edwin Gauld, August 2015.

17. Cliffonian Yearbook, 1954, 63. Etiquette writers, including Emily Post, recommended that widows continue to use their husband's entire name, while continuing to use the designation "Mrs." Meanwhile, divorcées should use the designation "Mrs.," followed by part or all of their given name and their husband's last name.

18. Lamson, *In the Vanguard*, 194.

19. Betty Liddick, "First Interview with Chief Justice Bird," *Los Angeles Times*, April 22, 1977, F1.

20. Cliffonian Yearbook, 1954, 11. Fifty-four seniors graduated in Bird's class. Sea Cliff High School shared facilities with lower grades K–8 as well.

21. Cliffonian Yearbook, 1954, 11.

22. Cliffonian Yearbook, 1954, 25.

23. Gene Blake, "Rose Bird: A New Dimension, Expected to Have Wide Impact on High Court," *Los Angeles Times*, February 13, 1977, A3.

24. Lamson, *In the Vanguard*, 194.

25. Lamson, *In the Vanguard*, 193.

26. Gorney, "Rose Bird and the Court of Conflict," C1.

27. Frank Clifford, "Lone Justice," *Los Angeles Times*, October 5, 1986.

28. Stephen Cook and K. Connie Kang, "Facing Judgement: The Rose Bird Court," *San Francisco Examiner*, January 5, 1986. The story is included in the collection on Bird's retention election at the California State Library, Sacramento CA.

29. Cairns, *Front-Page Women Journalists*, 2–4.

30. Rapoport, *California Dreaming*, 62.

31. Lamson, *In the Vanguard*, 195.

32. William Endicott, "Agricultural Chief Is No Farmer," *Los Angeles Times*, January 22, 1975, A18.

33. Gordon Winton, oral history interview conducted by Enid H. Douglas, 2004,

Oral History Program, Claremont Graduate School, for the California State Archives Oral History Program.

34. Boalt Hall class of 1965 roster, University of California, Berkeley; Rapoport, *California Dreaming*, 69; Martin and Jurik, "Women Entering the Legal Profession."
35. Heyman, "Tribute," 805.
36. Only the U.S. Supreme Court, the California Supreme Court, and the U.S. Court of Appeals counted as "prestigious," according to these criteria. Clerking for U.S. district courts, other state supreme courts, or on state intermediate appellate courts were not sufficient.
37. Bird, "3rd Year Girls Lament."
38. Roma Connable, "The Case for Girls in Law," *Mademoiselle*, May 1965, 190; Harris and Cohen, *Women Trailblazers of California*, 119–21.
39. The information about Bird's relationship with an Englishman comes from a college friend who met Bird on the Long Island Railroad when both traveled to Long Island University. The friend also recalled that Bird had been close to a man in her graduating class at Long Island University, though she did not specify the nature of the relationship. Email interview with Edwin Gauld, August 2015.
40. Lamson, *In the Vanguard*, 194.
41. Harry Bird's oldest daughter, Lottie, also never married and lived with her mother, Charlotte, until the latter's death in New Jersey in 1950.
42. Lamson, *In the Vanguard*, 193, 196. Philip Bird graduated from Santa Clara Law School in 1975 and went to work in Sacramento as a deputy state attorney.
43. Bowman, "Women in the Legal Profession," 10–12. Some very prominent female politicians graduated from law school in the 1960s, including former attorney general Janet Reno (Harvard, 1963); former Colorado congresswoman Patricia Schroeder (Harvard, 1964); and former North Carolina senator Elizabeth Dole (Harvard, 1964). All had difficulty finding jobs upon graduation.
44. Rice, *Defender of the Damned*.
45. Biff Barson, "More Clerkships," *The Writ*, n.d.
46. Blake, "Rose Bird: A New Dimension," A3.
47. Blake, "Rose Bird: A New Dimension," A3.
48. Lamson, *In the Vanguard*, 197.
49. Blake, "Rose Bird: A New Dimension."
50. Edwin Chen, "Rose Bird: A Study in Contrasts," *Los Angeles Times*, May 20, 1982, B1.
51. J. Anthony Kline, oral history interview (OH 92-7) conducted by Germaine La Farge, California Oral History Project, California State Archives, Sacramento. Kline later became a leading justice on the California Court of Appeal.
52. California v. Krivda, 409 U.S. 33 (1972). The case involved a search for marijuana.

Earlier the same year, the California Supreme Court had abolished the death penalty in the state, citing the California Constitution's ban on cruel *or* unusual punishment, which differed from the U.S. Constitution's proscription on cruel *and* unusual punishment. The U.S. high court followed suit nationally four months after California.

53. Clifford, "Lone Justice."
54. Cook and Kang, "Facing Judgement."
55. Clifford, "Lone Justice."
56. *State of California Commission on Judicial Performance Hearing in the Matter of Commission Proceedings Concerning the Seven Justices of the Supreme Court of California*, 1392 (June 26, 1979) (testimony of Rose Bird).
57. Amsterdam made this comment in an oral history interview as part of the Rule of Law Oral History Project at Columbia University. Myron O. Farber interviewed Amsterdam between April 1 and April 9, 2009, in New York City, where Amsterdam worked as a law professor at Columbia.
58. Cruden made his comments in "Learning a Passion for Law," 24.
59. Chen, "Rose Bird: A Study in Contrasts," B1.
60. Sugarman made his remarks at a memorial service for Bird in February 2000.
61. Cruden, "Learning a Passion for Law," 24.
62. Blake, "Rose Bird: A New Dimension."
63. Some sources on capital punishment in America include Banner, *The Death Penalty*; Bessler, *The Kiss of Death*; Bonner, *Anatomy of Injustice*; Cairns, *Proof of Guilt*; Cohen, *The Wrong Men*; and Dow, *The Autobiography of an Execution*. Evan Mandery's book *A Wild Justice* focuses significant attention on Anthony Amsterdam's role in temporarily ending capital punishment.
64. Blake, "Rose Bird: A New Dimension."
65. Edwin Chen, "Controversial Chief Justice," *Los Angeles Times*, May 20, 1982, B1.
66. Clifford, "Lone Justice."
67. Chen, "Rose Bird: A Study in Contrasts," B1.
68. Endicott, "Agriculture Chief Is No Farmer," A18.
69. Endicott, "Agriculture Chief Is No Farmer," A18.

2. A WOMAN IN CHARGE

1. William Endicott, "Brown Urged to Give Half of Posts to Women," *Los Angeles Times*, November 21, 1974, A24.
2. Robert Pack, "Brown Rides California Toward 'Revolution,'" *Los Angeles Times*, August 21, 1977, E1.
3. John Thurber, "Claire Dedrick, 74, Was Environmentalist, Member of Brown's Cabinet," *Los Angeles Times*, April 9, 2005, B1; Carlotta Mellon, oral history

interview conducted by Enid Douglass, 1990, Claremont Graduate School, for the California State Archives State Government Oral History Program, 54, 153.

4. Rapoport, *California Dreaming*, 57.

5. Edmund G. ("Pat") Brown has been the subject of numerous biographies. The best is probably Rarick's *California Rising*; Shirley Hufstedler discussed her judicial appointment in an oral history for the California Appellate Court Legacy Project, April 17, 2007.

6. Lamson, *In the Vanguard*, 200.

7. Rarick, *California Rising*, 63.

8. Rarick, *California Rising*, 57.

9. Pat Brown personally opposed the death penalty but feared the political consequences of commuting Chessman's death sentence. The case became a cause célèbre because Chessman had not committed murder, but he had been convicted of kidnapping under the state's "Little Lindbergh" law. At the time of Chessman's 1948 conviction, the time from trial and conviction to execution usually took from a few months to a year or two. But his trial had been riddled with problems that led to continual stays of execution. During his dozen years on death row, Chessman wrote four books and continually denied guilt. Brown allowed his execution to go forward, and in May 1960 he died in San Quentin's gas chamber.

10. Rapoport, *California Dreaming*, 113, 159.

11. The allegation that Brown was homosexual continued to be raised in political circles through the early years of his first term as governor, until journalists began to write about his relationships with celebrities. They included rock star Linda Ronstadt. Brown finally married when he was in his sixties.

12. Garcia, *From the Jaws of Victory*, 131.

13. Rarick, *California Rising*, 131.

14. Rarick, *California Rising*, 120–21.

15. Stolz, *Judging Judges*, 14. Stolz talks about the growing influence of urban areas in California.

16. Terkel, *Hard Times*, 71.

17. Levy, *Cesar Chavez*, 10.

18. The Taft-Hartley Act, passed by Congress over President Harry Truman's veto in the late 1940s, also specifically forbade secondary boycotts.

19. Garcia, *From the Jaws of Victory*, 128.

20. Willhoite, "The Story of the California Agricultural Labor Relations Act."

21. Eugene Chappie, oral history interview conducted by Donald B. Seney, 1990, California State University, Sacramento, for the California State Archives, State Government Oral History Project, 209.

22. Endicott, "Agriculture Chief Is No Farmer."

23. Lou Cannon, "Nancy Reagan, an Influential and Protective First Lady, Dies at 94," *New York Times*, March 7, 2016, 1.

24. Vuich came from a farming family in the San Joaquin Valley. She started her career as a tax accountant and stunned most observers in 1976 when she defeated a Republican incumbent. Three women served in the state assembly in 1975, all Democrats: Pauline Davis, Teresa Hughes, and Leona Egelode.

25. In 2014 Jerry Brown is again governor of California. In an interview during his 2010 campaign for a third term, he told one reporter: "I've got a wife. I don't try to close down the bars in Sacramento like I used to." Jesse McKinley, "Gaffe Puts Jerry Brown, Poetic and Profane, Under Fire Again," *New York Times*, October 9, 2010, A1.

26. Endicott, "Agriculture Chief Is No Farmer."

27. Lazzareschi, "Rose Bird, Criminal Lawyer," 88.

28. "Short-Handled Hoe Banned in California," 6.

29. Murray, "The Abolition of El Cortito," 26–39.

30. "Use of Short-Handled Hoe Banned by State," *Los Angeles Times*, April 8, 1975, A20; Bruns, *Cesar Chavez*, 93.

31. Willhoite, "The Story of the California Agriculture Labor Relations Act."

32. Jacques Levy, interview with LeRoy Chatfield for a book to be titled *Cesar Chavez' Guide to a Just Society*. Levy died before the book could be published. Information on meetings hosted by Jerry Brown is from Ferriss and Sandoval, *The Fight in the Fields*, 199.

33. Bion Milton Gregory, oral history interview conducted by Paul Ferrell, 2004, Oral History Program, Center for California Studies California State University, Sacramento, for the California State Archives State Government Oral History Program, 108–11.

34. Clifford, "Lone Justice."

35. Clifford, "Lone Justice."

36. Rapoport, *California Dreaming*, 159.

37. Rapoport, *California Dreaming*, 164.

38. Chappie, oral history interview, 209.

39. Clifford, "Lone Justice."

40. Kline, oral history interview, 70–73.

41. Senate Bill 813, Extraordinary Session 3, California State Senate Industrial Relations Committee, May 6, 1975, California State Archives, Sacramento.

42. John Dunlap, oral history interview conducted by Carole Hicke, 1988, Regional Oral History Office, University of California, Berkeley, for the California State Archives, State Government Oral History Program, 130.

43. Harry Bernstein, "Passage of Farm Labor Bill Predicted by Brown Aide," *Los Angeles Times*, April 12, 1975, G1; Harry Bernstein, "Agreement Reached on Farm Labor Bill," *Los Angeles Times*, May 20, 1975, B3; Harry Bernstein, "Senate Panel OKs Brown's Farm Bill," *Los Angeles Times*, May 8, 1975; D1; Wallace Turner, "California Farm Workers Law Passed," *New York Times*, May 30, 1975, 29.

44. Turner, "California Farm Workers Law Passed," 29.

45. California Labor Code Section 1140, Chapter 1 1975, Third Extraordinary Session, An Act to Add Part 3.5 to Division 2 of the Labor Code.

46. Keppel, "The Bitter Harvest," 377; Lamson, *In the Vanguard*, 202. Brown won three primaries—California, Nevada, and Maryland.

47. "Citizen Members Sought for Farm Market Boards," *Los Angeles Times*, June 10, 1975, B25.

48. "From Plant Pathologist to Vice President of Agriculture and Natural Resources at the University of California, 1947–86." James B. Kendrick, oral history interview conducted by Ann Lage, September 2, 1987, Regional Oral History Office, University of California, Berkeley, 216.

49. "Short-Handled Hoe Banned in California," 6.

50. Edwin Chen, "Dispute over Book on Bird Raises Issue of Writer's Bias," *Los Angeles Times*, December 13, 1981, A3.

51. Adriana Gianturco, oral history interview conducted by George Petershagen, 1994, California State University, Sacramento, for the California State Archives, State Government Oral History Program, 148.

52. Lazzareschi, "Rose Bird, Criminal Lawyer," 87.

53. In 1978 journalist Betty Rollin wrote *First You Cry*, possibly the earliest book about surviving breast cancer.

54. Orville Schell, *Brown*, 66.

55. Lazzareschi, "Rose Bird, Criminal Lawyer," 89.

56. "Magazine Gives Carter List of Eligible 'Ms.'-es," *Los Angeles Times*, November 22, 1976, A2. Carter did not choose Bird, but he had three women cabinet members: Juanita Morris Kreps as commerce secretary; Patricia Roberts Harris as secretary of health and human services; and Shirley Hufstedler as secretary of education.

57. Gene Blake, "Brown Picks Woman, Black for High Court," *Los Angeles Times*, February 13, 1977, A1.

58. Mellon, oral history interview, 153.

59. "Woman Chosen to Head Court," *New York Times*, February 14, 1977, 31.

60. Wallace Turner, "Brown Nominee for Chief Justice Sparks Partisan Fight in California," *New York Times*, February 24, 1977, 16.

61. Peter Bonventre and William J. Cook, "Ms. Chief Justice," *Newsweek*, February 28, 1977, 70.
62. "Woman Chosen to Head Court," 31.
63. "Rose Bird Confirmed," *San Francisco Chronicle*, March 27, 1977, 1.
64. The phrase "group called women" comes from Cott, *The Grounding of Modern Feminism*, 4.
65. Bonventre and Cook, "Ms. Chief Justice," 70.

3. THE MOST INNOVATIVE JUDICIARY

1. California Civil Code, Sections 60 and 69. California had barred interracial marriages since its beginning as a state in 1850.
2. Perez v. Sharp, 32 Cal.2d 711 (1948). W. G. Sharp was the county clerk for Los Angeles County. Lawrence E. Davies, "Mixed Marriages Upheld by Court," *New York Times*, October 2, 1948; "State High Court Rules Out Race as Barrier to Marriage," *Los Angeles Times*, October 2, 1948.
3. "Chief Justice Traynor," *New York Times*, May 17, 1983.
4. Starr, *Embattled Dreams*, 256. Radin backed state employees who refused to name names to a state assembly committee investigating communism.
5. "Rejected as State Justice," *Los Angeles Times*, July 22, 1940, A3.
6. Field, *Activism in Pursuit of the Public Interest*, xvi, 1.
7. Buntin, *L.A. Noir*, 212–13.
8. People v. Cahan, 44 Cal. 2d. 434 (1955).
9. Frank Clifford, "Stature of Honored Court Tested Amid Bird Debate," *Los Angeles Times*, September 14, 1986, A1.
10. People v. Dorado, 62 Cal. 2d 338 (1965). *Dorado* was particularly significant because the California high court ruled that suspects needed to be advised of their right to counsel even if they had not asked for an attorney. Earlier cases, most notably *Escobedo v. Illinois*, dealt with defendants whose requests to have attorneys present during questioning had been denied. The U.S. Supreme Court followed the same reasoning as *Dorado* in the Arizona case *Miranda v. Arizona* (1966).
11. People v. Belous, 71 Cal. 2d 438 (1969). In 1967 the California legislature enacted the Therapeutic Abortion Act, signed by Governor Reagan, which allowed doctors to perform abortions up to twenty-one weeks if the pregnancy came from rape or incest, or if it endangered the health of the mother; "Abortion Statutes: Are they Unconstitutional Per Se?," 444.
12. "California Court May Curb Abortion Prosecutions," *New York Times*, September 14, 1969, 66.
13. California v. Anderson, 6 Cal. 3d 628 (1972).
14. Marvin v. Marvin, 18 Cal. 3d 660 (1976). The court broke new legal ground with

its decision. Earlier courts had ruled against unmarried plaintiffs who sought enforcement of contractual agreements.

15. "Trailblazing Bench: California High Court Often Points the Way for Judges Elsewhere," *Wall Street Journal*, July 20, 1972.

16. Daryl Lembke, "State Supreme Court Faces New Barrage," *Los Angeles Times*, January 28, 1968, EB; "Chief Justice Traynor."

17. Lembke, "State Supreme Court Faces New Barrage," EB.

18. "Justice Assails Parker Raps at Cahan Ruling," *Los Angeles Times*, June 12, 1956, B1; "Impeaching of Traynor," *Los Angeles Times*, October 3, 1965, B1.

19. Richard Bergholz, "Knight Assails 4 Justices of California High Court," *Los Angeles Times*, July 25, 1965, B1.

20. Led by former California governor Earl Warren, the U.S. Supreme Court tackled a variety of controversial issues in the 1950s and 1960s, mostly related to civil rights. In 1954 for example, the court outlawed school segregation in *Brown v. Board of Education*. The following year it agreed with the U.S. district court ruling *Browder v. Gayle*, which ruled Alabama's segregated busing unconstitutional.

21. Robert E. Formichi, "Reports of Cases Determined in the Supreme Court of the State of California," Volume 37-3d, San Francisco, 1986, 958–59.

22. McGirr, *Suburban Warriors*, 205.

23. Burt A. Folkart, "Paul Peek Dies; Served in 3 Branches of Government," *Los Angeles Times*, April 9, 1987, C3.

24. Serrano v. Priest, 5 Cal. 3d 584 (1971). The case went through several iterations. Following the 1971 state supreme court ruling, the U.S. Supreme Court weighed in, ruling in a Texas case that using property taxes to finance schools was not unconstitutional. The California high court responded by citing the equal protection guarantee in the state constitution, an approach the U.S. high court deemed legitimate.

25. John D. Weaver, "Mister Chief Justice Traynor," *Los Angeles Times*, December 11, 1966, W28.

26. Thompson, "Judicial Retention Elections and Judicial Method."

27. Zeitlin v. Arneberg, 59 Cal. 2d 901 (1963). Zeitlin was the bookseller who wanted to sell *Tropic of Cancer*, and Arneberg was the city attorney of Los Angeles.

28. Bird, "Justice Mathew O. Tobriner," 162; the quote from Tobriner comes from Balabanian, "Justice Was More Than His Title," 880.

29. Cross-filing emerged as part of a much larger agenda designed to weaken political parties, which, progressives believed, had led to corruption and too much power held in too few hands. Enacted in 1919, cross-filing had garnered strong criticism by the 1950s, particularly from Democrats trying to regain power after ten years of Earl Warren's governorship and six years of his somewhat

less moderate successor, Goodwin Knight. Culver and Syer discuss cross-filing and its implications in *Power and Politics in California*.

30. Both McGirr's *Suburban Warriors* and Schuparra's *Triumph of the Right* place Southern California front and center in the rise of conservative politics in the post–World War II period. Orange County played perhaps the most significant role in this phenomenon, since it experienced explosive growth between the 1950s and 1980s. Though part of the extensive region was urban, until near the end of the twentieth century much of the land was covered by ever expanding suburbs, populated almost entirely by whites who resented social justice movements and feared "encroachment" by minority populations. Orange County is much less homogenous today and thus less reliably conservative.

31. Maury Beam, "Seven Men Guard John Doe's Rights," *Los Angeles Times*, November 8, 1954, 34; "Jesse Carter, 70, Justice on Coast," *New York Times*, March 16, 1970, 11.

32. Address by Mathew Tobriner to the meeting of California Attorneys for Criminal Justice, San Francisco, November 15, 1980.

33. Philip Hager, "Justice Defends Court's Ban on Death Penalty," *Los Angeles Times*, September 21, 1972, A3.

34. Banner, *The Death Penalty*, 264.

35. Dwight D. Eisenhower, like Ronald Reagan with Donald Wright, grew to regret choosing Earl Warren to head the U.S. Supreme Court. Within months of his appointment, Warren began leading the court toward rulings that supported the rights of minorities and criminal defendants.

36. Governor Jerry Brown made seven supreme court appointments in his first two terms in office, from 1975 to 1983. He began his third term in 2011 and thus far has made three appointments.

37. Medsger, *Framed*, 41–42.

38. Donald R. Wright, "A View of Reagan and the California Courts," interview conducted by Harvey P. Grody, 1984, for the California Government History Documentation Project: The Reagan Era, Oral History Program, California State University, Fullerton, 23.

39. Jerry Belcher, "Justice McComb, Forced Off the Court in '77, Dies," *Los Angeles Times*, September 7, 1981, A3.

40. Stanley Mosk, oral history interview conducted by Germaine LaBerge, 1998, Regional Oral History Office, University of California, Berkeley, for the California State Archives State Government Oral History Project, 25.

41. Many sources note the Bakke decision in Brown's appointment of Bird. They include Braitman and Uelmen's *Justice Stanely Mosk*. And Mosk himself seems to have believed this. Brown, however, has refuted this assertion.

42. Bakke v. Regents of the University of California, 18 Cal. 3d 34 (1976). Though the

U.S. Supreme Court did not agree with Mosk and ruled in favor of affirmative action in 1978, Bakke ultimately won admission to the medical school. Upon graduation, he became an anesthesiologist.

43. John Jacobs, "Rose Bird Paid the Price for Jerry Brown's Mistake," *San Francisco Examiner*, December 15, 1999, A29.

44. Mary McGrory, "What Clark Is Not: A Careerist, an Academic, an Ideologue; NICE," *Washington Post*, January 12, 1982, A3.

45. Philip Hager, "Clark Confirmed to High Court Despite Wright's Objection," *Los Angeles Times*, May 4, 1973, A1. The Commission on Judicial Appointments has only rejected one nominee, Max Radin.

46. The National Center for State Courts (NCSC) maintains a website that lists methods of judicial selection in all fifty states. It also includes news updates tracking changes, which occur with some regularity.

47. Stolz and Stolz, "Are the Voters Forcing Judges to Act Like Politicians?," 296–97.

48. Stolz, *Judging Judges*, 10–31. Stolz discussed some of the factors that led to changes in how judicial elections came to be contested in California.

49. Ed Meagher, "Death Penalty Ban Assailed by Reagan; State to Appeal," *Los Angeles Times*, February 19, 1972, 1.

50. Evan Mandery's book *A Wild Justice* offers a close and extensive view of the politics of capital punishment in the 1970s.

51. Robert Rawitch, "Prop. 17—Gut Issue for California Voters," *Los Angeles Times*, October 22, 1972, B1.

52. Winton, oral history interview, 166.

53. Gene Blake, "Cal. Death Penalty Upset," *Los Angeles Times*, December 7, 1976.

54. Jerry Gillam, "Brown Vows to Enforce Death Penalty Law," *Los Angeles Times*, February 23, 1977.

55. Mosk, oral history interview, 39.

56. Gene Blake and Jerry Gillam, "Pasadenan Appointed State High Court Chief," *Los Angeles Times*, April 7, 1970, 3.

57. In *Framed*, Medsger discusses the animosity that grew between Ronald Reagan and Chief Justice Donald Wright.

58. Grodin, *In Pursuit of Justice*, 5–13.

59. Mosk, oral history interview, 9–10.

60. Formichi, *Reports of Cases Determined in the Supreme Court*, 958–59.

61. Weaver, "Mr. Chief Justice Traynor."

62. Wright, "A View of Reagan and the California Courts."

4. BECOMING CHIEF JUSTICE

1. Gene Blake, "Judge Panel Hears Rose Bird," *Los Angeles Times*, March 8, 1977, 1.

2. Blake, "Judge Panel Hears Rose Bird," 1.

3. "Woman Chosen to Head Court," *New York Times*, February 14, 1977, 31.

4. Wright, "A View of Reagan and the California Courts," 65–66.

5. William Endicott, "Brown Seeks Advance OK of Woman Chief Justice," *Los Angeles Times*, February 12, 1977, 1.

6. Mosk, oral history interview, 56. Much later, Mosk acknowledged that he would have disliked being chief justice. "I don't think I would have liked it," he told interviewer Germaine LaBerge, "because of the requirement that you be effective as an administrator."

7. Mosk, "Chief Justice Donald R. Wright," 225–26.

8. Wright, "A View of Reagan and the California Courts," 66.

9. Kang, "The Decline of California's Vendetta-Ridden Supreme Court," 346.

10. Kang, "The Decline of California's Vendetta-Ridden Supreme Court," 346.

11. Bonventre and Cook, "Ms. Chief Justice," 70.

12. Gene Blake, "GOP Opposition to Rose Bird Appointment as Chief Justice Grows in Legislature," *Los Angeles Times*, February 19, 1977, B1.

13. Wright, "A View of Reagan and the California Courts," 66.

14. "Opposition to Chief Justice Nominee Voiced," *Los Angeles Times*, February 16, 1977, D1; Turner, "Brown Nominee for Chief Justice Sparks Partisan Fight," 16.

15. Wallace Turner, "Coast Hearing Today on a Chief Justice," *New York Times*, March 7, 1977, 16.

16. Turner, "Brown Nominee for Chief Justice Sparks Partisan Fight," 16; Blake, "GOP Opposition to Rose Bird Appointment."

17. Peter J. Belton, "A Senior Staff Attorney Reflects on Four Decades with the California Supreme Court, 1960–2001, and a Lifetime with Disability," oral history interviews conducted by Germaine LaBerge, 1999–2001, Regional Oral History Office, Bancroft Library, University of California, Berkeley, 2003, 135.

18. Nathan Lewin, "Judicial Experience—How Valuable Is It Really?," *Los Angeles Times*, February 20, 1977, H3.

19. "State Agriculture Chief Quits," *Los Angeles Times*, January 5, 1977, D4.

20. Kline, oral history interview, 70–73.

21. Blake, "Rose Bird: A New Dimension," A3.

22. Hogan, *The Judicial Branch of State Government*, 175.

23. He also removed the Industrial Relations Department from the larger agency and made its director Don Vial a cabinet member. Within months, the newly reconstituted agency had been renamed the state Consumer Services Agency.

24. "Younger's Shocker on Rose Bird," *San Francisco Chronicle*, February 19, 1977, 1.

25. Evelle J. Younger, "Nomination of Rose Bird," *Los Angeles Times*, March 11, 1977, B6; Stolz, *Judging Judges*, 89.

26. George Skelton, "Younger 'Job Application' Form Sent to Rose Bird," *Los Angeles Times*, March 4, 1977, B1.

27. Grodin, *In Pursuit of Justice*, 55.

28. Harry Bernstein, "Bishop's Letter on Rose Bird Stirs Furor," *Los Angeles Times*, March 5, 1977, OC8.

29. Bernstein, "Bishop's Letter on Rose Bird," OC8.

30. Gene Blake, "Ex-Brown Aide Opposes Rose Bird for High Court," *Los Angeles Times*, February 24, 1977, B3.

31. Turner, "Brown Nominee for Chief Justice Sparks Partisan Fight."

32. Harry Bernstein, "2 Members Roughed Up, Farm Board Says," *Los Angeles Times*, October 1, 1975, B1.

33. Russell Chandler, "New Archbishop Often Outspoken," *Los Angeles Times*, July 17, 1985, 18.

34. Clifford, "Lone Justice."

35. Mahony eventually faced the same kind of pummeling negative publicity that Rose Bird experienced. In the 1970s and 1980s, he rose rapidly through the Catholic Church hierarchy, becoming archbishop of Los Angeles and then a cardinal. When the priest abuse scandal broke in the 1990s, Mahony claimed he had done everything possible to root out pedophile priests from his diocese. However, subsequent investigations unearthed evidence that, while Mahony may have privately agonized over the abuse, he did little to stop it. Paul Conrad's cartoon is mentioned in Lamson, *In the Vanguard*, 189.

36. Lillie brushed off the suggestion that gender had played a role in her "unqualified" rating, but others believed it played a significant one. Myrna Oliver, "Mildred Lillie, 87; Appeals Court Justice, Pioneer in Legal Field," *Los Angeles Times*, October 29, 2002, A2.

37. Brazil, "Why the ALRB Is Under Constant Attack," 195.

38. Bernstein, "Bishop's Letter on Rose Bird."

39. Kenney, *Gender and Justice*, 149–59.

40. Resnick, "On the Bias," 1878.

41. Medsger, *Framed*, 15–16.

42. Hager, "Clark Confirmed to High Court," 1; Wright, "A View of Reagan and the California Courts," 20–21.

43. Bonventre and Cook, "Ms. Chief Justice."

44. Clifford, "Lone Justice." Ken Maddy, oral history interview (OH 2001-2) conducted by Donald Seney, 1999, Oral History Program, Center for California Studies, California State University, Sacramento, for the California State Archives State Government Oral History Program, 411.

45. Skelton, "Younger 'Job Application' Form Sent to Rose Bird."

46. Gene Blake, "Bar Group Backs Rose Bird for High Court," *Los Angeles Times*, March 2, 1977, B26.

47. Phil Gibson, "Recollections of a Chief Justice of the California Supreme Court," interview conducted by Gabrielle Morris, 1980, Governmental History Project, Goodwin Knight/Edmund Brown Sr. Era, Regional History Office, University of California, Berkeley.

48. Rose Bird's remarks appeared in a booklet issued by the California Supreme Court, "In Memoriam: Honorable Phil S. Gibson," June 7, 1984, 955.

49. Wallace Turner, "Coast Court Nominee Defends Her Record," *New York Times*, March 8, 1977, 17.

50. Gene Blake, "Rose Bird Testifies before Judicial Panel," *Los Angeles Times*, March 8, 1977, B1.

51. Gene Blake, "Non-lawyers to Join Bar Board," *Los Angeles Times*, September 22, 1975, B1.

52. Gene Blake, "Non-Lawyers on State Bar: A Year of Trial," *Los Angeles Times*, September 17, 1977, 14.

53. Blake, "Rose Bird Testifies before Judicial Panel."

54. "Younger's Shocker on Rose Bird."

55. Blake, "Rose Bird Testifies before Judicial Panel."

56. Gene Blake, "Rose Bird OKd as Chief Justice," *Los Angeles Times*, March 12, 1977, A1.

57. Blake, "Rose Bird OKd as Chief Justice."

58. Blake, "Rose Bird OKd as Chief Justice."

59. "Younger's Shocker on Bird."

60. Blake, "Rose Bird OKd as Chief Justice."

61. Blake, "Rose Bird OKd as Chief Justice."

62. "Rose Bird Confirmed," *San Francisco Chronicle*, March 27, 1977, 1.

63. People v. Hall (1854). The case determined that Chinese people could not testify against whites in California legal cases. Using tortured reasoning, the judge declared Chinese to be similar to "Indians." Since Indians, people of mixed race, and African Americans could not testify in trials, the decision meant that Chinese could not either.

64. "Rose Bird Sworn In as Chief Justice," *Los Angeles Times*, March 27, 1977, A3.

65. "Rose Bird Sworn In as Chief Justice," A3.

66. Medsger, *Framed*, 52.

67. "Rose Bird Sworn In as Chief Justice," A3.

68. "Rose Bird Sworn In as Chief Justice," A3.

69. Medsger, *Framed*, 54.

5. HAIL TO THE CHIEF

1. Liddick, "First Interview with Chief Justice Bird," F1.
2. Liddick, "First Interview with Chief Justice Bird."
3. *Commission on Judicial Performance Hearing*, 1521 (testimony of Rose Bird).
4. Liddick, "First Interview with Chief Justice Bird."
5. *Commission on Judicial Performance Hearing*, 1521 (testimony of Rose Bird).
6. Both former chief justice Donald Wright and staff attorney Peter J. Belton discussed Roger Traynor in oral histories. Wright noted that Traynor took the most interesting cases for himself. Wright, "A View of Reagan and the California Courts." Belton made his comments in "A Senior Staff Attorney Reflects," 135.
7. Braitman and Uelmen, *Justice Stanley Mosk*, 186.
8. Braitman and Uelmen, *Justice Stanley Mosk*, 187.
9. Stolz, *Judging Judges*, 115–16.
10. Jeffrey Toobin, *The Nine*, 29. Woodward and Armstrong's *The Brethren* reveals both Burger and Douglas as venal, petty, and arrogant.
11. Medsger, *Framed*, 55.
12. Medsger, *Framed*, 53–58.
13. Peter J. Belton, "A Senior Staff Attorney Reflects," 135.
14. Medsger, *Framed*, 57.
15. Medsger, *Framed*, 58; Stolz, *Judging Judges*, 109; Vile, *Great American Judges*, 69.
16. Kleps, "A Tribute to Chief Justice Donald R. Wright," 683.
17. Kleps, "A Tribute to Chief Justice Donald R. Wright," 683.
18. Joy Horowitz, "An Ex-Judge Asks: Who Writes Law?," *Los Angeles Times*, August 6, 1980, H1.
19. Stolz, *Judging Judges*, 109–10.
20. Nancy Baltad, "Job Equality for Women Still Lags, Rose Bird Says," *Los Angeles Times*, April 17, 1977, A2.
21. Stolz, *Judging Judges*, 109.
22. Bird's comments about the table are from *Commission on Judicial Performance Hearing*, 1398; Medsger, *Framed*, 66.
23. California Appellate Court Legacy Project, Reminiscences of Justice Richard Abbe, Video Interview of Justice Steve Stone and Justice Arthur Gilbert, July 30, 2007, 4–5.
24. Medsger, *Framed*, 66.
25. Stolz, *Judging Judges*, 114.
26. Medsger, *Framed*, 67.
27. Belton, "A Senior Staff Attorney Reflects," 213.
28. Winton, oral history interview, 265–66.
29. Salzman, "Second-Hand Rose," 157–59.

30. Frank Newman, oral history interview conducted by Carole Hicke, 1989–91, Regional Oral History Office, University of California, Berkeley, for the California State Archives State Government Oral History Program, 140–45; Newman's focus on human rights is discussed in Braitman and Uelmen's *Justice Stanley Mosk*.

31. William Endicott, "Personal Hostilities Tear at Supreme Court Fabric," *Los Angeles Times*, November 23, 1978, 1.

32. Endicott, "Personal Hostilities Tear at Supreme Court Fabric," 1; Medsger, *Framed*, 64.

33. Medsger, *Framed*, 251.

34. Gene Blake, "A Chiding Word from Ms. Bird," *Los Angeles Times*, October 7, 1977, A3.

35. Newman, oral history interview, 153.

36. Belton, "A Senior Staff Attorney Reflects," 96–97.

37. California Supreme Court Historical Society, "In Memoriam: Honorable Rose Elizabeth Bird, 1936–1999," *CSCHS Newsletter*, March 6, 2000.

38. Stolz discussed the process of vote-taking in *Judging Judges*.

39. Belton, "A Senior Staff Attorney Reflects," 97–102.

40. Bailey v. Superior Court, 19 Cal. 3d. 970 (1977).

41. Varjabedian v. Madera, 20 Cal. 3d. 285 (1977).

42. Bailey v. Superior Court, 19 Cal. 3d. 970 (1977).

43. Stolz, *Judging Judges*, 44.

44. McGirr's *Suburban Warriors* details the rise of conservatism as a force, particularly in Southern California.

45. William Endicott, "Media Blitz Against Chief Justice Bird Planned," *Los Angeles Times*, September 15, 1978, B3; Stolz, *Judging Judges*, 49–50.

46. William Endicott, "Rose Bird: Prop. 13 Adds Fuel to Fire," *Los Angeles Times*, June 20, 1978.

47. Wahl ended up winning her retention election in 1978 and went on to serve more than two decades; Sturdevant, *Her Honor*. Kenney also discusses Wahl in *Gender and Justice*, 52–60.

48. Salzman, "Reviewing the Record," 254.

49. Jerry Brown did win reelection in a landslide, beating Evelle Younger by twenty points—56 percent to 36 percent. Minor party candidates made up the difference.

50. Brenda Farrington Myers, "Rose Bird and the Rule of Law" (master's thesis, California State University, Fullerton, 1991); Mellencamp v. Bank of America, 21 Cal. 3d. 943 (1978).

51. Tribe, "Trying California's Judges on Television," 1175.

52. Medsger, *Framed*, 77.

53. California Penal Code Section 12022.7 defines great bodily harm as more

substantial injuries than those ordinarily suffered by victims of specific crimes, including rape. It covered physical injuries, not emotional or financial ones.

54. People v. Caudillo, 21 Cal. 3d 562 (1978).

55. Jonathan Kirsch, "Rose Bird and the Politics of Rape," *New West*, July 31, 1978, 30.

56. Braitman and Uelmen, *Justice Stanley Mosk*, 192.

57. Because of a change in sentencing laws, Daniel Caudillo was released in fall 1978, several months before Richardson's prediction. Due to the high-profile nature of his case, he was soon re-arrested, and he remained in prison until 1982.

58. Endicott, "Rose Bird: Prop. 13 Adds Fuel to the Fire"; Stolz, *Judging Judges*, 30.

59. Stolz, *Judging Judges*, 30; Tom Wicker, "A 'New Revolution,'" *New York Times*, June 9, 1978, A27.

60. While known as the Proposition 13 case, its actual title was Amador Valley Joint Union High School District v. State Board of Equalization, 22 Cal. 3d 208 (1978). Over the decades, there have been many efforts to revise Proposition 13, but all have failed.

61. William Endicott, "State High Court Upholds Prop. 13," *Los Angeles Times*, September 23, 1978, A1.

62. Stolz, *Judging Judges*, 52–58; Lamson also discusses the Richardson-backed ad in *In the Vanguard*, 213.

63. Stolz, *Judging Judges*, 58.

64. William Endicott, "Three Groups Join in Backing Bird," *Los Angeles Times*, October 27, 1978, B3.

65. Stolz, *Judging Judges*, 58–62.

66. Stolz, *Judging Judges*, 52–62.

67. Stolz, *Judging Judges*, 60; "The Attacks on Rose Bird," *Los Angeles Times*, October 1, 1978, F4.

68. Stolz, *Judging Judges*, 60.

69. Stolz, *Judging Judges*, 52.

70. Robert Fairbanks, "Leaked Letter Hints Mosk May Not Back Rose Bird," *Los Angeles Times*, November 3, 1978, A3; William Endicott, "Justice Bird Speaks Out on Ouster Bid," *Los Angeles Times*, A1.

71. Fairbanks, "Leaked Letter," A3; Endicott, "Justice Bird Speaks Out," A1.

72. William Endicott and Robert Fairbanks, "Supreme Court Decision to Reverse Gun Law Reported," *Los Angeles Times*, November 7, 1978, A1.

73. Stolz, *Judging Judges*, 136–37.

74. Frank Richardson won 72 percent of the vote, Frank Newman won 65 percent, and Wiley Manuel won nearly 62 percent.

6. DISORDER IN THE COURT

1. Newman, oral history interview, 161–73.
2. Kang, "The Decline of California's vendetta-ridden Supreme Court," 343.
3. When the state supreme court heard oral arguments on *People v. Tanner* in February 1978, the author of the "use a gun" measure, George Deukmejian, was a state senator running for state attorney general. In November 1978 he was elected to that office.
4. People v. Tanner, 23 Cal. 3d 16 (1978).
5. Medsger, *Framed*, 109.
6. George Nicholson, Edwin Meese III, and William James, "Court Decisions, Practices Hamper Prosecutorial Efforts," *Los Angeles Daily Journal*, September 11, 1978; *Commission on Judicial Performance Hearing*, exhibit 427.
7. Stolz, *Judging Judges*, 124–25.
8. There were a few exceptions. In 1972 Associate Justice Marshall McComb let slip the information that the court was about to overturn the death penalty in California. The vote was 6–1 with McComb as the lone dissenter. He was, however, in the grip of senility when he revealed this information.
9. Stolz, *Judging Judges*, 126.
10. Stolz, *Judging Judges*, 129. Mosk denied ever speaking to reporters about the *Tanner* case.
11. McGrory, "What Clark Is Not," A3.
12. Michael Kennedy, "Clark Sees High Court's Credibility on Line," *Los Angeles Times*, December 1, 1978, A6; Maureen Dowd, "The Man with the President's Ear," *Time*, August 8, 1983, 27.
13. Wright, "A View of Reagan and the California Courts," 21.
14. Robert Fairbanks and William Endicott, "Dissent Critical of Rose Bird May Have Delayed Ruling," *Los Angeles Times*, November 15, 1978, B7.
15. Robert Fairbanks and William Endicott, "Justices Asked to Sign Statement in Gun Use Case," *Los Angeles Times*, November 16, 1978, 1.
16. Stolz, *Judging Judges*, 150.
17. Insults have continued to fly in the country's highest court. In June 2015, when Associate Justice Anthony Kennedy wrote the landmark decision legalizing same-sex marriage nationally, his colleague Antonin Scalia angrily characterized the opinion as "couched in a style that is as pretentious as it content is egotistic." Discussion of insulting language in earlier courts is contained in Robert Fairbanks, "Anatomy of a Duel: A Court amid Turmoil," *Los Angeles Times*, March 6, 1979, B1. Medsger talks about Cannon's interest in the California court in *Framed*, 51, 88.
18. Fairbanks, "Anatomy of a Duel."

19. *Commission on Judicial Performance Hearing*, exhibit 529.

20. Medsger, *Framed*, 95.

21. Tribe, "Trying California's Judges on Television," 1177.

22. Other cases included *Fox v. City of Los Angeles*, in which plaintiffs charged that a large cross displayed on the grounds of City Hall violated the separation of church and state. Because most of the hearing focused on *Tanner*, I have chosen to focus almost exclusively on that case.

23. William Endicott, "Public Inquiry OKd on Gun Law Ruling," *Los Angeles Times*, January 17, 1979, A5.

24. Stolz, *Judging Judges*, 177.

25. People v. Tanner, 23 Cal. 3d 16 (1978).

26. Philip Hager, "Court Upsets Mandatory Sentencing," *Los Angeles Times*, December 23, 1978, 1.

27. The decision to rehear the *Tanner* was unusual, but not unprecedented. Stanley Mosk also changed his vote in a 1982 case.

28. Hager, "Court Upsets Mandatory Sentencing."

29. Medsger, *Framed*, 107.

30. Stolz, *Judging Judges*, 269; Medsger, *Framed*, 108–9.

31. Medsger, *Framed*, 107.

32. Medsger, *Framed*, 115.

33. Medsger, *Framed*, 121.

34. *Commission on Judicial Performance Hearing*, 638 (June 21, 1979) (testimony of Mathew Tobriner).

35. *Commission on Judicial Performance Hearing*, 599–602 (June 21, 1979) (testimony of Mathew Tobriner).

36. Philip Hager, "Clark Suggested Delaying Tanner Ruling—Tobriner," *Los Angeles Times*, June 22, 1979, A20.

37. Wallace Turner, "Coast Court Member Questioned On Friendship With Chief Justice," *New York Times*, June 22, 1979, D15; Stolz, *Judging Judges*, 287.

38. *Commission on Judicial Performance Hearing*, 1672 (June 28, 1979) (testimony of Rose Bird).

39. *Commission on Judicial Performance Hearing*, 1419 (June 27, 1979) (testimony of Rose Bird).

40. *Commission on Judicial Performance Hearing*, 1617–27 (June 28, 1979) (testimony of Rose Bird).

41. *Commission on Judicial Performance Hearing*, 1617–21 (June 28, 1979) (testimony of Rose Bird. Bird argued that the *Caudillo* rape case dealt with legislative intent, while the *Tanner* dealt with the legislature's constitutional right to tell judges how to do their jobs.

42. Stolz, *Judging Judges*, 305.

43. Stolz, *Judging Judges*, 309.

44. Myrna Oliver, "Ms. Bird Cites Effort to Embarrass Her," *Los Angeles Times*, June 29, 1979, B3; Wallace Turner, "California Court's Chief Tells of Cautious Confrontation With Top Critic," *New York Times*, June 30, 1979, 45; Stolz, *Judging Judges*, 309–10.

45. *Commission on Judicial Performance Hearing*, 2172–84 (July 3, 1979) (testimony of William Clark).

46. *Commission on Judicial Performance Hearing*, 2214–56 (July 3, 1979) (testimony of William Clark).

47. *Commission on Judicial Performance Hearing*, 2184 (July 3, 1979) (testimony of William Clark).

48. Larry Stammer, "Has No Proof of Political Delay of Ruling, Clark Says," *Los Angeles Times*, July 10, 1979, B3; Wallace Turner, "California Panel Delays Decision On Action Against Chief Justice," *New York Times*, July 4, 1979, A9; Stolz, *Judging Judges*, 319–24.

49. *Commission on Judicial Performance Hearing*, 2507 (July 3, 1979) (testimony of William Clark).

50. Bella Stumbo, "Court Inquiry Degenerates Into a Disaster," *Los Angeles Times*, July 15, 1979, A3.

51. Stolz, *Judging Judges*, 317.

52. Belton, "A Senior Staff Attorney Reflects," 218.

53. Stumbo, "Court Inquiry Degenerates Into a Disaster."

54. Myrna Oliver, "Mosk Asks Court Order Excusing Him From Inquiry," *Los Angeles Times*, July 7, 1979, 1; Stolz, *Judging Judges*, 338.

55. Mosk v. Superior Court, 25 Cal. 3d 474 (1979) sought to have the subpoena quashed that ordered Mosk to testify. He later castigated the commission for gathering "irrelevant information." This included "corridor gossip among law clerks: and "the rankest type of hearsay." Mosk, "Chilling Judicial Independence," 2–3.

56. Stanley Mosk discussed the hearings and his successful effort to close them in Mosk, oral history interview, 58–59.

57. Fox v. City of Los Angeles, 22 Cal. 3d 792 (1978).

58. *Commission on Judicial Performance Hearing*, 1444 (June 27, 1979) (testimony of Rose Bird).

59. Stolz, *Judging Judges*, 314; Kang, "The Decline of California's Vendetta-Ridden Supreme Court," 346.

60. Medsger, *Framed*, 146–47.

61. Robert Fairbanks and Philip Hager, "Court Wasn't Exonerated, Judicial Panel Member Says," *Los Angeles Times*, November 7, 1979, B1.

62. Tom Goldstein, "Coast Inquiry Stirring Fear of Politicizing the Judiciary," *New York Times*, September 20, 1979, D22.

63. Gene Blake, "Rose Bird Outlines Judiciary Problem," *Los Angeles Times*, October 27, 1979, C1.

64. Philip Hager, "State Supreme Court Cleared," *Los Angeles Times*, November 6, 1979, A8; Fairbanks and Hager, "Court Wasn't Exonerated."

65. It is unclear what caused Stolz's antipathy for Bird. He said he did not remember her as a law student, but it is possible that he saw her as a negative influence in the Brown administration, or that he honestly saw traits in her that were not conducive to leading a body of equals.

66. William Endicott, "Rose Bird Demands Changes in Book on Court," *Los Angeles Times*, May 16, 1981, A3.

67. Medsger, *Framed*, 1, 18.

68. Medsger, *Framed*, xii.

69. Newman, oral history interview, 162–67.

70. Kang, "The Decline of California's Vendetta-Ridden Supreme Court," 343.

71. Ross, "The Political Judiciary," 164.

7. THE POLITICS OF DEATH

1. Philip Hager, "State Supreme Court Upholds Death Penalty," *Los Angeles Times*, September 1, 1979, A1. Frierson was convicted and condemned a second time. The state supreme court upheld his conviction but overturned his death sentence because the defense had failed to offer a diminished-capacity defense. The third time both his sentence and conviction were upheld, but in 2006 a federal court overturned his conviction, citing Frierson's mental retardation (463 F. 3d 982 [9th Cir. 2006]).

2. People v. Frierson, 25 Cal. 3d 142 (1979); Jerry Gillam, "Assembly Overrides Brown's Veto of Death Penalty Bill," *Los Angeles Times*, August 12, 1977, A3. Other discussions of California's death penalty politics can be found in Cairns, *Proof of Guilt*; Bakken, *Invitation to an Execution*; and Hamm, *Rebel and a Cause*.

3. Shatz and Dalton discuss the Briggs initiative in "Challenging the Death Penalty with Statistics," 1258. In 2012 Briggs's son Ron and Donald Heller, the attorney who crafted Proposition 7 for the 1978 ballot, advocated the passage of Proposition 34, a measure to end capital punishment in California. The death penalty cost taxpayers nearly $200 million annually and could not be justified on that basis, Prop. 34 adherents argued. The measure failed by a 52–48 margin.

4. Shatz and Dalton, "Challenging the Death Penalty with Statistics," 1258.

5. Uelmen, "California Death Penalty Laws and the California Supreme Court."

6. Briggs also garnered a reputation for being "colorful." He once sought protection

from police, claiming that terrorists were after him. The "terrorists" proved to be tax auditors from the IRS.

7. James Richardson discusses George Deukmejian's career in *Willie Brown: A Biography*. Brown, an African American from San Francisco, became arguably the most powerful Democrat in California during his tenure as speaker of the state assembly in the 1980s and 1990s.

8. Hager, "State Supreme Court Upholds Death Penalty," A1; Parker and Hubbard discuss Deukmejian's legislation in "The Evidence for Death," 977–79.

9. "California's High Court Upholds The State's Death Penalty, 5 to 2," *New York Times*, September 1, 1979, 17; Hager, "State Supreme Court Upholds Death Penalty."

10. The last execution in California before the 1972 invalidation of capital punishment laws occurred in 1967. Aaron Mitchell had been condemned in 1963 for murdering a Sacramento policeman. Ronald Reagan proclaimed himself a death penalty advocate, but Mitchell's was the only execution during his tenure as governor. He reprieved the only other condemned man to seek clemency.

11. Chen, "Rose Bird, a Study in Contrasts," B1.

12. Chen, "Rose Bird, a Study in Contrasts," B1.

13. People v. Jackson, 28 Cal. 3d 264 (1980).

14. People v. Harris, 28 Cal. 3d 935 (1981).

15. Jerry Brown appointees on the ballot were Allen Broussard, who replaced Wiley Manuel; Otto Kaus, who replaced William Clark; and Cruz Reynoso, who replaced Mathew Tobriner. Reagan appointee Frank Richardson also was on the November 1982 ballot.

16. Claudia Luther, "Effort to Recall Bird Dropped by Richardson," *Los Angeles Times*, July 9, 1982, B1.

17. Wallace Turner, "California's Chief Justice Is Facing a Recall Move," *New York Times*, November 13, 1982, A13.

18. All together, six recall efforts were filed in 1982 against Bird. Besides those organized by Rackauckus and Richardson, another was created by George Nicholson, a prosecutor who, with Edwin Meese, penned the September 1978 *Los Angeles Daily Journal* article suggesting the supreme court had withheld the *Tanner* decision. California Secretary of State, Complete List of Recall Attempts, accessed at www.sos.ca.gov.

19. Tobriner made his comments in his *Harris* dissent.

20. Beverly Beyette, "NOW and Equal Rights: No More Ms. Nice Guy," *Los Angeles Times*, July 14, 1982, F1.

21. Uelmen, "California Death Penalty Laws and the California Supreme Court."

22. Philip Hager, "30 Murderers to Require New Penalty Trials, Officials Say," *Los*

Angeles Times, January 27, 1982, B3; People v. Morse, 70 Cal. 2d 711 (1964) forbade the jury instruction about a governor's ability to commute a sentence of life without parole to life with parole.

23. Kelso and Bass, "The Victims' Bill of Rights," 845–65. Kelso and Bass argue that the measure represented a response to the 1960s focus on the rights of criminals and the fact that the California Constitution could be more liberally construed than the U.S. Constitution.

24. Goldberg, "The Impact of Proposition 8," 619–32.

25. Philip Hager, "Victims' Bill of Rights Upheld," *Los Angeles Times*, September 3, 1982, A1.

26. Robert Fairbanks, "Deukmejian: How to Stay in the Spotlight," *Los Angeles Times*, June 9, 1980, B3.

27. Philip Hager, "Kaus, Broussard Confirmed for State High Court," *Los Angeles Times*, July 18, 1981, A1. Broussard, Reynoso, and Kaus received between 53 and 56 percent of the votes. Reagan appointee Richardson received 76 percent.

28. Judith Michaelson, "Deukmejian Assails Rose Bird as Elitist, No Believer in Democracy," *Los Angeles Times*, October 22, 1980, A20; Nancy Skelton, "Rose Bird's Remarks Rapped by Deukmejian," *Los Angeles Times*, August 5, 1981, B3.

29. Skelton, "Rose Bird's Remarks Rapped by Deukmejian," B3.

30. Philip Hager, "Court Bars Hypnosis-Induced Testimony," *Los Angeles Times*, March 12, 1982, B1.

31. The best-known book about this phenomenon is still Faludi's *Backlash*. Antifeminist books from the era include Marabel Morgan's *The Total Woman*, possibly the first of a long list of books encouraging wives to defer to their husbands.

32. Jerry Hicks, "Not 1st Choice, but Bird's a Hit with Her Talk," *Los Angeles Times*, October 16, 1983, A1.

33. Bird, "Mathew Tobriner: The Heart of a Lion, the Soul of a Dove," 871–75.

34. Wright, "A View of Reagan and the California Courts," 75.

35. Chen, "Rose Bird, a Study in Contrasts."

36. Alexandra Leichter, "The Rose Bird I Knew," *Palo Alto Weekly*, January 5, 2000, accessed at www.paloaltoonline.com.

37. Chen, "Rose Bird, a Study in Contrasts."

38. People v. Jackson, 28 Cal. 3d 264 (1980); Harry Bernstein, "Right Wing Trying to Pack State Courts, Bird Warns," *Los Angeles Times*, July 20, 1982, B3.

39. Frank Richardson, Reagan's last appointee, left the court in December 1983.

40. For much of the twentieth century, California used indeterminate sentencing. This policy reflected a time when authorities saw prisons as places for rehabilitation. Thus, when an inmate was considered "rehabilitated," he or she could be released, often after serving a few years of a potentially lengthy sentence. The

growing emphasis on punishment, rather than rehabilitation, resulted in a shift to determinate sentencing in 1977. Even Jerry Brown supported this change.

41. Cairns, *Proof of Guilt* discusses the abolition movement in California and nationally during the 1950s and 1960s. California abolitionists included former San Quentin warden Clinton Duffy, whose book *88 Men and 2 Women* discusses executions during his tenure. Following his retirement, Duffy traveled the country lobbying against capital punishment.

42. Dan Morain, "Both Sides Point to Death Penalty Decision of 1972," *Los Angeles Times*, February 18, 1986, A1.

43. People v. Jackson, 28 Cal. 3d 264 (1980).

44. Mark A. Stein, "Why More Killing? Authorities Baffled," *Los Angeles Times*, January 11, 1981, VI.

45. The best discussion of the Manson case is Bugliosi and Gentry's *Helter Skelter*. It focuses on the Tate killings but also discusses Manson's life and his evolution as a cult figure, able to recruit young people—many from middle-class families—to his bizarre communal lifestyle and philosophy. The book appeared in 1974, two years after abolition of the death penalty.

46. Kathleen A. Cairns, "Victims' Kin Hope for Executions," *Long Beach Press-Telegram*, June 17, 1983, A1.

47. Larry Wellborn, "Mom: Murdered Son Will Always Be in Her Heart," *Orange County Register*, August 26, 2011.

48. People v. Frank, 38 Cal. 3d 711 (1985). The judge was only partly right. Frank remained on death row until 2001, when he died.

49. People v. Frank, 38 Cal. 3d 711 (1985).

50. Maura Dolan, "Voiding of Killer's Death Sentence Hit," *Los Angeles Times*, June 8, 1985, A1.

51. After the 1978 murder of her granddaughter, Patti Linebaugh took up the fight to protect other children from molesters. During the Vietnam War, groups such as Mothers for Peace navigated the halls of Congress and appeared at hearings, arguing against the conflict. Such groups might have paved the way for later victims' groups led by mothers.

52. Ronald J. Ostrow, "U.S. High Court Upholds Briggs Death Initiative," *Los Angeles Times*, July 7, 1983, A1.

53. Uelmen, "California Death Penalty Laws and the California Supreme Court."

54. Philip Hager, "Legal Questions Delay Use of California Death Penalty," *Los Angeles Times*, August 11, 1983, B1.

55. People v. Jackson, 28 Cal. 3d 264 (1980); Daily Opinions, *Los Angeles Daily Journal*, January 23, 2008.

56. Harris became California's first executed inmate in twenty-five years when he

went to the gas chamber in April 1992; People v. Harris, 28 Cal. 3d 935 (1981); 885 F. 2d 1354 (9th Cir. 1989).

57. Betty Goodwin, "Ten Distinguished Women Honored," *Los Angeles Times*, December 4, 1984, F4.

58. Rose Elizabeth Bird, "On the Bench, There's No 'Strike Four,'" *Los Angeles Times*, June 12, 1983, E5; "Letters to the Times," June 20, 1983, C4. Twenty years later, during his Senate confirmation hearing, U.S. Supreme Court chief justice John Roberts also compared judging to umpiring.

59. Uelmen, "California Death Penalty Laws and the California Supreme Court."

60. Hager, "Legal Questions Delay Use of California Death Penalty."

61. Newman, oral history interview, 177.

62. Belton, "A Senior Staff Attorney Reflects," 188–89.

63. Stevie Lamar Fields had been out of prison for two weeks in 1979 when he kidnapped a college librarian, held her hostage, forced her to write checks, and then killed her.

64. People v. Ramos, 30 Cal. 3d 553 (1982); People v. Ramos, 37 Cal. 3d 136 (1984).

65. Dan Morain, "Death Verdict Reversal Sparks Challenge to Justices," *Los Angeles Times*, November 11, 1984, A3.

66. John Balzar, "Bird's Opponents: Who Are They and What Do They Have to Say?," *Los Angeles Times*, January 20, 1986, A3.

8. BIG BUSINESS V. ROSE BIRD

1. Bigbee v. Pacific Telephone and Telegraph Co. 34 Cal. 3d 49 (1983).

2. Ruth Kwon, "Bigbee v. Pacific Telephone and Telegraph: Cramming Politics into a Phone Booth" (student paper, Berkeley Law, University of California, Berkeley), accessed at www.law.berkeley.edu/sugarman/Bigbee_42306_web _version.pdf.

3. Escola v. Coca Cola Bottling Company of Fresno, 24 Cal. 2d 458 (1944).

4. Field, *Activism in Pursuit of the Public Interest*, 108.

5. Greenman v. Yuba Power Products, 59 Cal. 2d 57, 377 (1963).

6. Barrera v. State Farm Insurance Co., 71 Cal. 2d 659 (1969).

7. Vesely v. Sager, 5 Cal. 3d 154 (1971). Sager owned a bar in San Bernardino County. He kept serving a patron drinks even after it became glaringly obvious that the man was drunk. The patron subsequently got into his car and drove recklessly down a narrow mountain road.

8. Vestermark v. Ford Motor Company, 61 Cal. 2d 256 (1964); the case is discussed in Wade, "Chief Justice Traynor," 456.

9. Dillon v. Legg, 68 Cal. 2d 728 (1968). The majority determined that it was foreseeable that an accident caused by a negligent driver would cause emotional distress.

10. Field, *Activism in Pursuit of the Public Interest*, 100.

11. Bogus, "Symposium: Introduction," 2–4.

12. Field, *Activism in Pursuit of the Public Interest*, xvi.

13. California Supreme Court Historical Society, "In Memoriam: Honorable Rose Elizabeth Bird."

14. Mullenix, "Aggregate Litigation," 521.

15. Sindell v. Abbott Laboratories, 26 Cal. 3d 588 (1980); Philip Hager, "State Justices Widen Product Liability Rules," *Los Angeles Times*, March 21, 1980, B1.

16. Assembly v. Deukmejian, 30 Cal. 3d 638 (1982). John Jacobs also discusses the reapportionment debacle in his book *A Rage for Justice*, 436–39.

17. Robert Naylor, "Reapportionment in California," *Los Angeles Times*, March 2, 1982, C4.

18. Legislature v. Deukmejian, 34 Cal. 3d 658 (1983); Philip Hager, "High Court Cancels Redistricting Vote," *Los Angeles Times*, September 16, 1983, B1.

19. Philip Hager, "Court OKs Punitive Damages in Firing," *Los Angeles Times*, June 3, 1980, B3.

20. Knight v. Hallsthammar, 29 Cal. 3d 46 (1981).

21. Philip Hager, "Tenants Win Fight on Substandard Housing," *Los Angeles Times*, February 14, 1981, A1.

22. Barela v. Superior Court of Orange County, 30 Cal. 3d 244 (1981); Jeffrey Perlman and Philip Hager, "High Court Upsets Eviction of Woman for Reporting Crime," *Los Angeles Times*, November 28, 1981, p. OCA1.

23. Marina Point Ltd. v. Wolfson, 30 Cal. 3d 721 (1982); Philip Hager, "Landlords Can't Bar Children, Court Says," *Los Angeles Times*, February 9, 1982, A1.

24. David Lane, "Landlord-Tenant Disputes Spur Further Litigation," *Los Angeles Times*, January 30, 1983, A4.

25. Maura Dolan, "Landlords, Tenants Split on Liability Ruling Effect," *Los Angeles Times*, May 1, 1985, B3; Becker v. IRM Corporation, 38 Cal. 3d 454 (1985); Mark A. Stein, "Court Widens Landlord Liability in Incidents of Injury to Tenants," *Los Angeles Times*, April 30, 1985, A3.

26. Becker v. IRM Corporation, 38 Cal. 3d 454 (1985); Stein, "Court Widens Landlord Liability," A3.

27. Dolan, "Landlords, Tenants Split on Liability Ruling Effect."

28. Koire v. Metro Car Wash, 40 Cal. 3d 24 (1985).

29. David L. Kirp, "Now Girls in Boys Clubs: Can't Anything Be Private?," *Los Angeles Times*, November 5, 1985, B5.

30. Molien v. Kaiser Foundation Hospitals, 27 Cal. 3d 916 (1980).

31. Philip Hager, "State High Court Expands Psychotherapists' Liability," *Los Angeles Times*, September 30, 1983, A6; Hedlund v. Superior Court, 34 Cal. 3d 695 (1983).

Bonnie Hedlund was one of two therapists treating La Nita Wilson and her boyfriend Steven Wilson.

32. Suastez v. Plastic Dress Up, 31 Cal. 3d 774 (1982); American National Insurance Co. v. Fair Employment and Housing Commission, 32 Cal. 3d 603 (1982).

33. Dan Morain, "UC Hospital Interns Can Unionize, Court Rules," *Los Angeles Times*, April 4, 1986, A3; Regents of University of California v. Public Employee Relations, 41 Cal. 3d 601 (1986).

34. County Sanitation District No. 2 v. Los Angeles County Employees Association, 38 Cal. 3d 564 (1985).

35. County Sanitation District No. 2 v. Los Angeles County Employees Association, 38 Cal. 3d 564 (1985).

36. "Public Right to Strike," Letters to the Editor, *Los Angeles Times*, May 30, 1985, p. OC12.

37. Dan Morain, "Government Workers Granted Right to Strike," *Los Angeles Times*, May 14, 1985, A1.

38. "The Case against Rose Bird," *Wall Street Journal*, October 20, 1986.

39. Ronald Reagan, "Remarks to Members of the American Tort Reform Association," May 30, 1986, accessed at www.presidency.ucsb.edu/ws/index.php?pid=37370. Reagan referenced the Bigbee decision and Rose Bird's role in "runaway" tort claims several times over the years, to a variety of organizations.

40. William Endicott, "Governor Cites Cases in Assailing State Court," *Los Angeles Times*, February 14, 1985, A3.

41. Dan Morain, "Governor's Criticism Coincides with Tempered Stand by Court," *Los Angeles Times*, February 19, 1985, B3.

42. Morain, "Governor's Criticism," B3.

43. American Bank & Trust Co. v. Community Hospital, 33 Cal. 3d 674 (1983); American Bank and Crust Co. v. Community Hospital of Los Gatos, 36 Cal. 3d 359 (1984).

44. Frank Clifford, "Campaign against Bird Grows Louder," *Los Angeles Times*, September 15, 1985, A1.

45. Bill Zimmerman, "The Campaign That Couldn't Win: When Rose Bird Ran Her Own Defeat," *Los Angeles Times*, November 9, 1986, H1.

46. Paul Obis, "Tipping the Scale: California Chief Justice Rose Elizabeth Bird on Diet and Cancer," *Vegetarian Times*, September 1985, 28–30.

47. Rose Bird, "Beating It," *Vegetarian Times*, September 1985, 31–32, 58.

48. Bird, "Beating It," 30–31, 58.

49. Sigelman, Sigelman, and Fowler, "A Bird of a Different Feather?," 32–43.

50. Burt Bailey, "Rose Bird Story Called Hype," Letters, *Vegetarian Times*, November 1985, 8.

9. THE PEOPLE V. ROSE BIRD

1. Dan Morain, "'Massive Executions' in State's Future, Bird Says," *Los Angeles Times*, November 9, 1985, A1.

2. "Rose Bird Foes Denounce Poison Pen Mail Assault," *Los Angeles Times*, March 23, 1985, 24.

3. Californians to Defeat Rose Bird, campaign material, 1986 election, California State Library, Sacramento CA.

4. Californians to Defeat Rose Bird, campaign material; John Balzar, "Computers Churning Out Anti-Bird Letters to Press," *Los Angeles Times*, December 8, 1985, A3. By fall 1986, the two main anti-Bird campaigns had joined forces. The combined campaign was led by Stu Spencer.

5. Clifford, "Campaign against Bird Grows Louder," A1.

6. Anthony Lewis, "Chief Justice Bird: Calm at the Center," *New York Times*, October 23, 1986, A27. Cranston won reelection to the U.S. Senate despite concerted efforts to link him to Bird.

7. Barry Keene, oral history interview conducted by Carole Hicke, 1994, Regional Oral History Office, University of California, Berkeley, for the California State Archives State Government Oral History Program, 212.

8. Zimmerman, "The Campaign That Couldn't Win," H1.

9. Clifford, "Lone Justice."

10. Many people have written about how civil rights and women's groups of the 1960s and 1970s redefined politics. Evans's *Personal Politics* perhaps best explains the beginnings of the transformation during Freedom Summer in 1964. Young women traveled south to help register African American voters. Rather than equals, male organizers treated them as inferiors, fueling anger and a reexamination of power relationships and how they worked out in everyday life, as well as in the larger political arena.

11. "Rose Bird at Home—Friends Call her Shy," *San Francisco Chronicle*, August 25, 1986.

12. Campaign material, California State Library.

13. Balzar and Morain, "Politically Reluctant Bird Hops Aboard," A1.

14. Edmund G. Brown Jr., "Law versus Mood: A Case for the Supreme Court," *Los Angeles Times*, March 2, 1986, H1.

15. Bergholz, "Looking to November 1986," 101.

16. Liebert, "Rose Bird and the Campaign of 1986," 493.

17. Zimmerman, "The Campaign that Couldn't Win."

18. Richardson, "Stalking the Wily Chief Justice," 452.

19. Dan Morain, "Bird Says She Won't Turn Tail and Run," *Los Angeles Times*, November 23, 1985, A1.

20. Richardson, "Stalking the Wily Chief Justice," 455.

21. Richardson, "Stalking the Wily Chief Justice," 455.

22. Morain, "Bird Says She Won't 'Turn Tail and Run.'"

23. Frank Clifford, "Opposition to Bird Strong and Relatively Static, Pollsters Find," *Los Angeles Times*, December 12, 1985, A36.

24. John Balzar and Frank Clifford, "Bird Adopts a Temperate Tone, Says She Rues Attack on Meese," *Los Angeles Times*, February 21, 1986, A3.

25. Frank Clifford and John Balzar, "$4.7 Million Contributed for High Court Campaign," *Los Angeles Times*, February 4, 1986, A1.

26. Eric Levin, "The New Look in Old Maids," *People*, March 31, 1986, 28–30. Two months later, *Newsweek* carried its own story on "The Marriage Crunch," which quickly went viral. Of particular note was the article's assertion that women over forty had a greater chance of being killed by terrorists than of finding a mate. Rose Bird was not featured in the *Newsweek* story. The research findings subsequently were debunked. Faludi discusses the debate over marriage in *Backlash*.

27. Clifford, "Lone Justice."

28. Gorney, "Rose Bird and the Court of Conflict," C1.

29. Frank Clifford, "Bird Rises above the Bitter Campaign on a Visit Down Under," *Los Angeles Times*, April 29, 1986, C3.

30. Clifford, "Bird Rises above the Bitter Campaign," C3.

31. Richardson, "Stalking the Wily Chief Justice."

32. Lanie Jones, "Bird Delivers Non-Political Talk in Irvine," *Los Angeles Times*, February 20, 1986, A1.

33. Balzar and Morain, "Politically Reluctant Bird Hops Aboard."

34. Dan Morain, "Bird Praised for Her Administration," *Los Angeles Times*, April 20, 1986, A1

35. *CBS Evening News*, May 21, 1986, accessed via You Tube, September 25, 2014.

36. Ellen Goodman, "Rose Bird's Plight Has a Lesson for the Country," *Los Angeles Times*, June 29, 1986, F5.

37. People v. Smallwood, 42 Cal. 3d 415 (1986).

38. Grodin, oral history interview, 61.

39. Winograd, "Are They a 'Gang of Three'?," 439–41.

40. "1986 Rose Elizabeth Bird Campaign 30 sec Spots.wmv," YouTube video, 4:43, compilation of television ads Bird made under the auspices of the Committee to Conserve the Courts, posted by "tt4jd," October 25, 2011, www.youtube.com /watch?v=YB8xFq3lGXI.

41. Barbara Allen Babcock, "Rose Bird Under Attack for Results, Not for Court's Judicial Reasoning," *Los Angeles Times*, August 31, 1986, E3.

42. Lewis, "Chief Justice Bird: Calm at the Center."

43. Tom Wicker, "In the Nation: A Naked Power Grab," *New York Times*, September 16, 1986.
44. Lewis, "Chief Justice Bird: Calm at the Center."
45. Frank Clifford, "Close Friend Calls Chief Justice 'Inept' in Politics," *Los Angeles Times*, September 21, 1986, A3.
46. Clifford, "Lone Justice."
47. Frank Clifford, "Bird Drives Home a Point in Dialogue," *Los Angeles Times*, September 27, 1986, A1.
48. Kathleen Cairns, "Bird: It's Politics, Not Executions That Is the Issue, She Says," *Long Beach Press-Telegram*, October 6, 1986, A3.
49. Kathleen Cairns, "Anti-Bird Ad Features Mom of Slain Girl," *Long Beach Press-Telegram*, October 8, 1986, A1.
50. Rita Ciolli, "Election '86 Judiciary," *Newsday*, October 2, 1986, 3.
51. Ciolli, "Election '86 Judiciary."
52. Frank Clifford, "Poor and Weak Will Suffer if Opponents Win, Bird Says," *Los Angeles Times*, October 27, 1986, SD3.
53. Deidre MacDonald, "The Penalty of Mercy," *London Times*, October 17, 1986.
54. George Skelton, "Deukmejian to Oppose Grodin and Reynoso," *Los Angeles Times*, August 26, 1986, A1; Grodin later said that he believed as early as fall 1985 that Deukmejian would ultimately oppose him and Reynoso.
55. Kathleen Cairns, "Mosk Rues Confirmation Hostilities," *Long Beach Press-Telegram*, October 24, 1986, E2.
56. Kathleen Cairns, "Poll Shows Support Dwindling for Justices Reynoso and Grodin," *Long Beach Press-Telegram*, October 30, 1986, A1.
57. Frank del Olmos, "Ugly or Polite, It's Racism," *Los Angeles Times*, October 30, 1986, B7.
58. Wallace Turner, "California GOP Candidate Dismayed by Aide's Racial Comment," *New York Times*, October 9, 1982, 8.
59. Kathleen Cairns, "Embattled Rose Bird Turns On Charm for the Senior Citizens," *Long Beach Press-Telegram*, September 27, 1986, A6.
60. Frank Clifford, "Lone Justice."
61. Deidre English, "The Ordeal of Rose Bird: California Chief Justice Is Caught in the Election Year Crossfire," *Ms.*, November 1986, 71–73.
62. Forfreedom, "Rose Bird Campaign," 31.
63. Frank Clifford, "NOW Leader Calls Anti-Bird Campaign 'Rampant Sexism,'" *Los Angeles Times*, September 17, 1986, A25.
64. Frank Clifford and Richard Paddock, "Deukmejian, Bird Sharpen Attacks as Vote Nears," *Los Angeles Times*, October 18, 1986, A1.
65. Clifford and Paddock, "Deukmejian, Bird Sharpen Attacks as Vote Nears," A1.

66. Clifford and Paddock, "Deukmejian, Bird Sharpen Attacks as Vote Nears," A1.
67. Frank Clifford, "Voters Repudiate 3 of Court's Liberal Justices," *Los Angeles Times*, November 5, 1986, A1. "Rose Bird, California Chief Justice Election Statement," KPIX Television, San Francisco CA, accessed via You Tube, September 26, 2014.
68. Paul Reidinger, "The Politics of Judging," *American Bar Association Journal*, April 1, 1987, 54.
69. Clifford, "Voters Repudiate 3 of Court's Liberal Justices."
70. Jacobs, "Rose Bird Paid the Price," A29.
71. Catherine Doyle, "Letter to the Editor," *Los Angeles Times*, November 11, 1986, B4.
72. Philip Hager," Lucas Sworn in as California Chief Justice," *Los Angeles Times*, February 6, 1987, B1.
73. Maddy, oral history interview, 651. Maddy was an iconoclastic Republican assembly member and state senator from Fresno.
74. Lynn O'Shaugnessy, "Bird Hits Deukmejian Appointees, Warns of Dangers Facing Courts," *Los Angeles Times*, January 5, 1987, 1.
75. Bird was not the only chief justice defeated in 1986. Ohio voters ousted Frank D. Celebrezze, who was first elected to the post in 1972. Celebrezze's campaign was accused of accepting contributions from groups linked to organized crime.

10. HIGH COURTS AND POLITICAL FOOTBALLS

1. James Gerstenzang, "Bork, Nominee for Supreme Court, Praised for His 'Judicial Restraint,'" *Los Angeles Times*, July 2, 1987, A1.
2. *Griswold v. Connecticut* (1965) is generally viewed as the first case explicitly decided on the right to privacy, though *Roe v. Wade* (1973) is usually the case most frequently cited with regard to privacy.
3. Kenneth Noble, "Bork Backers Flood Senate With Mail," *New York Times*, September 3, 1987, A16.
4. "Against Robert Bork: His Bill of Rights Is Different," *New York Times*, October 5, 1987, A22; "Scholar Warns of 'Chaos' With Bork on High Court," *Los Angeles Times*, September 22, 1987, A1.
5. "Excerpts From Debate in Senate over Bork Nomination to the High Court," *New York Times*, October 22, 1987.
6. David Broder, "Judicial Lynching, Left and Right," *Los Angeles Times*, October 6, 1987, D7; Letters to the Times, July 12, 1987, E4.
7. The Senate defeated the nominations of Clement Haynsworth in 1969 and Harrold Carswell in 1970. Nixon had appointed both men to fill the seat left vacant by the departure of liberal justice Abe Fortas. Reagan nominee Douglas Ginsburg withdrew his name in 1987 after it was revealed that he had smoked marijuana as a law student.

8. Linda Greenhouse, "Washington Talk: Court Politics; Nursing the Wounds from the Bork Fight," *New York Times*, November 30, 1987.

9. David Lauter, "Senate Rejects Bork for Supreme Court, 58–42," *Los Angeles Times*, October 24, 1987, 1.

10. Myrna Oliver, "Bork Assails Liberals for Court Defeat," *Los Angeles Times*, February 13, 1988, 37. Bork did write a book about his experience, *The Tempting of America: The Political Seduction of the Law*.

11. Grodin, *In Pursuit of Justice*, 163.

12. Claudia Luther, "Bork Says State Gun Laws Constitutional," *Los Angeles Times*, March 15, 1989, A5.

13. Andrew Cohen, "The Sad Legacy of Robert Bork," *The Atlantic*, December 19, 2012, accessed at www.theatlantic.com/politics. The story reprised Bork's nomination battle just after his death at the age of eighty-five.

14. Joel Sappell, "Death Penalty Controversy Trails Bird," *Los Angeles Times*, May 14, 1990, 1.

15. Steve Winstein, "Rose Bird Reflects on her Image on the Tube," *Los Angeles Times*, February 23, 1988, S1.

16. Katherine Bishop, "Ousted California Judge in Center of New Storm," *New York Times*, February 12, 1988.

17. Dan Morain, "Bird Tries Some Verse in TV Commentator Debut," *Los Angeles Times*, February 6, 1988, A10

18. Joel Sappell, "Court Tenure Shadows Life of Rose Bird," *Los Angeles Times*, May 14, 1990, A3; Dolan, "Rose Bird's Quest for Obscurity," A1; Adam Pertman, "Ex-State Supreme Court Chief's Fall Called an American Tragedy," *Los Angeles Daily News*, May 26, 1996, 26.

19. Kenney, *Gender and Justice*, 149.

20. Todd Purdum, "Rose Bird, Once California's Chief Justice, Is Dead at 63," *New York Times*, December 6, 1999, 1; Sappell, "Court Tenure Shadows Life of Rose Bird."

21. Rose Elizabeth Bird, "Unequal Partners: We Still Haven't Decided Whether All Women and Created Equal Too," *Washington Post Magazine*, June 28, 1987, 45; the other four contributors were historian Garry Wills, civil rights activist Roger Wilkins, appeals court justice Frank Easterbrook, and humorist Charlie Haas.

22. People v. Anderson, 43 Cal. 3d 1101 (1987).

23. Gerald Uelmen, "A Cure for the Court's Death Row Burnout," *Los Angeles Times*, November 29, 1989, B7.

24. Schmidt v. Superior Court (Valley Mobile Park), 48 Cal. 3d 370 (1989); the case pertained to a mobile home park that required residents to be age twenty-five and older.

25. Sands v. Morongo Unified School District, 53 Cal. 3d 863 (1991); Planned

Parenthood Shasta Diablo Inc. v. Williams, 7 Cal. 4th 860 (1994); Schmidt v. Superior Court, 13 Cal. 3d 1060 (1987); Warfield v. Peninsula Golf and Country Club, 10 Cal. 4d 1060 (1995); People v. Humphrey, 13 Cal. 4th 1073 (1996). Culver discusses the Lucas court's shift in "The Transformation of the California Supreme Court 1977–1997," 1461–90.

26. Philip Hager, "Decisions by State Supreme Court Decrease Sharply," *Los Angeles Times*, May 26, 1990, A37.

27. Philip Hager, "Kaufman Rips Bird Court on Death Penalty," *Los Angeles Times*, April 13, 1990, A1.

28. Philip Hager, "Kaufman's Bird Court Remarks Assailed," *Los Angeles Times*, April 14, 1990, A20.

29. Dolan, "Rose Bird's Quest for Obscurity," A1.

30. Dolan, "Rose Bird's Quest for Obscurity," A1.

31. Dolan, "Rose Bird's Quest for Obscurity," A1.

32. The average vote percentage of justices seeking retention on the California Supreme Court since 1988 has been slightly higher than 60 percent.

33. Pertman, "Ex-State Supreme Court Chief's Fall Called an American Tragedy."

34. Bai discusses Gary Hart's fall from grace during the run up to the 1988 Democratic presidential campaign and how the media covered it in *All the Truth Is Out*.

35. Richard L. Berke, "Judge Thomas Faces Bruising Battle With Liberals Over Stand on Rights," *New York Times*, July 4, 1991, A12; "Excerpts From Senate Hearings on the Thomas Nomination," *New York Times*, October 13, 1991, 30. In the end, no one emerged unscathed. Thomas was enraged and bitter, some male senators suggested they were skeptical of Hill's testimony, and the judiciary panel never called three other female witnesses with similar allegations. In 1992 five women were elected to the U.S. Senate, their elections attributed in part to the perception that male politicians were tone-deaf and insufficiently concerned about sexual harassment.

36. Jeffrey Toobin, "Judges for Sale," *The New Yorker*, August 14, 2012, 6.

37. Miller, *Direct Democracy and the Courts*, 213.

38. Diane Hartman, "Former Supreme Tells of Trials," *The Docket*, June 2000, http://www.denbar.org/docket/doc_articles.cfm?ArticleID=3626; Robert Houk, "Voters Should Question Motives for Targeting Justices," *Johnson City Press*, May 27, 2014. The three justices under attack in 2014 all retained their seats.

39. Rose Elizabeth Bird, "The Jury Did Its Job: Put Blame Where It Belongs," *Los Angeles Times*, October 18, 1995, A12.

40. Rose Elizabeth Bird, "Perspective on Public Life; Character Assassins Strike Again," *Los Angeles Times*, May 26, 1996, 5.

41. "Ex-Chief Justice Rose Bird Undergoes Second Mastectomy," *San Francisco*

Chronicle, November 8, 1996, 22; Bob Egelko, "Supreme Court Justice Broussard Lauded as a Law Scholar," *Orange County Register*, November 9, 1996, 31.

42. Rose Elizabeth Bird, "A Brutal Education Legacy," *San Francisco Examiner*, June 29, 1997, 7.

43. Rose Elizabeth Bird, "Thinking About Running for President? Think Again," *San Francisco Examiner*, April 7, 19.

44. John L. Mitchell, "Rose Bird Honored by ACLU," *Los Angeles Times*, April 3, 1998, 1.

45. George Skelton, "Lungren Without the Polish," *Los Angeles Times*, September 24, 1998, 1.

46. American Academy of Pediatrics, et al. v. Daniel E. Lungren, 16 Cal. 4th 307 (1997); two other justices, Stanley Mosk and Kathryn Werdegar, also appeared on the November 1998 ballot, but both had dissented from George's opinion.

47. Stephen Barnett, "The Court of Public Opinion Is Out of Order," *Los Angeles Times*, August 22, 1997, B9.

48. Maura Dolan, "California and the West: Judicial Hiring Freeze Lifts for Democrats," *Los Angeles Times*, January 9, 1999, 3.

49. Among Jewison's most significant films were *In the Heat of the Night*, starring Sidney Poitier; *A Soldier's Story*, featuring Denzel Washington; and *The Hurricane*, about boxer Ruben Carter.

50. Cooper, "Rose Bird: The Last Interview," 38.

51. Purdum, "Rose Bird, Once California's Chief Justice Is Dead," B18.

52. Larry D. Hatfield, "Ex-Chief Justice Rose Bird Dies," *San Francisco Examiner*, December 5, 1999, A1.

53. Richard Pearson, "Ousted Jurist Rose Bird Dies," *Washington Post*, December 6, 1999, B6; Harold Jackson and Christopher Reed, "Rose Bird: Trailblazing U.S. Judge Who Fought Death Penalty," *The Guardian*, December 8, 1999, 24.

54. Debra Saunders, "Rose Bird Was Courageous, and Wrong," *San Francisco Chronicle*, December 7, 1999, A27.

55. Peter H. King, "In Defense of the Late Rose Bird's View of Justice," *Orange County Register*, December 12, 1999, A3.

56. Morrison, "Bird Was Quixotic, Courageous, and a Little Too Naïve," A3.

57. Emily Gurnon, "Mourners Remember the Courage of Rose Bird," *San Francisco Examiner*, January 30, 2000, D1.

58. California Supreme Court Historical Society, "In Memoriam: Honorable Rose Elizabeth Bird."

11. PAYING FOR JUSTICE

1. Nathan Crabbe, "Former Iowa Chief Justice Discusses Influence of Special Interest Groups," *Gainesville (IA) Sun*, September 10, 2012, accessed at Gainesville.com.

2. "'Hot Coffee' Documents Chamber of Commerce Campaign to Unseat Judges Opposed to Tort Reform," *Democracy Now*, January 25, 2011, accessed at www .democracynow.org/appearances/oliver_diaz.

3. "No Opponent, But Big Money in Illinois Justice's Race," NPR *Morning Edition*, October 26, 2010; Monique Garcia, "State Supreme Court Justice Wins Retention Battle," *Chicago Tribune*, November 2, 2010, A1.

4. Lizette Alvarez, "Republican Party Aims to Remake Florida Supreme Court," *New York Times*, October 2, 2012, A20.

5. Bell, "Politics of Crime and Threat to Judicial Independence"; *Ballotpedia*, s.v. "Tennessee Supreme Court election, 2014," accessed at ballotpedia.org /Tennessee_Supreme_Court_elections,_2014.

6. Tim Potter, "Kansans Vote to Retain Justices Lee Johnson and Eric Rosen," *Wichita Eagle*, November 4, 2014, 3.

7. Toobin, "Judges for Sale," 6; Bert Brandenberg, "Justice for Sale: How Elected Judges Became a Threat to American Democracy," *Politico*, September 1, 2014, accessed at Politico.com.

8. Wiseman, "So You Want to Stay a Judge," 653.

9. A. J. Vicens, "7 Incredibly Sleazy Ads Targeting Justices," *Mother Jones*, October 28, 2014, accessed at www.motherjones.com/politics/2014/10.

10. Brandenburg and Schotland, "Keeping Courts Impartial amid Changing Judicial Elections," 105.

11. Wiseman, "So You Want to Stay a Judge."

12. Mildred Lillie, oral history interview conducted by Mary Louise Blackstone, 1989, for the Committee on the History of the California State Bar, 123.

13. Brandenberg, "Justice for Sale."

14. Brandenberg, "Justice for Sale."

15. Brandenberg, "Justice for Sale."

16. Olson made this comment while he was plaintiff's attorney in Caperton v. Massey Coal Co., Inc., 556 U.S. 868 (2009). Caperton sued Massey for using machinations to renege on a contract. After the original jury awarded Caperton $50 million, Massey appealed. To increase the odds of a sympathetic state high court, the company successfully spent $3 million to oust a sitting West Virginia justice. The justice who benefitted from Massey's largesse refused to recuse himself and provided the margin for overturning the initial verdict. Caperton then took his case to the U.S. Supreme Court. In a 5–4 decision authored by Anthony Kennedy, the court ruled for the plaintiff, declaring that the Constitution could require an elected judge to recuse her or himself in a case involving someone who donated money to a judicial campaign.

17. Sue Bell Cobb, "I Was Alabama's Top Judge. I'm Ashamed By What I Had

to Do to Get There," *Politico*, March/April 2015, www.politico.com/magazine
/story/2015/03/judicial-elections-fundraising-115503.

18. David Orr, "It's Time to Get Judicial Retention Elections off the Ballot," *The Blog*, March 18, 2010. Orr was the Cook County, Illinois, county clerk.

19. Sandra Day O'Connor, "Fair and Independent Courts: A Conference on the State of the Judiciary" (presentation to the Conference on the State of the Judiciary, sponsored by Georgetown Law and the American Law Institute, September 28–29, 2006).

20. Orr, "It's Time to Get Judicial Retention Elections off the Ballot"; Lillie, oral history interview, 4.

21. "A Judicial Campaign Rule Survives," *New York Times*, April 30, 2015, A30. The editorial declared the ruling "a surprise because unrestricted money in politics has had few friends as steadfast as the Supreme Court's current conservative majority."

22. Dunn and Hansen, "Judicial Retention Elections," 1429.

23. Maura Dolan, "Californians' Support for Death Penalty Goes Against Trend," *Los Angeles Times*, December 30, 2012, A1.

24. Maura Dolan, "Former Death Penalty Supporters Now Working against It," *Los Angeles Times*, September 23, 2012, A1.

25. Proposition 34 on the November 2012 ballot would have made California the eighteenth state to abolish capital punishment. It failed passage by four percentage points; Dan Morain, "Off Topic: California Supreme Court Chief Justice Tani Cantil-Sakauye," *Sacramento Bee*, January 26, 2014, 2.

26. "Chief Justice Ronald George Reflects on Death Penalty, Prop. 8," *The California Report*, KQED, San Francisco, December 6–8, 2013.

27. In re Marriages, 43 Cal. 4th 757 (2008). When the case went before the federal Ninth Circuit Court of Appeal in 2010, Governor Schwarzenegger refused to join the appeal, as did Attorney General Jerry Brown. In 2013 the U.S. Supreme Court ruled that the plaintiffs had no standing to file suit.

28. "Chief Justice Ronald George Reflects on Death Penalty, Prop. 8."

29. Cathleen Decker, "Brown and Whitman go head to head," *Los Angeles Times*, September 29, 2010, A1.

30. Adam Nagourney, "Jerry Brown, Governor of California, Takes Second Chance to Shape Court," *New York Times*, December 26, 2014, 1.

31. Bird, "The Instant Society and the Rule of Law."

32. Kenney, *Gender and Justice*, 150.

33. Maura Dolan, "Governor Chooses Moderate for Chief Justice," *Los Angeles Times*, July 22, 2010, A1.

34. Shane Goldmacher, "Gov. Lauds Chief Justice Choice; Tani Cantil-Sakauye

Is Called a 'Living, Breathing Example of the American Dream,'" *Los Angeles Times*, July 23, 2010, A4.

35. Goldmacher, "Gov. Lauds Chief Justice Choice," A4; Morain, "Off Topic."

36. Maura Dolan, "Death Penalty on Its Last Mile?," *Los Angeles Times*, December 24, 2011, A1.

37. Daniel B. Wood, "Why California's Chief Justice Is Taking On the Legislature," *Christian Science Monitor*, March 20, 2012, 9.

38. Maura Dolan, "Law License Ruling Breaks Ground for Immigrant Rights," *Los Angeles Times*, January 3, 2014, 4.

39. Morain, "Off Topic."

40. Bird, "The Instant Society and the Rule of Law."

BIBLIOGRAPHY

ARCHIVAL SOURCES

Bancroft Library, University of California, Berkeley, Regional Oral History Office
    Selected oral histories of the California Supreme Court
California State Archives, Sacramento
    California Oral History Project
    Election materials, November 1986
    Legislative bill files
State of California Commission on Judicial Performance Hearing in the Matter of Commission Proceedings Concerning the Seven Justices of the Supreme Court of California, 1979

PUBLISHED SOURCES

"Abortion Statutes: Are they Unconstitutional Per Se? People v. Belous." *Washington University Law Quarterly*, no. 4 (1969): 445–51.

Bai, Matt. *All the Truth Is Out: The Week Politics Went Tabloid*. New York: Alfred Knopf, 2014.

Bakken, Gordon Morris, ed. *Invitation to an Execution: The History of the Death Penalty in America*. Albuquerque: University of New Mexico Press, 2010.

Balabanian, David. "Justice Was More than His Title." *California Law Review* 70 (July 1982): 878–80.

Banner, Stuart. *The Death Penalty: An American History*. Cambridge MA: Harvard University Press, 2003.

Bell, Jeannine. "Politics of Crime and Threat to Judicial Independence." In *Justice in Jeopardy: Report of the Commission on the 21st Century Judiciary*. Chicago: American Bar Association, 2003.

Bergholz, Richard. "Looking to November 1986." *California Journal* (March 1985): 101.

Bessler, John. *The Kiss of Death: America's Love Affair with the Death Penalty*. Boston: Northeastern University Press, 2003.

Bird, Rose Elizabeth. "The Instant Society and the Rule of Law." *Catholic University Law Review* 31 (1982).

———. "Justice Mathew O. Tobriner: A Man of Uncommon Grace." *Hastings Constitutional Law Quarterly* 11 (Winter 1984): 161–64.

———. "Mathew Tobriner: The Heart of a Lion, the Soul of a Dove." *California Law Review* 70, no. 4 (1982): 871–75.

———. "3rd Year Girls Lament." *The Writ* (Spring 1965).

Bogus, Carl T. "Symposium: Introduction: Genuine Tort Reform." *Roger Williams University Law Review* 13 (Winter 2008): 1–7.

Bonner, Raymond. *Anatomy of Injustice: A Murder Case Gone Wrong*. New York: Vintage, 2013.

Bowman, Chris. "Brown's Farm-Labor Coup." *California Journal* 6 (June 1975): 190–92.

Bowman, Cynthia Grant. "Women in the Legal Profession from the 1920s–1970s: What Can We Learn about Law and Social Change?" *Maine Law Review* 61, no. 1 (2009).

Braitman, Jacqueline R., and Gerald F. Uelmen. *Justice Stanley Mosk: A Life at the Center of California Politics and Justice*. New York: McFarland, 2012.

Brandenburg, Bert, and Roy Schotland. "Keeping Courts Impartial amid Changing Judicial Elections." *Daedalus* 137, no. 4 (Fall 2008): 105.

Brazil, Eric. "Why the ALRB Is under Constant Attack." *California Journal* 10 (June 1979): 194–96.

Bruns, Roger. *Cesar Chavez: A Biography*. Westport CT: Greenwood, 2005.

Bugliosi, Vince, and Curt Gentry. *Helter Skelter: The True Story of the Manson Murders*. New York: W. W. Norton, 1974.

Buntin, John. *L.A. Noir: The Struggle for the Soul of America's Most Seductive City*. New York: Broadway Books, 2010.

Cairns, Kathleen A. *Front-Page Women Journalists, 1920–1950*. Lincoln: University of Nebraska Press, 2003.

———. *Proof of Guilt: Barbara Graham and the Politics of Executing Women in America*. Lincoln: University of Nebraska Press, 2013.

Cannon, Lou. *President Reagan: The Role of a Lifetime*. New York: Public Affairs, 2000.

Carrington, Paul. "Judicial Independence and Democratic Accountability in Highest State Courts." *Law and Contemporary Problems* 61, no. 3 (1998): 79–126.

Cohen, Lizabeth. *A Consumer's Republic: The Politics of Mass Consumption in Post War America*. New York: Vintage, 2003.

Cohen, Stanley. *The Wrong Men: America's Epidemic of Wrongful Death Row Convictions*. New York: Carrollton & Graf, 2003.

Coontz, Stephanie. *The Way We Never Were: American Families and the Nostalgia Trap*. New York: Basic Books, 1993.

Cooper, Claire. "Rose Bird." *California Journal* 20 (November 1999): 16–17.

———. "Rose Bird: The Last Interview." *California Lawyer* 20 (February 2000): 38.

Cott, Nancy. *The Grounding of Modern Feminism*. New Haven CT: Yale University Press, 1987.

Cruden, John. "Learning a Passion for Law." *Magazine of Santa Clara University School of Law* 17, no. 2 (Summer 2011): 24.

Culver, John H. "The Transformation of the California Supreme Court, 1977–1997." *Albany Law Review* 61, no. 5 (1998): 1461–90.

Culver, John H., and John C. Syer. *Power and Politics in California*. New York: Wiley, 1980.

Culver, John H., and John T. Wold. "Rose Bird and the Politics of Judicial Accountability in California." *Judicature* 70, no. 2 (1986): 80–89.

Cuordileone, K. A. *Manhood and American Political Culture in the Cold War*. New York: Routledge, 2006.

Dow, David R. *The Autobiography of an Execution*. New York: Twelve, 2010.

Dunn, B. Michel, and Randall M. Hansen. "Judicial Retention Elections." *Loyola Law Review* 34, no. 4 (2001): 1429–45.

Erlick-Martin, Susan, and Nancy C. Jurik. *Doing Justice, Doing Gender: Women in Legal and Criminal Justice Occupations*, 2nd ed. New York: Sage Publications, 2006.

Evans, Sara. *Personal Politics: The Roots of Women's Liberation in the Civil Rights Movement and the New Left*. New York: Vintage, 1980.

Faludi, Susan. *Backlash: The Undeclared War against American Women*. New York: Broadway Books, 2006.

Farrington-Myers, Brenda. "Rose Bird and the Rule of Law." Master's thesis, California State University, Fullerton, 1991.

Ferriss, Susan, and Ricardo Sandoval. *The Fight in the Fields: Cesar Chavez and the Farmworkers Movement*. New York: Mariner Books, 1998.

Field, Ben. *Activism in Pursuit of the Public Interest: The Jurisprudence of Chief Justice Roger J. Traynor*. Berkeley: Public Policy Press for the California Supreme Court Historical Society, 2003.

Forfreedom, Ann. "Rose Bird Campaign." *Off Our Backs* 15, no. 10 (November 1985): 31.

Formichi, Robert E. *Reports of Cases Determined in the Supreme Court of the State of California*. Vols. 8–30. San Francisco: Bancroft-Whitney, 1986.

Friedland, Diana. "27 Years of Truth-in-Evidence: The Expectations and Consequences of Proposition 8's Most Controversial Provision." *Berkeley Journal of Criminal Law* 14, no. 1 (2009): 1–33.

Garcia, Matt. *From the Jaws of Victory: The Triumph and Tragedy of Cesar Chavez and the Farm Worker Movement*. Berkeley: University of California Press, 2014.

Goldberg, Hank M. "The Impact of Proposition 8 on Prior Misconduct Impeachment Evidence in California Criminal Codes." *Loyola University Law Review* 24 (April 1991): 621–54.

Grisham, John. *The Appeal*. New York: Dell, 2012.

Grodin, Joseph. *In Pursuit of Justice: Reflections of a Supreme Court Justice*. Berkeley: University of California Press, 1991.

———. Oral history interview conducted by John K. Hanft for the California Bar Oral History Series. *Hastings Constitutional Law Quarterly* 16 (1988): 7–68.

Hamm, Ted. *Rebel and a Cause: Caryl Chessman and the Politics of the Death Penalty in Postwar California*. Berkeley: University of California Press, 2000.

Harris, Gloria G., and Hannah S. Cohen. *Women Trailblazers of California: Pioneers to the Present*. Charleston SC: The History Press, 2012.

Heyman, Ira Michael. "Tribute: Preble Stolz." *California Law Review* 80, no. 4 (July 1992).

Hogan, Sean O., ed. *The Judicial Branch of State Government: People, Process and Politics*. Santa Barbara CA: ABC-CLIO, 2006.

Jacobs, John. *A Rage for Justice: The Passion and Politics of Phillip Burton*. Berkeley: University of California Press, 1995.

Kang, K. Connie. "The Decline of California's Vendetta-Ridden Supreme Court." *California Journal* 10 (October 1979): 343–46.

———. "Why the Bird Court Is in Constant Turmoil." *California Journal* 10 (April 1979): 128–30.

Kelso, J. Clark, and Brigitte A. Bass. "The Victims' Bill of Rights: Where Did It Come From and How Much Did It Do?" *Pacific Law Review* 23, no. 3 (1992): 843–79.

Kenney, Sally J. *Gender and Justice: Why Women in the Judiciary Really Matter*. New York: Routledge, 2013.

Keppel, Bruce. "The Bitter Harvest." *California Journal* 6 (November 1975): 377–79.

Kleps, Ralph N. "A Tribute to Chief Justice Donald R. Wright." *Hastings Constitutional Law Quarterly* 4, no. 4 (1977): 683–87.

Lamson, Peggy. *In the Vanguard: Six American Women in Public Life*. New York: Houghton-Miflin, 1979.

Lazzareschi, Carla. "Rose Bird, Criminal Lawyer as the Compleat Bureaucrat." *California Journal* 7 (March 1976): 87–89.

Levy, Jacques, and Jacqueline Levy. *Cesar Chavez: Autobiography of La Causa*. Minneapolis: University of Minneapolis Press, 2007.

Liebert, Larry. "Rose Bird and the Campaign of 1986: A Thorny Issue for Democrats." *California Journal* 16 (March 1985): 493–95.

Lorenz, J. D. *Jerry Brown: The Man on the White Horse*. New York: Houghton-Mifflin, 1978.

Mandery, Evan. *A Wild Justice: The Death and Resurrection of Capital Punishment in America*. New York: W. W. Norton, 2014.

Martin, Susan E., and Nancy J. Jurik. "Women Entering the Legal Profession: Change and Resistance." In *Doing Justice, Doing Gender: Women in Legal and Criminal Justice Occupations*, 2nd ed. New York: Sage, 2006.

May, Elaine Tyler. *Homeward Bound: American Families in the Cold War Era*. New York: Basic Books, 1988.

McGirr, Lisa. *Suburban Warriors: The Origins of the New American Right*. Princeton NJ: Princeton University Press, 2002.

Medsger, Betty. *Framed: The New Right Attack on Chief Justice Rose Bird and the Courts*. New York: Pilgrim Press, 1983.

Merkel, Philip L. "California's Role in the Mid-20th Century Controversy over Pain and Suffering Damages: The NACCA, Melvin Belli and the Crusade for 'The Adequate Reward.'" *California Legal History* 5 (2010): 287–88.

Miller, Kenneth. *Direct Democracy and the Courts*. London: Cambridge University Press, 2009.

Mosk, Stanley. "Chief Justice Donald R. Wright." *California Law Review* 65, no. 2 (March 1977): 224–26.

———. "Chilling Judicial Independence—The California Experience." *Western New England Law Review* 3 (Summer 1980): 1–10.

Mullenix, Linda S. "Aggregate Litigation and the Death of Democratic Dispute Resolution." *Northwestern University Law Review* 107, no. 2 (2013): 511–62.

Murray, Douglas. "The Abolition of El Cortito, the Short-Handled Hoe." *Social Problems* 30, no. 1 (1982): 26–39.

Newton, Jim. *Justice for All: Earl Warren and the Nation He Made*. New York: Riverhead Books, 2007.

Parker, Scott G., and David P. Hubbard. "The Evidence for Death." *California Law Review* 78, no. 4 (July 1990): 973–1026.

Pawel, Miriam. *The Crusades of Cesar Chavez*. New York: Bloomsbury Press, 2015.

Price, Charles M. "Judicial Review." *California Journal* 20 (September 1999): 34–39.

Rapoport, Roger. *California Dreaming: The Political Odyssey of Pat and Jerry Brown*. Berkeley: Nolo Press, 1982.

Rarick, Ethan. *California Rising: The Life and Times of Pat Brown*. Berkeley: University of California Press, 2005.

Resnick, Judith. "On the Bias: Feminist Reconsideration of the Aspiration for Our Judges." *Southern California Law Review* 61, no. 1 (1988): 1877–944.

Rice, Cy. *Defender of the Damned: Gladys Towles Root*. New York: Citadel Press, 1964.

Richards, David A. J. *The Sodomy Cases: Bowers v. Hardwick and Lawrence v. Texas*. Lawrence: University of Kansas Press, 2009.

Richardson, James. "Stalking the Wily Chief Justice." *California Journal* 17 (September 1986): 452–55.

————. *Willie Brown: A Biography*. Berkeley: University of California Press, 1997.

Rosen, Ruth. *The World Split Open: How the Modern Women's Movement Changed America*. New York: Viking, 2000.

Ross, David R. "The Political Judiciary." *California Journal* 11 (April 1980): 164.

Salzman, Ed. "Reviewing the Record of a Beleaguered Chief Justice." *California Journal* 9 (August 1978): 252–54.

————. "Second-Hand Rose: Chief Justice Bird—Elevating the Law of the Masses." *California Journal* 8 (May 1977): 157–59.

Schell, Orville. *Brown*. New York: Random House, 1978.

Schuparra, Kurt. *Triumph of the Right: The Rise of the California Conservative Movement, 1945–1966*. Armonk NJ: M. E. Sharpe, 1998.

Shatz, Steven, and Terry Dalton. "Challenging the Death Penalty with Statistics: Furman, McClesky and a Single County Case Study." *Cardozo Law Review* 34, no. 4 (2013): 1227–82.

"Short-Handled Hoe Banned in California." *Labor Occupational Health Project Monitor* 2, no. 3 (April–May 1975): 6.

Sigelman, Lee, Carol K. Sigelman, and Christopher Fowler. "A Bird of a Different Feather? An Experimental Investigation of Physical Attractiveness and the Electability of Female Candidates." *Social Psychology Quarterly* 50, no. 1 (March 1987): 32–43.

Speich, Jeremy. "Joyce Kennard: An Independent Streak on California's Highest Court." *Albany Law Review* 65, no. 4 (2002): 1181.

Starr, Kevin. *Embattled Dreams: California in War and Peace, 1940–1950*. New York: Oxford University Press, 2003.

Stolz, Preble. *Judging Judges: The Investigation of Rose Bird and the California Supreme Court*. New York: Free Press, 1981.

Stolz, Preble, and Kit Stolz. "Are the Voters Forcing Judges to Act Like Politicians?" *California Journal* 9 (September 1978): 252–54.

Sturdevant, Lori. *Her Honor: Rosalie Wahl and the Minnesota Women's Movement*. Minneapolis: Minnesota Historical Society Press, 2014.

Terkel, Studs. *Hard Times: An Oral History of the Great Depression*. New York: Pantheon Books, 1970.

Thompson, Robert S. "Judicial Retention Elections and Judicial Method: A Retrospective." *Southern California Law Review* 61, no. 1 (1987): 1429–45.

Toobin, Jeffrey. *The Nine: Inside the Secret World of the Supreme Court*. New York: Anchor, 2008.

Tribe, Laurence H. "Trying California's Judges on Television: Open Government or Judicial Intimidation." *American Bar Association Journal* 65 (August 1979): 1175–79.

Uelmen, Gerald F. "California Death Penalty Laws and the California Supreme Court: A Ten Year Perspective." *Crime and Social Justice* 25 (1986): 78–93.

Vile, John R. *Great American Judges: An Encyclopedia, Vol. 1.* New York: ABC-CLIO, 2003.

Wade, John W. "Chief Justice Traynor and Strict Tort Liability for Products." *Hofstra Law Review* 2, no. 2 (1974): 455–67.

Willhoite, David. "The Story of the California Agricultural Labor Relations Act." *California Legal History* 7 (December 2012): 409–23.

Winograd, Barry. "Are They a 'Gang of Three'?" *California Journal* 17 (September 1986): 439–41.

Wiseman, Rebecca. "So You Want to Stay a Judge: Name and Politics of the Moment May Decide Your Future." *Journal of Law and Politics* 18 (Summer 2002): 643–56.

Woodward, Bob, and Scott Armstrong. *The Brethren: Inside the Supreme Court.* New York: Simon and Schuster, 1979.

INDEX

Abbe, Richard, 107

ABC television, 225–27

abortion: attitudes toward, 55; in California, 7, 58–60, 251, 265n11; Clarence Thomas on, 233; parental consent for, 237–38; protection of patients seeking, 229; U.S. Supreme Court on, 3, 5, 60, 222

Abrahamson, Shirley, 90, 252, 253

affirmative action: and California court, 71, 251; Clarence Thomas on, 233; legislation on, 236; at University of California, 69–70, 267nn41–42. *See also* minorities; women

African Americans: in California legislature, 279n7; on California Supreme Court, 54, 78, 148, 159–60, 251; civil rights movement of, 18; as defendants, 235; education of, 236; in governor's race, 214; marriages of, 57–58; and right to testify, 271n63; Rose Bird's association with, 13–14, 26; support of, of Rose Bird, 211; on

U.S. Supreme Court, 232; as voters, 285n10. *See also* race

age discrimination, 182, 190, 229, 289n24. *See also* equal protection

agribusiness: attempts to remove judges by, 62–63, 114–15, 120, 218; citizens' role in, 49; legislation affecting, 37–49, 73, 161; power of, 36–37, 84. *See also* farmworkers; food crops

Agriculture Labor Relations Act (ALRA), 46–51, 82–88, 115, 161, 239

Agriculture Labor Relations Board (ALRB), 48–49, 75–76, 85–89

Agriculture Workers Organizing Committee (AWOC), 38

AIDS epidemic, 183, 222

Alabama, 247, 266n20

Alameda County, 148, 174

Alatorre, Richard, 38

Alcala, Rodney, 212

Allred, Gloria, 118, 220

All the Truth Is Out (Bai), 290n34

California: Brown family in, 34–35; business opportunities in, 190; election (1986) in, 200–201; oversight of court system in, 103–5; population distribution in, 37; redistricting in, 178, 225; Rose Bird's law career in, 24–31; state employee salaries in, 33, 45, 53; Tani Cantil-Sakauye's family in, 254; women lawyers in, 23

California Agriculture and Services Agency: responsibilities of, 36, 161; Rose Bird as secretary of, 30–56, 73, 83–87, 100, 101, 121, 163, 239, 254; Rose Bird's transition from, 103, 104

California Appellate Project, 206

California Assembly Education Committee, 19

California Attorneys for Criminal Justice, 81

California bar association, 49, 79, 92–94, 133, 200, 231. *See also* attorneys; bar associations

California bar exam, 70, 90–91

California Board of Equalization, 64

California Chamber of Commerce, 127

California Constitution: and abortion, 238; and ballot measures, 112; on death penalty, 150–58, 230, 280n23; on due process guarantees, 167; on equal protection, 266n24; as extension of federal constitution, 61; on interracial marriage, 57; justices' respect for, 5, 66, 163, 170; on prayer, 229; precedence of, 26, 260n52; on property taxes, 119; on redistricting, 179; revision of, 109; on sentencing discretion, 134, 138, 276n41

California Consumer Services Agency, 269n23

California Department of Industrial Relations, 50, 87–88, 269n23

California Department of Transportation, 33, 50

California District Attorneys Association, 81

California Employment Development Department, 84

California Farm Bureau Federation, 83

California Food and Agriculture Department, 49, 84

California Franchise Tax Board, 36

California Industrial Safety Board, 42

California Journal, 50–52, 108, 115, 201, 208

California Judicial Council, 104, 132–33, 206, 210, 215–16, 254

California Labor Federation, 161

California legislature: on abortion, 265n11; on court budget, 103, 255; creation of investigative commission by, 132; on death penalty, 72–73, 149, 150–53, 158, 167–68, 170; farm bill in, 39, 46–49, 239; farmworker allies in, 38; George Deukmejian in, 159; Gordon Winton in, 41; on "great bodily injury," 117–18, 273n53; and gun law, 123, 127, 134–35, 275n3; on housing discrimination, 63; on liability damages, 178, 188, 191; Paul Peek in, 64; on pedophiles, 166; political composition of, 178–80; on property taxes, 119; redistricting of, 178, 225; relationship of, with judiciary, 61, 65; on Rose Bird's appointment, 82, 91; on state bar association, 93–94; and tort reform, 176; Willie Brown in, 279n7; women in, 40, 263n24

Law School Aptitude Test (LSAT), 19–20

law schools, 5, 19–23, 61, 219, 220, 230, 260n43. *See also* attorneys; Boalt Hall

Lear, Norman, 200

Legal Aid Society of Los Angeles, 181

Leichter, Alexandra, 163

letters: to Cruz Reynoso, 217; to judicial appointment commission, 82, 85–88, 90, 94, 95; to justices, 61, 196, 239, 240; on *People v. Tanner* decision, 125, 126, 131, 132; on Robert Bork, 222; on Rose Bird's retention, 122, 211; to *Times* regarding Rose Bird, 169, 219

lettuce growers, 38, 42, 43. *See also* food crops

Levy, Jacques, 263n32

Lewin, Nathan, 83

Lewinsky, Monica, 236

Lewis, Anthony, 146–47, 209–10

Lewis, R. Fred, 244

liability: California Supreme Court on, 58, 59, 174–75; costs of, 189–91; for emotional distress, 175–76, 185; insurance against, 176, 183–84, 187–88; of landlords, 183–84, 229. *See also* consumers' rights

Liddick, Betty, 100–101

Lillie, Mildred, 88, 246, 270n36

Linebaugh, Patti, 166, 167, 281n51

"Little Lindbergh" law, 262n9. *See also* kidnapping

Liu, Goodwin, 251

lobbyists, 41

Lockwood, Lorna, 54, 253

London School of Economics, 148, 208

Long Island University, 16–17, 260n39

Lorenz, Jim, 84

Los Angeles CA: Alexandra Leichter in, 163; attorneys from, 93, 95, 171; bookmaker in, 58–59; court facilities in, 107, 193, 217; cross display in, 132, 144, 276n22; education funding trial in, 63; farmworker allies in, 38; Florence Bernstein in, 210–11; housing shortage in, 181; Manson killings in, 165; marriage licenses in, 57; mayor of, 160, 198; obscenity case in, 65, 266n27; opposition to Rose Bird in, 203; oral arguments in, 78, 111; Otto Kaus in, 148; racial violence in, 35; renters' rights in, 181–83; Roger Mahony in, 270n35; Ronald George in, 232; Rose Bird's home near, 44; Rose Bird's memorial in, 241–42; Rose Bird's speeches in, 196, 220, 237; Seth Hufstedler in, 133; Stanley Mosk in, 76; support for Rose Bird in, 211; women lawyers in, 23

Los Angeles City Hall, 173

Los Angeles Community College District Board, 35

Los Angeles County, 186–87, 219

Los Angeles Daily Journal, 105, 128, 141, 279n18

Los Angeles Police Department, 58–59, 61, 66, 82, 197. *See also* police

Los Angeles Press Club, 213

Los Angeles Superior Court, 33, 69, 70, 262n5

Los Angeles Times: on court operations, 275n17; coverage of Rose Bird by, 80, 83, 85, 88, 100–101, 121, 169, 205, 211, 219, 226, 241; on crime increase, 165; on gun law case, 123–26, 129, 138, 141–42, 144; on housing discrimination, 182–83; on O.J. Simpson trial,

217; Marshall McComb during, 68; for *People v. Caudillo*, 117; for *People v. Tanner*, 127, 128, 275n3; in Sacramento, 76–78

Orange County: gender discrimination case in, 184; John Briggs in, 151; opposition to Rose Bird in, 156, 197–98; political leanings in, 65, 67, 267n30; renters' rights in, 181–82; Theodore Frank's sentence in, 166; women's organization in, 33

Orange County Register, 241

Packwood, Robert, 222

palimony, 60, 265n14

Palo Alto CA: Anne Walsh in, 154, 196; robbery in, 127; Rose Bird in, 5, 28, 31, 41, 108–9, 196, 227, 231, 236, 239; Rose Bird's memorial in, 241–42

Pandol, Jack, 84

Panelli, Edward, 214, 217

Pariente, Barbara, 247

Parker, William, 58–59, 61, 66

parole, 151–52, 157, 160, 167, 171, 229, 279n22

Peek, Paul, 62, 63, 64

Penal Code section 461, 118

People magazine, 203–4

People v. Anderson, 60, 73

People v. Belous, 59–60

People v. Caudillo: and attack on Rose Bird, 117–20; reference to, in *People v. Tanner* dissent, 139–41, 145; sentence in, 131, 134, 139, 276n41. *See also* Caudillo, Daniel; rape

People v. Hall, 97, 271n63

People v. Morse, 151–52, 279n22

People v. Ramos, 171

People v. Tanner: decision on, 123–29,

132, 135, 279n18; description of, 127–28, 275n3; investigation regarding, 133–47; rehearing of, 135, 276n27; sentence in, 139, 276n41; William Clark's dissent on, 130–31. *See also* gun laws

Perez, Andrea, 57–58

Perez v. Sharp, 57–58, 250

personal injury cases, 174–75

Personal Politics (Evans), 285n10

Peters, Raymond, 60, 62, 64, 148

Philibosian, Robert, 171

Poche, Marc, 91

Polanski, Roman, 165

police: apprehension of Harold Tanner by, 127; coercion by, 59; in death penalty case, 155; drug raid by, 159; murders of, 151, 164, 279n10; "reasonable suspicion" of, 114; relationship of, with Rose Bird, 95, 154; in renters' rights case, 181–82; Tani Cantil-Sakauye on shootings of, 255. *See also* Los Angeles Police Department

politics: conservatives' power over California, 65, 67, 68, 114–17, 161–64, 169–72, 200, 202, 210, 225–29, 237, 250, 251, 267n30; of court investigation, 132–33, 143, 147, 149; of death penalty in California, 176; and delay of *People v. Tanner* decision, 123–24, 128–29, 132, 139–41; effect of, on justices, 62, 65–74, 82, 92–99, 114–19, 122–23, 137–38, 145, 153, 157, 160–64, 170, 177, 210–14, 223–25, 232–33, 238, 245–48, 253, 266n29; fundraising in, 114–15, 119–22, 156–57, 192, 197–98, 200–209, 212, 213, 218, 223, 227; influences on American, 199, 285n10;

politics (*continued*)

 Jerry Brown's interest in, 18, 29–30, 35, 36, 90; media coverage of, 50–51, 233, 290n34; Rose Bird's disdain for, 191–92, 199, 208–11, 216, 218, 234, 236–37, 239–40; Rose Bird's effect on, 6, 163, 227–28; Rose Bird's interest in, 15–18, 24, 30, 225–26; in Sacramento, 40; sex in, 233, 236–37; Stanley Mosk on, 69; of victims' rights groups, 166; of William Clark, 129–30

Polk, George, 16

Polytechnic Institute (Brooklyn), 17

Pomona College, 33, 208

Portman, Sheldon, 24, 25, 81

poverty, 19, 21, 25, 29, 35, 206, 231–32

Powell, Gregory, 164

Powell, Lewis, 221

prison sentences: and death penalty, 72, 150, 177, 278n1; for gun possession, 127–29, 134, 135; indeterminate, 164, 280n40; parole in, 151–52, 157, 160, 167, 171, 229, 279n22; for pedophiles, 166; and "three strikes" law, 238

privacy, 222, 238, 288n2

proplaintiff rulings: California court's history of, 174–75, 187–88, 190; in Mississippi, 7, 243; objections to, 176, 187–88, 209; of Rose Bird, 4, 177; in Texas, 233

Proposition 6, 152

Proposition 7. *See* Briggs Initiative

Proposition 8 (1982), 158–59, 280n23

Proposition 8 (2008), 250–51, 293n27. *See also* same-sex marriage

Proposition 13, 117–20, 159, 197, 274n60. *See also* taxes, property

Proposition 14, 63, 66, 67

Proposition 17, 72. *See also* death penalty

Proposition 34, 249, 278n3, 293n25. *See also* death penalty

Proposition 209, 236. *See also* affirmative action

Quinn, Tom, 30

Racanelli, John, 135, 147

race: California Supreme Court on issues of, 61; in death penalty case, 168; George Deukmejian on, 160, 214; and housing laws, 63; and marriage, 57–58; in O.J. Simpson trial, 235; political division over, 67; Robert Bork on, 221; and violence, 35; Wiley Manuel on, 79. *See also* African Americans; Latinos; minorities

racial inequality, 3, 13, 18, 19, 29, 97, 216, 228, 236, 266n20, 271n63. *See also* equal protection

Rackauckas, Anthony, 156–57, 279n18

Radin, Max, 58, 265n4

rape: and abortion, 265n11; of Amy Sue Seitz, 166; death penalty for, 151, 155, 233, 234; injuries from, 117–18, 273n53; justices "soft" on, 115, 131; sentencing for, 134, 276n41; threats to Rose Bird, 196, 240. *See also People v. Caudillo*

Rarick, Ethan, 262n5

Rather, Dan, 6

Ray, Vance, 254

Reagan, Ronald: on abortion, 265n11; appointments by, 4, 6, 60, 67, 74, 90–91, 95, 102, 113, 119, 134, 136, 167,

Werdegar, Kathryn, 291n46
West Virginia, 246–47
White, Penny, 7, 234
Whitman, Meg, 1
Wicker, Tom, 119, 210
Wilkins, Roger, 289n21
Willoughby, Thomas, 146
Wills, Garry, 289n21
Wilson, La Nita, 185, 283n31
Wilson, Pete, 18, 82, 85, 97, 227, 231, 232, 236–38
Wilson, Steven, 185, 283n31
wine, 36, 43. *See also* grape growers
Winton, Gordon, 19, 41, 108
Wisconsin, 16, 252
women: attitudes toward powerful, 88–89, 93, 204–6, 215–16; books about, 280n31; California court on issues relating to, 55–56; in California politics, 40–41, 47, 240; cancers in, 177–78; cases involving, 113, 184; on Clarence Thomas, 233; as commentators, 226; as court staff, 106; on death row, 249; experiences of, in courtrooms, 228; housing for, at Berkeley, 18; Jerry Brown's appointment of, 32–33, 36, 53–54, 69, 88; Jimmy Carter's appointment of, 53, 264n56; job market for, 11, 16, 17, 23, 113, 260n43; as justices, 8, 71, 74–75, 78, 79, 88–91, 95, 97, 101–2, 104, 116, 121, 127, 145–47, 154, 157, 161–62, 166–67, 169, 215–20, 228–30, 239–40, 243, 247, 250–56, 270n36; as "old maids," 203–4, 286n26; opportunities for, 4–5, 19–24, 31, 240, 260n43; professional conduct of, 24–28, 232; self-sufficiency of, 9–10; stereotypes of, 12, 14, 30, 116–17, 161–62,

166, 258n12, 280n31; support of Rose Bird by, 52–53, 96–99, 121, 157, 200, 216; in U.S. Senate, 290n35; victims' rights groups of, 166–67, 281n51; vulnerability of, 4, 8, 215, 220, 252. *See also* affirmative action; feminism; gender discrimination; minorities

Women in Business, 169, 205–6
women's rights: and abortion, 60; in American politics, 199, 285n10; attitudes toward, 117; Robert Bork on, 6; and Rose Bird, 28, 55, 89, 106, 216, 228, 239–40. *See also* equal protection; feminism; gender discrimination

Wood, Parker, 78–80, 90, 94–96
Woodford, Jeanne, 249
Woodward, Bob, 103, 272n10
workers' rights: and affirmative action, 236; attitudes toward, 55; cases involving, 185–90, 238; comparison of, with renters' rights, 183; and farm bill, 47, 49, 87; Phil Gibson on, 62–63; Rose Bird on, 42, 45, 216. *See also* labor unions

World War I, 10
World War II, 11, 12, 16, 19–20, 226, 230, 254, 258n12
Wright, Donald: appointment of, as chief justice, 60, 80, 267n35; collegiality of, 104, 105, 108; on death penalty, 73, 74, 164; on Judicial Council, 132; male networks of, 76–77; on Marshall McComb, 68; on opposition to Rose Bird, 162; professional conduct of, 103; on renters' rights, 180–81; retirement of, 53, 69, 80; on Roger Traynor, 272n6;

Wright, Donald (*continued*)
on Rose Bird, 79, 81–82, 157; on William Clark, 70, 90–91, 130
The Writ, 21

Yale Law School, 28, 34–35, 75, 204
Younger, Evelle: as attorney general, 54; at confirmation hearings, 78, 79, 82, 83, 85, 86, 90–92, 94, 96; gubernatorial bid of, 115, 128, 152, 273n49; on *People v. Tanner*, 128, 140

Zeitlin v. Arneberg, 65, 266n27
Zenoff, David, 24, 93
Zimmerman, Bill, 191–92, 199, 201
Zschau, Ed, 198

CPSIA information can be obtained
at www.ICGtesting.com
Printed in the USA
LVOW11*2018300117

522619LV00004B/60/P